LOUISIANA LIGHT

Books by Roy F. Guste, Jr.

ANTOINE'S RESTAURANT COOKBOOK

THE RESTAURANTS OF NEW ORLEANS

THE 100 GREATEST DISHES OF LOUISIANA COOKERY

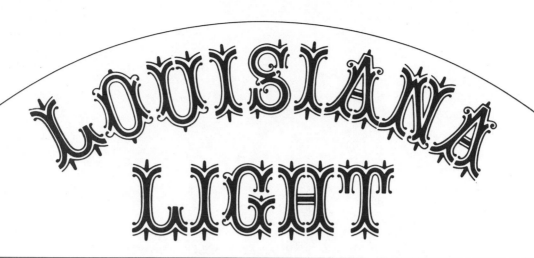

LOUISIANA LIGHT

LOW-FAT · LOW-CALORIE LOW-CHOLESTEROL · LOW-SALT

CAJUN AND CREOLE COOKERY

by

ROY F. GUSTE, JR.

with

THE OCHSNER MEDICAL INSTITUTIONS

With a Foreword by

JOHN L. OCHSNER, M.D.

W · W · NORTON & COMPANY · NEW YORK · LONDON

Printed in the United States of America.

The text of this book is composed in Garamond,
with display type set in Avant-Garde Extra Light.
Composition and
manufacturing by the Haddon Craftsmen Inc.
Book design by Jacques Chazaud.
Illustrations by Maura Conron.

First Edition

Library of Congress Cataloging-in-Publication Data

Guste, Roy F. Jr.
"Louisiana light": low-fat, low-calorie, low-cholesterol, low-salt
Cajun & Creole cookery / by Roy F. Guste, Jr., with the
Ochsner Medical Institutions; with a foreword by John L. Ochsner.—
1st ed.
p.   cm.
1. Cookery, American—Louisiana style. 2. Cookery, Creole.
I. Ochsner Medical Institutions. II. Title.
TX715.2.L68G87 1990
641.5'63—dc19   89–30237

ISBN 0-393-02714-7

W. W. Norton & Company, Inc., 500 Fifth Avenue, New York, N. Y. 10110
W. W. Norton & Company Ltd., 37 Great Russell Street, London WC1B 3NU

1 2 3 4 5 6 7 8 9 0

To my parents,

Roy and Beverly,

who first taught me how to eat well . . . I return the favor.

CONTENTS

SOUPS, BISQUES, AND GUMBO

FISH AND SEAFOOD

CHICKEN AND DUCK

MEAT

SPECIALTIES

SALADS

VEGETABLES

DESSERTS

APPENDIX

STATEMENT FROM THE DIETITIANS

As practicing dietitians (nutritionists) in an area of the country which has a high incidence of cardiovascular disease, diabetes and hypertension, and yet an area where the people are lovers of good food, we find this cookbook especially appealing. The combination of high quality food prepared in an uncomplicated, appetizing way and using the favorite foods of New Orleans is going to interest everyone. The fact that these foods are good for us and fit into several modified diets is a bonus, or as we may say here in Louisiana, lagniappe.

We have enjoyed reviewing the recipes and participating in their development and can recommend them to anyone who enjoys good food.

The Staff of the Departments of Dietetics
The Ochsner Medical Institutions

FOREWORD

Food is the first pleasurable experience of life, and in Louisiana this enjoyment continues throughout life. Dining in Louisiana is almost considered a spiritual occurrence; hence, the state is renowned for its cookery and chefs. Louisiana cooking is exceptionally rich, and traditionally much of the rich taste results from the use of saturated fats, cholesterol, sugar, and salt. Each of these ingredients can be harmful in certain quantities, especially for people with risk factors for heart disease.

As a heart surgeon, I am painfully aware of the harmful effects of exogenous substances that elevate the blood lipids, add excessive calories, or create fluid retention. Such adverse effects tax the cardiovascular system, and in those with inherent risk factors, the effects can be catastrophic. Today, one in three American adults can be expected to die of a heart attack. Therefore, we should all be cognizant of the various risk factors and control them as much as possible. One needs to exercise aerobically, control blood pressure, not smoke, and eat healthy, low-saturated-fat and low-cholesterol meals—all of which are factors in determining heart disease risk. The incidence of coronary-artery disease is high in North America and particularly in the state of Louisiana where the intake of saturated fat and cholesterol is excessive. Conversely, in areas of the world where the average intake of cholesterol and saturated fats is low, the incidence of coronary-artery disease is nearly zero. This is no mere coincidence.

Louisiana Light is not a fad-diet book. It is a book in which Roy Guste has produced new recipes and altered traditional Louisiana ones in order to control saturated fat and cholesterol and to eliminate sugar and salt. He has analyzed each recipe with a computerized program to calculate its nutritional value. The dietitians of The Ochsner Medical Institutions have reviewed the contents of the recipes to insure that each one meets the appropriate guidelines for lowering cholesterol, losing weight, and controlling blood pressure. Thus, this book is for cooks who love to cook and are concerned with the health of those they serve.

John L. Ochsner, M.D.
The Ochsner Medical Institutions

INTRODUCTION

Eating well and staying healthy is what this book is all about. The recent national interest in Louisiana cookery—Cajun and Creole—has brought a greater percentage of American cooks a more extensive general knowledge of these cuisines. This knowledge is part of a unique culinary heritage in which all of us can share. But of what good is this knowledge of Cajun and Creole cookery if, in fact, it is always presented as a too-rich and all-too-often fattening and cholesterol-filled affair? It does not and should not have to be this way for those of us who are health- and diet-conscious and those of us who want to maintain a sound internal and external physical condition.

It is no secret that some of Louisiana's culinary representatives are not exactly the picture of health, but they are the exceptions. Most individuals involved with the food industry are conscious of their responsibility to the public and its dietary welfare, and do provide alternate, or in some cases complete, menus prepared in a manner that helps to reduce excess fats and cholesterol. This attitude is fast becoming more widespread as the public demands it more and more as part or all of their restaurant and home dining experiences.

When I passed into my thirty-sixth year, I began to gain weight and became less able to keep up with my exercise. I also became concerned about cholesterol in the fabulous Creole and Cajun foods of New Orleans.

In an attempt to lose some of the weight I was gaining and at the same time have dishes and meals that were satisfying both in quantity and taste, I decided to rework some of my favorite Louisiana recipes into versions that did not use added fat. As I began to develop these recipes I had to change my own view of the foods I could eat.

Because of my recent weight gain and what I perceived as a change in my metabolism, I decided to pursue a more balanced diet, adding the dietary fiber I had been missing. I wanted to lower my caloric intake so I decided to limit fat as much as possible. I know that all fats do not raise cholesterol levels, but I also wanted to balance my calories against the fiber and carbohydrates that I now considered good and necessary to any balanced diet.

I also became concerned about salt. I used a lot of it, a result of growing up in an area where many of our foods are highly salted by almost all cooks. Boiled seafood, for example, would not be considered properly prepared if it were not "good and salty." "Salty" oysters is the way we traditionally describe the most delectable oysters.

My first step in developing low-fat, low-calorie, low-cholesterol, and low-salt dishes was to examine the individual ingredients, eliminate those which are highest in those areas, and rebalance the remaining ingredients with seasonings and vegetables that give a more fully rounded, satisfying flavor. In this way I was endeavoring not merely to replace the undesirable ingredients, but rather to expand the base of flavor so that those ingredients containing unnecessary fat, calories, cholesterol and sodium became expendable.

It is important for me to say that in the first month of developing and eating only these recipes I lost 15 pounds.

This book and these recipes will give you, as they have given me, delicious and healthful meals with the true flavor of traditional Louisiana cookery—Creole and Cajun. These dishes will help you to achieve a proper diet and will be savored by everyone who enjoys good food.

ACKNOWLEDGMENTS

My thanks go first to John Ochsner, who understood what I wanted to do and gave me the help, assistance, and support I needed to get the job done.

Secondly, I want to thank the staff of the Ochsner Medical Institutions with whom I worked to develop this collection of recipes; they instilled in me a great respect for the importance of proper diet and gave me the tools to do the job. In particular, I want to thank Chris Welton, Registered Dietitian and Director of Clinical Nutrition Services for Ochsner, and Charlotte Sovic of the Ochsner Weight Control Clinic.

Lastly, I want to thank Martha Jones, Registered Dietitian, Clinical Dietitian Nutrition Clinic and most charming and knowledgeable friend, whose ideas and thoughts and warm good humor in addition to her clinical knowledge added greatly to this work and to its completion.

OVERVIEW

Our bodies manufacture *some* cholesterol, which is a necessary part of many functions such as the hormone system and brain and nerve function. But when we ingest too much cholesterol and saturated fat, the excess may be deposited on the inner walls of the blood vessels, which then become thickened and narrowed. If they are blocked completely, heart attacks (sometimes called myocardial infarcts) or strokes may occur, often fatal.

So—do we want to keep the amount of saturated fat and cholesterol in our diets at the lowest level? Absolutely!

The general guidelines for keeping a desirable cholesterol level—in the range of 180–200 mg/dl—is to limit your total intake of fat to 30% of total daily calories as opposed to the 40% that is the norm for most Americans. Along with the reduction of total fat intake you should try to replace the saturated fat with polyunsaturated and monounsaturated fats. The Recommended Dietary Allowance, RDA, for cholesterol is 300 milligrams (mg) daily. Try not to exceed this amount.

To understand these terms that we hear so often and which can be so confusing, let's look at the three types of dietary fat.

Saturated fats are usually of animal origin such as meat and other flesh, dairy fats, lard, bacon fat, and variety meats. Vegetable fats can become saturated by being hydrogenated, or solidified. Some vegetable fats such as palm kernel oil, palm oil, coconut oil, and cocoa butter (chocolate) are naturally saturated. These saturated fats cause an increase in blood cholesterol just as animal fats do.

Polyunsaturated fats such as safflower, sunflower, corn and soybean oils, and monounsaturated fats such as canola (rapeseed), olive, peanut (in moderation) and cottonseed oils are beneficial and can even help to lower blood cholesterol. They still should not be used in excessive amounts—remember, no more than 30% of the day's calories (ideally divided into 10% sat, 10% poly, 10% mono).

Cholesterol is found only in foods of animal origin. Especially rich sources are egg yolk and organ meats. Dietary cholesterol should not exceed 300 milligrams per day. It is especially harmful when accompanied by saturated fat.

Another type of beneficial fatty acid, called Omega-3, is found in fish and many good fish recipes are included in this book. At least two fish meals weekly are recommended.

Even though sugar does not affect blood cholesterol, it can add to your total caloric intake and may not be tolerated well by those people with elevated blood sugar and/or triglycerides. The recipes in this book have no added sugar.

People who are salt sensitive, which can lead to blood pressure elevation, will be pleased to see that there is no salt added in the recipes. The Recommended Dietary Allowance, RDA, for daily sodium (salt) intake for most people is 2200 milligrams (mg). Try not to exceed that amount.

The recipes for alcoholic beverages may be enjoyed by anyone who has not been told by a physician to avoid alcohol. Remember that alcohol *does* contain calories and can affect some medical conditions such as diabetes, hypertension, elevated triglycerides, etc.

Among the foods that should be increased in fat-controlled, cholesterol-lowering cooking are those that are high in fiber and complex carbohydrates, namely oats, beans, fruits, and vegetables for *soluble* fiber. These fibers have cholesterol-lowering properties. *Insoluble* fiber, such as that found in whole-wheat and other whole grains, is necessary along with an adequate fluid intake for prevention of constipation and other digestive problems.

The recipes in this book can help you meet the goals set forth in U.S.D.A. Dietary Guidelines for Americans:

1. Eat a variety of foods.
2. Maintain your ideal weight.
3. Avoid too much fat, too much saturated fat, and too much cholesterol.
4. Eat foods with adequate starch and fiber.
5. Avoid too much sugar.
6. Avoid too much sodium.
7. If you drink alcoholic beverages, do so in moderation.

As simple as these seven statements may sound, it is necessary to be aware of what makes up the foods you eat in order to follow them. These recipes, their analyses, and the appendix of analyses of principle foods used here will help you to know what you are eating and how to maintain a proper diet.

A proper diet is all important in living a long and healthy life.

LOUISIANA LIGHT

THE BASICS

Changing the ground rules

    1)   Eliminate the oil

        a.   The "Dry Roux"

        b.   Comparison of fats and oils

    2)   The onion-and-garlic base

        a.   Cooking the onions

        b.   The changing flavors of onions and garlic

Portions

Stock

Salt substitutes

Artificial sweeteners

Cooking with wine

Condiments

On the matter of the egg

Utensils

Interpreting the recipe analyses

CHANGING THE GROUND RULES

Changing the ground rules is the key to these recipes and to converting any dish that you yourself would love to enjoy healthfully. It is simple! The two key elements to my approach are the following:

1) Eliminate the fats and oils.
2) Use a richly flavored vegetable base: onion and garlic.

That's all there is to it.

ELIMINATE THE OIL

One primary means of eliminating calories and cholesterol is to eliminate any unnecessary fat altogether. Just say NO!!! Don't add that butter or oil and try your favorite recipes without it.

There is no denying that cooking in oil and butter adds a marvelous taste to foods and makes the work of cooking easier. But it is not necessary.

Physically, oils let you cook more easily by helping to prevent foods from sticking to the pan: when you stir foods with oil, the heat is distributed upward from the bottom. It is not necessary, though. And you don't need to run out and buy a whole set of nonstick pots and pans, although I do like a nonstick baking sheet for my "fried" dishes, which actually are baked. All you really have to do is pay attention to the cooking and continue to move the foods around in the pan regularly so that things don't stick and burn. This is not difficult, but it does take a bit more attention than you may be used to.

The "Dry Roux."

The traditional roux is an important element of many Cajun and Creole dishes. It is a mixture of half flour and half fat (oil or butter) cooked to progressive degrees of color from blond to brown depending on the richness and the "smokiness" of the flavor you are striving to achieve, the brown roux being the richest. This typical ingredient is a problem to low-fat, low-calorie, low-cholesterol cookery because of its high oil content, but making a "roux" without the oil is simple.

DRY "ROUX"

INGREDIENTS:

1 cup all-purpose flour

PREPARATION:

Put the flour in a heavy skillet and place over moderate heat.
Stir the flour around often with a wooden spoon as it cooks.
Pay attention to the cooking because the flour will take a few minutes, 5 or 7, to begin coloring. At this point you have a blond "roux." For the next 5 or 7 minutes it will darken until it reaches a light wood color. Stir constantly to keep the flour in the bottom of the skillet moving so it will not burn, and so all the flour in the pan will color evenly. The whole process takes about 15 minutes of close attention to get a good rich "roux."
Whether or not you are familiar with cooking a roux with oil, you must pay attention to the color here because when the flour is cooked without oil it will not become as brown as we eventually want it to. That is, not until you mix it with an equal amount of liquid to add it to a dish. At that point the moisture will cause it to darken properly.
The recipes call for "dry roux" in quantities of a tablespoon or so at a time. What you don't use immediately can be stored unrefrigerated in a tightly capped jar almost indefinitely.

Comparison of fats and oils.

Even though I have used no added fats or oils in this collection of recipes and have spoken only of eliminating them, I thought that you might find a comparison of them as interesting as I have.

I have used the measurement of 10 grams, which is the approximate weight of one teaspoon (9/10 of a teaspoon).

10 Grams (9/10th tsp.)	Fats					
	Sat	Mono	Poly	Chol	Sod	Cal
almond	0.826 g	6.97 g	1.74 g	0	—	88.4
butter:						
salted	5.07 g	2.34 g	0.300 g	21.9 mg	68.2 mg	71.6
unsalted	5.07 g	2.34 g	0.300 g	21.9 mg	1.10 mg	71.6
clarified	6.209 g	2.87 g	0.369 g	26.8 mg	—	87.6
cocoa-butter oil	5.96 g	3.29 g	0.298 g	0 mg	—	88.4
coconut	8.67 g	0.583 g	0.179 g	0 mg	—	88.4
corn	1.27 g	2.42 g	5.87 g	0 mg	0 mg	88.4
cottonseed	2.59 g	1.78 g	5.18 g	0 mg	—	88.4
lard	3.92 g	4.51 g	1.12 g	9.51 mg	.001 mg	90.2
margarine:						
salted 80% fat	1.58 g	3.58 g	2.54 g	0 mg	94.3 mg	71.8
soft-low fat 40% fat	0.771 g	1.57 g	1.38 g	0 mg	95.9 mg	34.6
olive	1.35 g	7.36 g	0.838 g	0 mg	0 mg	88.4
palm	4.91 g	3.70 g	0.931 g	0 mg	—	88.4
palm kernel	8.12 g	1.14 g	0.156 g	0 mg	—	88.4
peanut	1.69 g	4.62 g	3.20 g	0 mg	0 mg	88.4
rapeseed/canola	.555 g	6.24 g	2.77 g	0 mg	—	88.4
safflower	.908 g	1.21 g	7.43 g	0 mg	0 mg	88.4
sesame	1.42 g	3.97 g	4.17 g	0 mg	—	88.3
soybean	1.49 g	4.30 g	3.76 g	0 mg	0 mg	88.4
sunflower	1.03 g	1.95 g	6.56 g	0 mg	0 mg	88.4
walnut	.908 g	2.28 g	6.33 g	0 mg	—	88.4
wheat-germ	1.91 g	1.54 g	6.18 g	0 mg	—	88.2

THE ONION-AND-GARLIC BASE

Cooking the onions.

There are two principle methods of cooking onions at the beginning of the preparation of dishes using the onion and garlic base. Each renders a different taste with exactly the same product.

The first method is to add the chopped onions to the pan and then heat them. When you do this the onions give up their liquid and cook, for the most part, more slowly. They will begin to color, or change from white to an opalescent beige, and their taste becomes mild and loses the initial harsh pungency that is onion.

The second method is to heat the saucepan or skillet very hot and add the chopped onions. This sears the onions immediately and begins a caramelization which results in a sweeter and richer flavor. The edges of the onions will become dark brown and give off a rich, "smoky" aroma; it is this aroma that tells you that you are getting to the point which will give you the richest taste, that point and that taste you want to achieve. This is an important step. It is important because it is the base of many of the recipes here and it is important because you must pay attention to the cooking. Do not throw in the onions and walk away from the pan: the onions will burn. You must stir them around while they are cooking to be sure that they are all cooking evenly and you must constantly scrape the bottom and sides of the pan to loosen any pieces that stick. These pieces will burn and flavor your whole dish if you don't keep things moving around in the pan. This whole process only takes a minute or so, so pay attention.

The next most important step in these recipes is in blending in the "dry roux" so it is thoroughly combined with the other ingredients and no lumps form.

The changing flavor of onions and garlic.

I have found in using onions as my most important base in cooking many of the recipes included here, and in cooking them in the different ways I suggest, that they differ from time to time. The ones I generally use are large yellow onions that I occasionally interchange with large white onions, for no other reason than which look best at the store that day. I prefer not to use red onions in cooking but rather raw in salads, and perhaps when I use them chopped as a garnish for Red Beans and Rice. The obvious fact remains that the flavor of the onions changes from day to day and the way they cook also changes. To begin with, the most pungent onions are the freshest onions. It happens that the longer they sit in the grocery or the longer they travelled to get there seems to have caused them to lose some of their pungency and to sweeten somewhat more than when they were fresh. The sweet taste is quite delicious generally except when you might be attempting some sauce for, say, a fish dish and want a rich taste without a sweet taste.

Garlic is the same way. The longer it sits the less pungent it becomes. It also seems to become bitter as it ages. It is necessary to note also that not all garlic is the same. There are a number of varieties and they all vary somewhat in taste and cook somewhat differently. In my experience I have found that most of the regular size garlics are similar in pungency to one another while the very large or elephant garlic has less pungency, less of the strong garlic taste. Because of this difference I prefer to use regular garlic rather than the large garlic for cooking.

PORTIONS

Portion size has been determined to aid in weight reduction and cholesterol control. These portions—generally 3 ounces of cooked product—are quite suitable and filling when served as part of a complete balanced meal.

I found in testing all the recipes for this book that just as it does not take long for us to become accustomed to the absence of fat and salt, so does it not take long for us to become quite satisfied with a three-ounce portion of fish or meat or other food. If you are determined to use larger portions, remember to increase the analysis figures accordingly.

All of the principle foods used in these recipes are analyzed in the appendix. Use these analyses to determine your own figures and to create your own healthful adaptations of these recipes or of others that are already your favorites.

STOCK

When using stock in recipes it is very important to know what it is that you are adding to that recipe. Dry or canned stocks or stocks made from cubes are generally very highly salted. If you are watching your salt intake it would be better if you made your own stock from scratch, or purchase low-sodium stock-base products.

In these recipes I use water but you can use stock, provided you make your own without salt or fat. In a chicken dish, for example, I usually buy a whole chicken so I will have the carcass to make a stock. What I do is remove and discard all fat and skin, then I remove the breasts and meat from the carcass, and remove the bones from the legs and wings. I then reserve the meat for the dish and make a stock with the bones.

To make the stock I simply split the bones into pieces with a heavy knife and put them in a small saucepan with two cups of water and bring all to a boil; cover the pan, lower the heat, and simmer for fifteen minutes. When that is done I spoon off and discard any oil globules that may float on the surface, and strain the remaining liquid, now stock.

SALT SUBSTITUTES

My thoughts on salt substitutes are that they are unnecessary and should be avoided. It is a rethinking of the way we prepare food that needs to be approached. If you begin your rethinking and reworking you will find that the substitutes rarely do satisfy the desire for the taste of salt. Why develop a taste for potassium, which is the principle ingredient of most salt substitutes?

It takes time to stop missing the salt taste, but as your taste buds become accustomed to not being barraged by salt they will wake up to the real flavor of the foods that you eat and not the salt.

ARTIFICIAL SWEETENERS

Artificial sweeteners are an ingredient to which we must also pay close attention. Not all sweeteners are alike and you must read what they can and cannot do. For example, sweeteners containing aspartame lose their sweetening power when added to dishes and cooked for longer periods of time, as you would in baking. These same sweeteners can, however, be used quite successfully when added to hot foods or beverages that are not kept cooking.

Not all packets of sweetener are the equivalent of the same measure of sugar. Some sweetener packets are designed to give you the sweetness of two teaspoons of sugar and others to give you the sweetness of one teaspoon of sugar.

Some sweeteners do contain a form of sugar and you should add them to the calorie and carbohydrate count of the analysis of the recipe you are using. Some sweeteners to count calories of are fructose, dextrose, maltose and lactose.

Read what is written on the package to find out what your sweetener is adding to your diet.

COOKING WITH WINE

When wine is added to a sauce or a dish, you may think you're adding the same amount of calories you would if you drank the same amount of wine. This is not the case. When the mixture is boiled or simmered the alcohol will evaporate and so will the calories in that alcohol. The resulting caloric content is comparable to vinegar. However this is not true for sweet wines, which are high in sugar. And cooking wines should be avoided because of their high sodium content.

CONDIMENTS

Condiments can play an important part in adjusting the final taste of the dish to suit the individual palate.

The condiments I use most are vinegar, lemon juice, mustards, hot pepper sauce, and horseradish. Other commercially available condiments—combinations of herbs and spices—can also add greatly to a dish. Some commercial herb mixtures, and some Louisiana mixtures, have a high percentage of salt, so it's best to look for low-sodium products as indicated on the label.

Mustards are good flavorants as are hot sauces. Although I call for Creole mustard in these recipes, you can use any whole-grain mustard as a substitute. Unless the mustard is labeled "sweet" it will be low in calories, and mustards contain no cholesterol. Hot sauces are made with salt but they are used so sparingly that they are not a threat.

Fresh herbs are also another marvelous way to give that extra taste-punch to your dishes. It may turn out to be well worth your while to actually grow yourself a small herb garden, indoors or outdoors. They are very easy to grow and are a delight to have available. As you try different things for yourself, always be sure to know the salt content of what you are adding. Some prepared condiments may be high in salt, sugar, or fat.

Even though I don't call for all the condiments included in the following comparison, I want you to understand the differences in some of the more commonly used preparations such as mayonnaise and ketchup. I have used the measure of one teaspoon for the sake of comparison. This is a random selection, the breakdowns of the prepared products do vary with different manufacturers.

Comparison of Simple Condiments

1 Teaspoon	Sodium	Fat	Calories	Cholesterol
horseradish	4.67 mg	.010 g	1.35	0
Tabasco	34.44 mg	.020 g	.560	0
ketchup	59.3 mg	.023 g	6.04	0
fresh lemon juice	.042 mg	.015 g	1.25	0
mayonnaise	26.0 mg	3.65 g	32.9	2.71 mg
mustard	65.2 mg	.229 g	3.92	0
cider vinegar	.042 mg	0 g	.604	0

ON THE MATTER OF THE EGG

One of the most treacherous foods we can eat is the egg yolk; it is extremely high in cholesterol. It should be used sparingly and carefully. There are egg substitutes on the market to replace the egg; they are made of egg whites and other ingredients and flavorants without the cholesterol.

In this collection I have not used even a single egg yolk. Often I use egg whites to bind stuffings, make meringues, and as deviled eggs. Egg whites are a marvel to the cook while the yolks are a hazard to the cholesterol-conscious, health-conscious individual.

This following comparison will give you the clear picture. Remember it is recommended that we limit our daily cholesterol intake to 300 milligrams. Do you really want to spend close to your whole daily allowance on one egg yolk? Besides, the American Heart Association recommends no more than three yolks a week, including those used in cooking and baking.

Comparison of the Yolk to the White of a Hard-Boiled Egg

1 Egg—Hard Boiled	Fats			Chol	Sod	Cal
	Sat	Mono	Poly			
yolk	1.69 g	2.05 g	.770 g	208 mg	9 mg	63
white	0 g	0 g	0 g	0 mg	50 mg	16

UTENSILS

Do utensils make a difference? Sure they do, but there's no reason that the ones you have always used won't work here. The trick to cooking these recipes is in watching the cooking and stirring regularly. When you prepare your first recipe without the use of oil you will understand exactly what I mean. Don't be frightened by the process. Pans with a nonstick surface are helpful, though I have found that some brands do not wear well.

The only recommendation I make is that you use heavy cookware for the same reason that you should always use heavy cookware—even heat distribution. When I say heavy I don't necessarily mean weight. There are many very fine thick-walled aluminum pots on the market today, some anodized, that cook as well as the traditional heavy copper pots and are a fraction of the cost.

The real matter of importance is to pay attention as you cook, and stir the ingredients often.

INTERPRETING THE RECIPE ANALYSES

The analysis of each recipe provides a breakdown of the measures of the elements listed. When these measurements are compared to the RDA, or Recommended Dietary Allowance, of the same elements, you can understand what that particular recipe is doing for you, what these foods bring to your body, and how a serving portion of the recipe compares to the total RDA.

As a general example for all body weights and types I have used the median weight and height of the American female—120 pounds, 5'4" height—with a lightly active lifestyle, in three progressive ages of 25, 50 and 75 years. I have used the same three ages for the median American male—154 pounds, 5'10" height— who also have a lightly active lifestyle. These analyses give you the RDAs and allow you to make your own comparisons from one age group to the next. It is most important to remember that this is an average and will not apply precisely to every individual. Consult your physician for a dietitian or nutritionist who can help you determine your precise RDA.

With a review of the following charts and the analysis of each recipe you can determine how these recipes can fit into your own dietary plans and goals.

Recommended Dietary Allowances for Women

Age: 25 yrs.

Calories	1946*	Cobalamin-B12	3.00 mcg
Protein	43.6 g	Folacin	400 mcg
Carbohydrates	282 g**	Pantothenic	7.00 mg*
Dietary Fiber	38.9 g#	Vitamin C	60.0 mg
Fat-Total	64.8 g**	Vitamin E	10.0 mg
Fat-Saturated	21.6 g**	Calcium	800 mg
Fat-Mono	21.6 g**	Copper	2.50 mg*
Fat-Poly	21.6 g**	Iron	10.0 mg
Cholesterol	300 mg**	Potassium	3750 mg*
Vitamin A	800 re	Magnesium	350 mg
Thiamin-B1	1.00 mg	Phosphorus	800 mg
Riboflavin-B2	1.20 mg	Selenium	125 mcg*
Niacin-B3	13.0 mg	Sodium	2200 mg*
Pyridoxine-B6	2.00 mg	Zinc	15.0 mg

Age: 50 yrs.

Calories	1778*	Cobalamin-B12	3.00 mcg
Protein	43.6 g	Folacin	400 mcg
Carbohydrates	258 g**	Pantothenic	7.00 mg*
Dietary Fiber	35.6 g#	Vitamin C	60.0 mg
Fat-Total	59.4 g**	Vitamin E	10.0 mg
Fat-Saturated	19.8 g**	Calcium	800 mg
Fat-Mono	19.8 g**	Copper	2.50 mg*
Fat-Poly	19.8 g**	Iron	10.0 mg
Cholesterol	300 mg**	Potassium	3750 mg*
Vitamin A	800 re	Magnesium	350 mg
Thiamin-B1	1.00 mg	Phosphorus	800 mg
Riboflavin-B2	1.20 mg	Selenium	125 mcg*
Niacin-B3	13.0 mg	Sodium	2200 mg*
Pyridoxine-B6	2.00 mg	Zinc	15.0 mg

Age: 75 yrs.

Calories	1611*	Cobalamin-B12	3.00 mcg
Protein	43.6 g	Folacin	400 mcg
Carbohydrates	234 g**	Pantothenic	7.00 mg*
Dietary Fiber	32.2 g#	Vitamin C	60.0 mg
Fat-Total	53.7 g**	Vitamin E	10.0 mg
Fat-Saturated	17.9 g**	Calcium	800 mg
Fat-Mono	17.9 g**	Copper	2.50 mg*
Fat-Poly	17.9 g**	Iron	10.0 mg
Cholesterol	300 mg**	Potassium	3750 mg*
Vitamin A	800 re	Magnesium	350 mg
Thiamin-B1	1.00 mg	Phosphorus	800 mg
Riboflavin-B2	1.20 mg	Selenium	125 mcg*
Niacin-B3	13.0 mg	Sodium	2200 mg*
Pyridoxine-B6	2.00 mg	Zinc	15.0 mg

*Suggested values; within recommended ranges
**Dietary goals
#Fiber = 2 gram/100 kcal

Recommended Dietary Allowances for Men

Age: 25 yrs.

Calories	2502*	Cobalamin-B12	3.00 mcg
Protein	56.0 g	Folacin	400 mcg
Carbohydrates	363 g**	Pantothenic	7.00 mg*
Dietary Fiber	50.0 g#	Vitamin C	60.0 mg
Fat-Total	83.4 g**	Vitamin E	10.0 mg
Fat-Saturated	27.8 g**	Calcium	800 mg
Fat-Mono	27.8 g**	Copper	2.50 mg*
Fat-Poly	27.8 g**	Iron	10.0 mg
Cholesterol	300 mg**	Potassium	3750 mg*
Vitamin A	1000 re	Magnesium	350 mg
Thiamin-B1	1.25 mg	Phosphorus	800 mg
Riboflavin-B2	1.50 mg	Selenium	125 mcg*
Niacin-B3	16.5 mg	Sodium	2200 mg*
Pyridoxine-B6	2.20 mg	Zinc	15.0 mg

Age: 50 yrs.

Calories	2261*	Cobalamin-B12	3.00 mcg
Protein	56.0 g	Folacin	400 mcg
Carbohydrates	328 g**	Pantothenic	7.00 mg*
Dietary Fiber	45.2 g#	Vitamin C	60.0 mg
Fat-Total	75.4 g**	Vitamin E	10.0 mg
Fat-Saturated	25.1 g**	Calcium	800 mg
Fat-Mono	25.1 g**	Copper	2.50 mg*
Fat-Poly	25.1 g**	Iron	10.0 mg
Cholesterol	300 mg**	Potassium	3750 mg*
Vitamin A	1000 re	Magnesium	350 mg
Thiamin-B1	1.13 mg	Phosphorus	800 mg
Riboflavin-B2	1.36 mg	Selenium	125 mcg*
Niacin-B3	14.9 mg	Sodium	2200 mg*
Pyridoxine-B6	2.20 mg	Zinc	15.0 mg

Age: 75 yrs.

Calories	2019*	Cobalamin-B12	3.00 mcg
Protein	56.0 g	Folacin	400 mcg
Carbohydrates	293 g**	Pantothenic	7.00 mg*
Dietary Fiber	40.4 g#	Vitamin C	60.0 mg
Fat-Total	63.7 g**	Vitamin E	10.0 mg
Fat-Saturated	22.4 g**	Calcium	800 mg
Fat-Mono	22.4 g**	Copper	2.50 mg*
Fat-Poly	22.4 g**	Iron	10.0 mg
Cholesterol	300 mg**	Potassium	3750 mg*
Vitamin A	1000 re	Magnesium	350 mg
Thiamin-B1	1.01 mg	Phosphorus	800 mg
Riboflavin-B2	1.21 mg	Selenium	125 mcg*
Niacin-B3	13.3 mg	Sodium	2200 mg*
Pyridoxine-B6	2.20 mg	Zinc	15.0 mg

*Suggested values; within recommended ranges
**Dietary goals
#Fiber = 2 gram/100 kcal

COCKTAILS

Brandy Skim-Milk Punch

Mint Julep

Gin Fizz

Brandy Skim-Milk Punch *Makes 1 cocktail*

INGREDIENTS:

1/2 cup cold skim milk
1/3 cup crushed ice
1 tablespoon brandy
1/4 teaspoon vanilla extract

Artificial sweetener equivalent
of 1 teaspoon sugar
Freshly grated nutmeg

PREPARATION:

Put the skim milk, crushed ice, brandy, vanilla, and sweetener in a cocktail shaker.

Shake briefly and pour into a highball glass.

Sprinkle with freshly grated nutmeg and enjoy.

NOTES:

Enjoy your eating and drinking as much as you should so long as it is properly prepared and your alcohol intake is moderate and allowed.

VARIATION:

Bourbon in place of the brandy makes an excellent Milk Punch.

BRANDY SKIM-MILK PUNCH *One serving*

Calories	78.4	Calcium	154 mg
Protein	4.18 g	Iron	0.063 mg
Carbohydrates	11.3 g	Sodium	65.8 mg
Dietary Fiber	0.006 g		
Fat-Total	0.273 g		
Fat-Saturated	0.181 g		
Fat-Mono	0.063 g		
Fat-Poly	0.008 g		
Cholesterol	2.00 mg		

Calories from protein:	21%	Poly/Sat	=	0.0:1
Calories from carbohydrates:	58%	Sod/Pot	=	0.3:1
Calories from fats:	3%	Ca/Phos	=	1.2:1
Other calories (i.e. alcohol):	18%	CSI	=	0.3

Mint Julep

Makes 1 cocktail

INGREDIENTS:

6 *fresh mint leaves*　　　　　　　1 *ounce bourbon (2 tablespoons)*
Artificial sweetener equivalent of　*Crushed ice*
　2 *teaspoons sugar*　　　　　　1 *fresh mint sprig*

PREPARATION:

Put the mint leaves and the sweetener in the bottom of a heavy glass. Crush the leaves with a wooden spoon.

Add the bourbon and ice and stir to blend the ingredients.

Garnish the Mint Julep cocktail with the mint sprig and enjoy.

NOTE:

You should stir the ice around in the glass for a while so frost will form on the outside of the glass.

VARIATIONS:

Vodka, rum and gin all make excellent Juleps.

MINT JULEP　　　　　　　　　　　　　　　　　　　　　*One serving*

Calories	63.6	Calcium	4.42 mg
Protein	0.016 g	Iron	0.018 mg
Carbohydrates	0.039 g	Sodium	5.32 mg
Dietary Fiber	0.020 g		
Fat-Total	0.001 g		
Fat-Saturated	0.000 g		
Fat-Mono	0.000 g		
Fat-Poly	0.000 g		
Cholesterol	0 mg		

Calories from protein:	0%	Poly/Sat	=	1.2:1
Calories from carbohydrates:	0%	Sod/Pot	=	1.3:1
Calories from fats:	0%	Ca/Phos	=	10.6:1
Other calories (i.e. alcohol):	100%	CSI	=	0.0

Gin Fizz

Makes 1 cocktail

INGREDIENTS:

1 egg white
½ cup crushed ice
¼ cup skim milk
½ ounce gin (1 tablespoon)
2 teaspoons fresh lemon juice

4 drops orange-flower water
Artificial sweetener equivalent
of 2 teaspoons sugar
¼ cup cold soda water

PREPARATION:

Pour all the ingredients except the soda water into a cocktail shaker and shake vigorously for 2 minutes.

Pour into a cocktail glass, add the soda water, and serve.

NOTE:

The shaking is tiresome but it helps the egg whites to become frothy.

VARIATION:

Other liquors can be used in place of the gin to make your own brand of fizz.

GIN FIZZ

One serving

Calories	72.1		Calcium	83.1 mg
Protein	5.48 g		Iron	0.068 mg
Carbohydrates	4.28 g		Sodium	94.1 mg
Dietary Fiber	0.036 g			
Fat-Total	0.140 g			
Fat-Saturated	0.076 g			
Fat-Mono	0.030 g			
Fat-Poly	0.013 g			
Cholesterol	1.00 mg			

Calories from protein:	30%		Poly/Sat	=	0.2:1
Calories from carbohydrates:	24%		Sod/Pot	=	0.6:1
Calories from fats:	2%		Ca/Phos	=	1.3:1
Other calories (i.e. alcohol):	44%		CSI	=	0.1

APPETIZERS

Shrimp Rémoulade

Crayfish Cardinal

Deviled Eggs

Stuffed Mushrooms

Italian Shrimp

Baked Oyster and
  Crabmeat Casserole

Crabmeat Ravigote

Shrimp Rémoulade

Serves 2

INGREDIENTS FOR RÉMOULADE SAUCE:

1/4 cup Creole mustard
1 tablespoon minced green
onion
1 tablespoon minced fresh
parsley

1 tablespoon minced celery
1 tablespoon fresh lemon juice
1 1/2 teaspoons paprika
Scant 1/4 teaspoon cayenne

INGREDIENTS TO BOIL SHRIMP:

2 cups water
1/4 teaspoon cayenne
4 bay leaves

8 medium-size shrimp, shell on
(about 4 ounces)

2 leaves lettuce, washed

PREPARATION:

In a bowl combine all the sauce ingredients, cover, and refrigerate while preparing the shrimp.

In a saucepan bring the water, cayenne, and bay leaves to a boil.

Let the water boil for 2 minutes for the cayenne and bay leaves to release their flavors, then add the shrimp.

Turn off the heat immediately and let the shrimp steep in the water as it cools. This only takes about 2 minutes; they will become a lovely pink color as they become done.

Remove the shrimp from the liquid and let them cool.

When they are cool enough to handle, peel the shrimp and discard the shells.

Fold the shrimp into the Rémoulade Sauce, being sure they are well coated; cover tightly, and refrigerate several hours.

To Serve:

Place the lettuce leaves on chilled salad plates and spoon the Shrimp Rémoulade onto them.

Note:

Some cooks prefer to let the assembled Shrimp Rémoulade chill overnight so the shrimp will acquire more of the sauce taste. I feel this also toughens the shrimp so I prefer to chill it only long enough to get the shrimp good and cold.

Variations:

This sauce is quite spicy and can hold its own with no further garnish, though many people like to serve lemon quarters with the Shrimp Rémoulade.

Chopped hard-boiled egg white could be sprinkled over the Shrimp Rémoulade to add both color and texture contrast.

SHRIMP RÉMOULADE   *One serving*

Calories	92.9	Calcium	222 mg
Protein	15.3 g	Iron	2.35 mg
Carbohydrates	3.80 g	Sodium	499 mg
Dietary Fiber	0.714 g		
Fat-Total	2.38 g		
Fat-Saturated	0.182 g		
Fat-Mono	1.42 g		
Fat-Poly	0.534 g		
Cholesterol	83.3 mg		

Calories from protein:	63%	Poly/Sat	=	2.9:1
Calories from carbohydrates:	16%	Sod/Pot	=	1.4:1
Calories from fats:	22%	Ca/Phos	=	1.2:1
		CSI	=	4.4

SUGGESTED MENU: *One serving*

Shrimp Rémoulade
Okra, Chicken, and Crab Gumbo
Tomato and Green Onion Citronette
Ambrosia

Calories	505		Calcium	396 mg
Protein	45.3 g		Iron	7.08 mg
Carbohydrates	65.9 g		Sodium	662 mg
Dietary Fiber	8.39 g			
Fat-Total	6.42 g			
Fat-Saturated	1.12 g			
Fat-Mono	2.55 g			
Fat-Poly	1.65 g			
Cholesterol	159 mg			

Calories from protein:	36%	Poly/Sat	=	1.5:1
Calories from carbohydrates:	52%	Sod/Pot	=	0.5:1
Calories from fats:	11%	Ca/Phos	=	0.8:1
		CSI	=	9.1

Crayfish Cardinal

Serves 2

INGREDIENTS:

½ cup chopped green onion
1 tablespoon dry blond "roux"
¼ cup white wine
¼ cup skim milk
2 teaspoons tomato paste

⅛ teaspoon freshly ground
   black pepper
Pinch of cayenne
4 ounces cooked washed crayfish
   tails

PREPARATION:

Cook the green onion in a heavy saucepan over medium heat for 2 minutes while stirring regularly.

Blend the "roux" with the wine, then stir into the milk. Add this mixture to the saucepan with the green onion.

Add the tomato paste, pepper, and cayenne.

Simmer for 2 minutes.

Add the crayfish tails and simmer for 2 minutes more, or until hot.

Serve in heated ramekins.

NOTE:

Keep stirring the onions while you are cooking them so nothing sticks to the pan and burns.

VARIATION:

Crab and shrimp substituted for the crayfish both make excellent versions of this dish.

CRAYFISH CARDINAL   *One serving*

Calories	82.6	Calcium	102 mg
Protein	11.6 g	Iron	1.93 mg
Carbohydrates	9.73 g	Sodium	134 mg
Dietary Fiber	1.17 g		
Fat-Total	1.07 g		
Fat-Saturated	0.245 g		
Fat-Mono	0.274 g		
Fat-Poly	0.271 g		
Cholesterol	31.7 mg		

Calories from protein:	49%	Poly/Sat	=	1.1:1
Calories from carbohydrates:	41%	Sod/Pot	=	0.4:1
Calories from fats:	10%	Ca/Phos	=	0.6:1
		CSI	=	1.8

SUGGESTED MENU: *One serving*

Crayfish Cardinal
Chicken Roasted with Garlic Cloves
Steamed Spinach with Onion
Bananas Foster

Calories	507	Calcium	460 mg
Protein	49.0 g	Iron	7.63 mg
Carbohydrates	52.2 g	Sodium	372 mg
Dietary Fiber	9.89 g		
Fat-Total	7.04 g		
Fat-Saturated	2.25 g		
Fat-Mono	1.95 g		
Fat-Poly	1.53 g		
Cholesterol	108 mg		

Calories from protein:	39%	Poly/Sat	=	0.7:1
Calories from carbohydrates:	41%	Sod/Pot	=	0.2:1
Calories from fats:	13%	Ca/Phos	=	0.8:1
Other calories (i.e. alcohol):	8%	CSI	=	7.7

Deviled Eggs

Serves 2

INGREDIENTS:

6 eggs
1 tablespoon minced sweet pickle
1 tablespoon minced green onion
1 tablespoon minced celery

1 tablespoon Creole mustard
1 teaspoon minced fresh parsley
1/2 teaspoon fresh lemon juice

PREPARATION:

Simmer the eggs for 12 minutes. Remove them from the water, let them cool, and peel them.

Cut the eggs in half lengthwise and discard the yolks.

Chop the whites of 4 halves.

Blend the chopped whites with the pickle, green onion, celery, mustard, parsley, and lemon juice.

Stuff the mixture 1 teaspoon at a time into the remaining 8 egg-white halves.

NOTE:

If you refrigerate the Deviled Eggs before you serve them, be sure they are tightly covered with wrap so the air will not discolor them.

VARIATION:

Paprika sprinkled over the eggs adds a nice touch of color.

DEVILED EGGS   *One serving*

Calories	75.1		Calcium	26.2 mg
Protein	10.6 g		Iron	0.616 mg
Carbohydrates	7.48 g		Sodium	353 mg
Dietary Fiber	0.501 g			
Fat-Total	0.404 g			
Fat-Saturated	0.017 g			
Fat-Mono	0.316 g			
Fat-Poly	0.029 g			
Cholesterol	0 mg			

Calories from protein:	56%	Poly/Sat	=	1.7:1
Calories from carbohydrates:	39%	Sod/Pot	=	1.7:1
Calories from fats:	5%	Ca/Phos	=	1.2:1
		CSI	=	0.0

SUGGESTED MENU: *One serving*

Deviled Eggs
Shrimp Etouffée
Creole Tomatoes with Basil, Garlic, and Green Onion Dressing
Cherries Jubilee

Calories	590		Calcium	290 mg
Protein	37.2 g		Iron	7.27 mg
Carbohydrates	99.0 g		Sodium	558 mg
Dietary Fiber	7.00 g			
Fat-Total	3.74 g			
Fat-Saturated	0.946 g			
Fat-Mono	1.01 g			
Fat-Poly	1.02 g			
Cholesterol	115 mg			

Calories from protein:	26%	Poly/Sat	=	1.1:1
Calories from carbohydrates:	68%	Sod/Pot	=	0.4:1
Calories from fats:	6%	Ca/Phos	=	0.7:1
		CSI	=	6.7

Stuffed Mushrooms

Serves 2

INGREDIENTS:

2 ounces ground white turkey
   meat
¼ cup chopped onion
¼ cup chopped green onion
¼ cup water
2 tablespoons dry sherry
2 teaspoons chopped fresh
   parsley
¼ teaspoon thyme
1 tablespoon dry blond "roux"
⅛ teaspoon freshly ground

black pepper
2 tablespoons bread crumbs
1 egg white
2 ounces crabmeat, cartilage
   removed
4 large stuffing mushrooms,
   stems removed
1 tablespoon grated Parmesan
   cheese
1 tablespoon bread crumbs

PREPARATION:

Put the turkey meat, the onion, and green onion in a saucepan and cook over medium heat while stirring regularly for 5 minutes, or until they begin to brown slightly.

Pour the water and Sherry into the saucepan and add the parsley and thyme.

Whisk a few tablespoons of the liquid into the "roux," then return the mixture to the pan. Season with the pepper, bring to a simmer, and continue simmering for 10 minutes.

Preheat the oven to 400 degrees.

Remove the stuffing mixture from the heat, and let cool slightly.

Fold in the 2 tablespoons bread crumbs, the egg white, and the crabmeat.

Spoon the stuffing into the mushroom caps.

Blend the cheese with the tablespoon bread crumbs and sprinkle over the tops of the stuffed mushrooms.

Arrange the mushrooms in a baking pan and bake for 5 to 7 minutes, or until the topping on the Stuffed Mushrooms is browned and the stuffing is bubbling hot.

NOTE:

This dish also makes an excellent entree for 1.

VARIATION:

The crabmeat could be replaced with chopped cooked shrimp.

STUFFED MUSHROOMS

One serving

Calories	177	Calcium	85.3 mg
Protein	18.1 g	Iron	2.19 mg
Carbohydrates	14.5 g	Sodium	434 mg
Dietary Fiber	2.11 g		
Fat-Total	3.04 g		
Fat-Saturated	1.06 g		
Fat-Mono	0.719 g		
Fat-Poly	0.759 g		
Cholesterol	50.4 mg		

Calories from protein:	41%	Poly/Sat	=	0.7:1
Calories from carbohydrates:	33%	Sod/Pot	=	1.2:1
Calories from fats:	16%	Ca/Phos	=	0.4:1
Other calories (i.e. alcohol):	11%	CSI	=	3.6

SUGGESTED MENU:

One serving

Stuffed Mushrooms
Spicy Roasted Chicken Breasts
Country Rice
Green Salad with Creamy Creole Dressing
Hot Apple Soufflé

Calories	556	Calcium	206 mg
Protein	52.7 g	Iron	5.18 mg
Carbohydrates	64.0 g	Sodium	676 mg
Dietary Fiber	6.87 g		
Fat-Total	7.94 g		
Fat-Saturated	2.30 g		
Fat-Mono	2.42 g		
Fat-Poly	1.83 g		
Cholesterol	122 mg		

Calories from protein:	39%	Poly/Sat	=	0.8:1
Calories from carbohydrates:	48%	Sod/Pot	=	0.6:1
Calories from fats:	13%	Ca/Phos	=	0.4:1
		CSI	=	8.4

Italian Shrimp

Serves 2

INGREDIENTS:

1 cup chopped onion
1/2 cup white wine
4 cloves garlic, minced
1/2 teaspoon thyme
1/2 teaspoon rosemary

1/2 teaspoon oregano
1/4 teaspoon freshly ground
   black pepper
6 ounces peeled uncooked
   shrimp

PREPARATION:

In a saucepan combine all the ingredients except the shrimp and simmer for 2 minutes.

Add the shrimp, cover the pan, and continue simmering for 2 minutes longer. Spoon the shrimp and sauce into small bowls.

NOTE:

Don't overcook the shrimp! You want them to have a nice texture and a snap to the bite.

VARIATION:

This dish can be cooked with shell-on shrimp which you peel at the table as you eat. Remember the finger bowls!

ITALIAN SHRIMP

One serving

Calories	157		Calcium	110 mg
Protein	17.2 g		Iron	2.89 mg
Carbohydrates	10.8 g		Sodium	143 mg
Dietary Fiber	1.49 g			
Fat-Total	1.54 g			
Fat-Saturated	0.309 g			
Fat-Mono	0.251 g			
Fat-Poly	0.521 g			
Cholesterol	113 mg			

Calories from protein:	44%	Poly/Sat	=	1.7:1
Calories from carbohydrates:	28%	Sod/Pot	=	0.4:1
Calories from fats:	9%	Ca/Phos	=	0.5:1
Other calories (i.e. alcohol):	20%	CSI	=	6.0

SUGGESTED MENU:

One serving

Italian Shrimp
Chicken with Potatoes and Petits Pois
Green Salad with Creamy Creole Dressing
Strawberry Bavarian Cream

Calories	562		Calcium	371 mg
Protein	59.4 g		Iron	6.54 mg
Carbohydrates	58.7 g		Sodium	393 mg
Dietary Fiber	10.3 g			
Fat-Total	6.57 g			
Fat-Saturated	1.60 g			
Fat-Mono	1.98 g			
Fat-Poly	1.68 g			
Cholesterol	186 mg			

Calories from protein:	45%	Poly/Sat	=	1.0:1
Calories from carbohydrates:	44%	Sod/Pot	=	0.2:1
Calories from fats:	11%	Ca/Phos	=	0.5:1
		CSI	=	10.9

Baked Oyster and Crabmeat Casserole

Serves 2

INGREDIENTS:

1/4 cup white wine
1/8 teaspoon white pepper
6 shucked oysters
1 tablespoon flour
1/4 cup chopped onion
1/4 cup chopped green onion

1 teaspoon chopped fresh parsley
2 ounces crabmeat, cartilage removed
2 teaspoons grated Parmesan cheese
2 teaspoons bread crumbs

PREPARATION:

Pour the wine into a saucepan and add the pepper. Bring to a boil and reduce to a simmer.

Poach the oysters in the liquid for 1 minute. Remove the oysters and set them aside. Reserve the poaching liquor.

Put the flour in a mixing bowl and whisk in the hot poaching liquor a little at a time, until smooth and well blended. Pour the mixture back into the saucepan and bring to a simmer. Simmer for 5 minutes.

Add the onion, green onion, and parsley. Return to a simmer, and continue cooking for 15 minutes.

Preheat the oven to 500 degrees.

Remove sauce from the heat and stir in the reserved oysters and the crabmeat.

Spoon the mixture into small ovenproof casseroles or soufflé dishes.

Combine the cheese and bread crumbs and sprinkle over the top.

Bake for 5 minutes, or until the top is browned and the sauce is bubbling hot.

NOTE:

If the sauce becomes too dry, add a tablespoon of water when adding the oysters and crabmeat.

Variations:

Use shrimp instead of either oysters or crabmeat. This recipe is also done successfully with just oysters, crabmeat, or shrimp.

BAKED OYSTER AND CRABMEAT CASSEROLE   *One serving*

Calories	122		Calcium	113 mg
Protein	12.5 g		Iron	4.61 mg
Carbohydrates	9.07 g		Sodium	107 mg
Dietary Fiber	0.866 g			
Fat-Total	2.03 g			
Fat-Saturated	0.774 g			
Fat-Mono	0.410 g			
Fat-Poly	0.565 g			
Cholesterol	51.7 mg			

Calories from protein:	41%	Poly/Sat	=	0.7:1
Calories from carbohydrates:	30%	Sod/Pot	=	0.4:1
Calories from fats:	15%	Ca/Phos	=	0.6:1
Other calories (i.e. alcohol):	14%	CSI	=	3.4

SUGGESTED MENU: *One serving*

Baked Oyster and Crabmeat Casserole
Braised Pork Tenderloin
Cauliflower and Dill Pickle Salad
Pear Compote with Brandied Vanilla Cream

Calories	500		Calcium	255 mg
Protein	44.7 g		Iron	7.67 mg
Carbohydrates	51.0 g		Sodium	386 mg
Dietary Fiber	9.26 g			
Fat-Total	12.1 g			
Fat-Saturated	3.99 g			
Fat-Mono	4.64 g			
Fat-Poly	1.97 g			
Cholesterol	136 mg			

Calories from protein:	36%	Poly/Sat	=	0.5:1
Calories from carbohydrates:	42%	Sod/Pot	=	0.3:1
Calories from fats:	22%	Ca/Phos	=	0.5:1
		CSI	=	10.8

Crabmeat Ravigote

Serves 2

INGREDIENTS:

1 tablespoon minced green bell
   pepper
1 tablespoon minced green onion
1 tablespoon minced pimiento
1 teaspoon fresh lemon juice

¼ teaspoon freshly ground
   black pepper
Pinch cayenne
6 ounces lump crabmeat,
   cartilage removed

PREPARATION:

Combine all the vegetables and seasonings, then gently fold in the crabmeat, being careful not to break it up too much.

NOTE:

This is a delightful summer salad or appetizer.

VARIATIONS:

Artificial crabmeat can be used, as can small shrimp or crayfish tails boiled without salt.

CRABMEAT RAVIGOTE

One serving

Calories	78.4	Calcium	54.2 mg
Protein	17.9 g	Iron	0.972 mg
Carbohydrates	2.01 g	Sodium	48.4 mg
Dietary Fiber	0.621 g		
Fat-Total	1.21 g		
Fat-Saturated	0.231 g		
Fat-Mono	0.298 g		
Fat-Poly	0.524 g		
Cholesterol	65.7 mg		

Calories from protein:	79%	Poly/Sat	=	2.3:1
Calories from carbohydrates:	9%	Sod/Pot	=	0.1:1
Calories from fats:	12%	Ca/Phos	=	0.3:1
		CSI	=	3.5

SUGGESTED MENU:

One serving

Crabmeat Ravigote
Jambalaya
Red and White Bean Salad
Turnips and Greens
Raisin Oat-Bran Cookies

Calories	660	Calcium	292 mg
Protein	50.6 g	Iron	9.49 mg
Carbohydrates	106 g	Sodium	316 mg
Dietary Fiber	14.4 g		
Fat-Total	6.11 g		
Fat-Saturated	1.32 g		
Fat-Mono	1.71 g		
Fat-Poly	2.25 g		
Cholesterol	91.5 mg		

Calories from protein:	30%	Poly/Sat	=	1.7:1
Calories from carbohydrates:	62%	Sod/Pot	=	0.2:1
Calories from fats:	8%	Ca/Phos	=	0.4:1
		CSI	=	5.9

SOUPS, BISQUES, AND GUMBO

Crab and Corn Bisque

Oyster and Artichoke Soup

Creole Chicken Soup

Red Bean Soup

Tomato Bisque

Creole Fish Stew

Okra, Chicken, and Crab Gumbo
   with Rice

Crab and Corn Bisque

Serves 2

INGREDIENTS:

1/2 cup chopped onion
1 cup fresh corn kernels
2 cups water or chicken stock
  (see recipe page 30)
2 tablespoons dry blond "roux"
1/4 teaspoon thyme

Freshly ground black pepper to
  taste
4 ounces lump crabmeat,
  cartilage removed
2 teaspoons chopped fresh
  parsley

PREPARATION:

In a saucepan cook the onion, stirring regularly over medium heat, until it just begins to color, about 2 minutes.

Add the corn and continue cooking for 2 minutes, or until the kernels are cooked but not mushy.

Whisk a few tablespoons water or stock into the "roux," then stir into the pan.

Add all remaining ingredients except the crabmeat and parsley and bring to a simmer. Simmer for 15 minutes.

Just before serving, fold in the crabmeat and heat only long enough to be sure that all is piping hot.

Stir in the parsley and serve in warmed bowls.

NOTE:

It is important that you use fresh corn in this recipe to get a full-flavored bisque.

VARIATION:

Shrimp or crayfish tails could be used here in place of the crabmeat. If using uncooked shrimp, simmer them in the Bisque for 2 minutes.

CRAB AND CORN BISQUE

One serving

Calories	157	Calcium	55.8 mg
Protein	15.6 g	Iron	1.57 mg
Carbohydrates	23.9 g	Sodium	52.2 mg
Dietary Fiber	5.08 g		
Fat-Total	1.84 g		
Fat-Saturated	0.316 g		
Fat-Mono	0.480 g		
Fat-Poly	0.818 g		
Cholesterol	43.8 mg		

Calories from protein:	36%	Poly/Sat	=	2.6:1
Calories from carbohydrates:	55%	Sod/Pot	=	0.1:1
Calories from fats:	9%	Ca/Phos	=	0.2:1
		CSI	=	2.5

SUGGESTED MENU:

One serving

Crab and Corn Bisque
Jambalaya
Leeks Vinaigrette
Hot Apple Soufflé

Calories	525	Calcium	131 mg
Protein	32.3 g	Iron	5.38 mg
Carbohydrates	94.6 g	Sodium	152 mg
Dietary Fiber	13.1 g		
Fat-Total	5.03 g		
Fat-Saturated	1.08 g		
Fat-Mono	1.37 g		
Fat-Poly	1.70 g		
Cholesterol	69.1 mg		

Calories from protein:	23%	Poly/Sat	=	1.6:1
Calories from carbohydrates:	68%	Sod/Pot	=	0.1:1
Calories from fats:	8%	Ca/Phos	=	0.3:1
		CSI	=	4.5

Oyster and Artichoke Soup   *Serves 4*

INGREDIENTS:

2 large artichokes
1 1/2 quarts water, or to cover
1/2 cup chopped onion
1/2 cup chopped green onion
1/4 cup chopped celery
1 clove garlic, minced
1 tablespoon minced fresh
   parsley

1/4 teaspoon thyme
1 bay leaf
Freshly ground black pepper to
   taste
8-ounce container fresh oysters
   in their liquor

PREPARATION:

Put the artichokes into a saucepan and add 1 1/2 quarts of water, or enough to cover them. Cover and simmer for 40 minutes, or until the leaves are tender and can easily be removed from the choke.

Remove the artichokes from the water and let them cool on a plate. Reserve 1 quart of the cooking liquor.

Meanwhile, make the soup:

Put the onion, green onion, celery, and garlic in a saucepan and cook them over medium heat, stirring constantly, until the vegetables just begin to acquire a light brownish color.

Blend in the reserved artichoke cooking liquor.

Add all remaining ingredients except the artichokes and oysters and simmer for 10 minutes.

When the artichokes are cool enough to handle, remove the leaves from the choke and scrape the meat from the leaves. Save the meat and the heart. Discard the scraped leaves and the center of the choke. Slice the hearts into strips about 1/3 inch wide.

Two or 3 minutes before serving, blend the artichoke meat into the soup. Add the heart strips and the oysters and their liquor and cook only long enough for the edges of the oysters to begin to curl.

Serve in warm bowls, being sure that each person has a proper share of the oysters and artichoke strips.

NOTE:

You may want your oysters cooked longer but don't let overcooking toughen them.

VARIATIONS:

One or 2 teaspoons of fresh lemon juice stirred in just before serving adds a nice touch.

This soup can be made with crabmeat or shrimp in place of the oysters.

If you want a thicker soup, blend 2 tablespoons dry blond ''roux'' into some of the liquid, then blend that into the soup 5 minutes or so before you add the oysters.

OYSTER AND ARTICHOKE SOUP   *One serving*

Calories	77.2		Calcium	101 mg
Protein	6.69 g		Iron	5.03 mg
Carbohydrates	10.9 g		Sodium	95.9 mg
Dietary Fiber	2.82 g			
Fat-Total	1.14 g			
Fat-Saturated	0.372 g			
Fat-Mono	0.133 g			
Fat-Poly	0.410 g			
Cholesterol	28.3 mg			

Calories from protein:	33%	Poly/Sat	=	1.1:1
Calories from carbohydrates:	54%	Sod/Pot	=	0.3:1
Calories from fats:	13%	Ca/Phos	=	0.8:1
		CSI	=	1.8

SUGGESTED MENU: *One serving*

Oyster and Artichoke Soup
Iceberg Lettuce with Onion and Parmesan Dressing
Baked Breaded Chicken
Rice Pudding

Calories	623		Calcium	360 mg
Protein	66.2 g		Iron	9.32 mg
Carbohydrates	53.0 g		Sodium	482 mg
Dietary Fiber	5.48 g			
Fat-Total	15.3 g			
Fat-Saturated	4.68 g			
Fat-Mono	5.04 g			
Fat-Poly	3.47 g			
Cholesterol	180 mg			

Calories from protein:	43%	Poly/Sat	=	0.7:1
Calories from carbohydrates:	34%	Sod/Pot	=	0.4:1
Calories from fats:	22%	Ca/Phos	=	0.5:1
		CSI	=	13.7

Creole Chicken Soup

Serves 2

INGREDIENTS:

½ cup chopped onion
¼ cup chopped celery
1 clove garlic, minced
3 cups water or chicken stock
(see recipe page 30)
1 cup chopped tomato

6 ounces lean chicken meat,
cooked or raw
¼ teaspoon thyme
¼ teaspoon marjoram
2 bay leaves
Freshly ground black pepper to
taste

PREPARATION:

Cook the onion, celery, and garlic over high heat for 2 minutes, stirring constantly until they begin to color.

Add all remaining ingredients.

Cover the pot and simmer gently for 30 minutes.

TO SERVE:

Ladle into warm soup bowls and serve piping hot.

NOTES:

This is a very simple and basic preparation, an excellent way to create a thrifty meal or first course from small amounts of leftover poultry. It can of course be made from scratch by simply using uncooked poultry meat. I prefer to cut leftover bird parts into pieces with the bone still in and add them to the pot. However, this does require the sometimes inelegant exercise of dealing with the bones as you eat.

VARIATIONS:

Any poultry can be used, from chicken or turkey to Cornish hen or squab, and from wild duck, or *poule d'eau,* to snipe, quail, or pheasant. The meat of the bird can be cooked or raw. A tablespoon of blond "roux" mixed with some of the stock and stirred into the soup a few minutes before the simmering is complete adds a silky texture to the dish.

CREOLE CHICKEN SOUP

One serving

Calories	198	Calcium	49.3 mg
Protein	26.1 g	Iron	2.00 mg
Carbohydrates	8.03 g	Sodium	105 mg
Dietary Fiber	2.38 g		
Fat-Total	6.66 g		
Fat-Saturated	1.79 g		
Fat-Mono	2.31 g		
Fat-Poly	1.57 g		
Cholesterol	75.9 mg		

Calories from protein:	53%	Poly/Sat	=	0.9:1
Calories from carbohydrates:	16%	Sod/Pot	=	0.2:1
Calories from fats:	31%	Ca/Phos	=	0.2:1
		CSI	=	5.6

SUGGESTED MENU:

One serving

Creole Chicken Soup
Fillet Marchand de Vin
Leeks Vinaigrette
Boiled New Potatoes
Strawberry Bavarian Cream

Calories	564	Calcium	225 mg
Protein	62.9 g	Iron	7.79 mg
Carbohydrates	48.7 g	Sodium	228 mg
Dietary Fiber	9.18 g		
Fat-Total	16.1 g		
Fat-Saturated	4.88 g		
Fat-Mono	6.12 g		
Fat-Poly	2.18 g		
Cholesterol	159 mg		

Calories from protein:	43%	Poly/Sat	=	0.4:1
Calories from carbohydrates:	33%	Sod/Pot	=	0.1:1
Calories from fats:	24%	Ca/Phos	=	0.4:1
		CSI	=	12.9

Red Bean Soup

Serves 2

INGREDIENTS:

4 cups water
½ cup dried red kidney beans
¼ cup chopped onion
2 tablespoons chopped green
    bell pepper
2 tablespoons chopped celery
1 clove garlic, minced

1 bay leaf
1 teaspoon cider vinegar
⅛ teaspoon thyme
⅛ teaspoon chili powder
⅛ teaspoon freshly ground
    black pepper

PREPARATION:

Put all ingredients in a pot and bring to a boil. Reduce to a simmer, cover the pot, and continue cooking for 2 hours, stirring occasionally to make sure that nothing sticks to the bottom of the pot.

When the beans are very soft and tender, mash them through a strainer or puree them in a blender or processor along with the liquids from the pot.

Put the soup back on the heat, and simmer for 15 minutes.

Ladle into warm soup bowls.

NOTE:

If the soup is too thick for you—even though this should be a thick soup—thin it with a little water.

VARIATIONS:

Either white or black beans can be used in place of the red in this recipe.
Add a dash of sherry to each bowl before serving the soup.
A squeeze of lemon in the soup at the table adds a marvelous touch of tartness.

RED BEAN SOUP
One serving

Calories	160	Calcium	66.7 mg
Protein	10.5 g	Iron	3.56 mg
Carbohydrates	27.6 g	Sodium	17.5 mg
Dietary Fiber	10.6 g		
Fat-Total	0.644 g		
Fat-Saturated	0.084 g		
Fat-Mono	0.076 g		
Fat-Poly	0.409 g		
Cholesterol	0 mg		

Calories from protein:	26%	Poly/Sat	=	4.9:1
Calories from carbohydrates:	70%	Sod/Pot	=	0.0:1
Calories from fats:	4%	Ca/Phos	=	0.3:1
		CSI	=	0.1

SUGGESTED MENU:
One serving

Red Bean Soup
Creole Tomatoes with Basil, Garlic, and Green-Onion Dressing
Daube Glacé
Pineapple with Port Wine

Calories	606	Calcium	188 mg
Protein	51.1 g	Iron	8.26 mg
Carbohydrates	64.8 g	Sodium	165 mg
Dietary Fiber	17.8 g		
Fat-Total	9.23 g		
Fat-Saturated	3.11 g		
Fat-Mono	3.38 g		
Fat-Poly	1.09 g		
Cholesterol	78.8 mg		

Calories from protein:	34%	Poly/Sat	=	0.4:1
Calories from carbohydrates:	43%	Sod/Pot	=	0.1:1
Calories from fats:	14%	Ca/Phos	=	0.3:1
Other calories (i.e. alcohol):	10%	CSI	=	7.1

Tomato Bisque

Serves 2

INGREDIENTS:

2 cups chopped onion

2 cloves garlic, minced

1 tablespoon dry brown "roux"

2 cups chopped peeled and
  seeded tomato

1 cup water or chicken stock (see
  recipe page 30)

2 tablespoons minced celery

1 tablespoon minced fresh
  parsley

2 bay leaves

¼ teaspoon thyme

Freshly ground black pepper to
  taste

PREPARATION:

Puree the onion and garlic and simmer over medium heat for 10 minutes, stirring frequently, until it begins to darken to a beige color.

Carefully blend in the "roux."

Add remaining ingredients and simmer covered for 20 minutes.

NOTE:

This bisque is going to be very thick. If you prefer it thinner, add more chicken stock or some water.

VARIATION:

Adding a few shrimp or some pieces of leftover fish make this bisque a delightful seafood dish.

TOMATO BISQUE

One serving

Calories	110		Calcium	66.6 mg
Protein	4.20 g		Iron	2.05 mg
Carbohydrates	24.0 g		Sodium	26.2 mg
Dietary Fiber	5.73 g			
Fat-Total	0.888 g			
Fat-Saturated	0.141 g			
Fat-Mono	0.123 g			
Fat-Poly	0.354 g			
Cholesterol	0 mg			

Calories from protein:	14%		Poly/Sat	=	2.5:1
Calories from carbohydrates:	79%		Sod/Pot	=	0.0:1
Calories from fats:	7%		Ca/Phos	=	0.7:1
			CSI	=	0.1

SUGGESTED MENU:

One serving

Tomato Bisque
Red and White Bean Salad
Poached Trout with Lemon and Horseradish
Boiled New Potatoes
Pear Compote with Brandied Vanilla Cream

Calories	618		Calcium	273 mg
Protein	41.1 g		Iron	8.81 mg
Carbohydrates	111 g		Sodium	136 mg
Dietary Fiber	20.2 g			
Fat-Total	6.88 g			
Fat-Saturated	1.28 g			
Fat-Mono	2.29 g			
Fat-Poly	2.11 g			
Cholesterol	54.1 mg			

Calories from protein:	24%		Poly/Sat	=	1.7:1
Calories from carbohydrates:	66%		Sod/Pot	=	0.1:1
Calories from fats:	9%		Ca/Phos	=	0.4:1
			CSI	=	4.0

Creole Fish Stew

Serves 2

INGREDIENTS:

1 ½ cups chopped onion
¼ cup minced celery
1 ½ cups chopped peeled and
   seeded tomato
1 cup water or fish stock (see
   recipe page 89)
4 cloves garlic, minced
1 tablespoon minced fresh
   parsley

2 × 1" strip orange peel, without
   white pith
2 bay leaves
½ teaspoon thyme
⅛ teaspoon cayenne
⅛ teaspoon freshly ground
   black pepper
2 three-ounce fresh fish fillets,
   any fish

PREPARATION:

Cook the onion and celery in a saucepan over high heat, stirring regularly for 3 minutes. It is important that you stand over the cooking at this step because when you are cooking without oil as in this recipe, you must stir often while you are browning the vegetables or they will stick to the bottom of the pan and burn. Use a wooden spoon and scrape the bottom and sides as you stir to keep all pieces free.

Add all remaining ingredients except the fish.

Cover and simmer gently for 20 minutes.

Add the fish and simmer for 5 minutes.

Serve in warm soup bowls.

NOTE:

The vegetables themselves create the thickness of this stew.

VARIATION:

Any seafood, cooked or uncooked, can be added to this stew when you add the fish, be it oysters, crabmeat, shrimp, or scallops. Use your imagination and the availability of local seafood to make this a magnificent dish.

CREOLE FISH STEW
One serving

Calories	168	Calcium	122 mg	
Protein	19.4 g	Iron	2.21 mg	
Carbohydrates	17.7 g	Sodium	82.6 mg	
Dietary Fiber	4.57 g			
Fat-Total	3.68 g			
Fat-Saturated	0.519 g			
Fat-Mono	1.20 g			
Fat-Poly	1.05 g			
Cholesterol	56.1 mg			

Calories from protein:	43%	Poly/Sat	=	2.0:1
Calories from carbohydrates:	39%	Sod/Pot	=	0.1:1
Calories from fats:	18%	Ca/Phos	=	0.4:1
		CSI	=	3.3

SUGGESTED MENU:
One serving

Creole Fish Stew
Mirliton Stuffed with Shrimp
Celery Rémoulade
Orange Flip

Calories	409	Calcium	394 mg	
Protein	38.7 g	Iron	5.87 mg	
Carbohydrates	55.2 g	Sodium	596 mg	
Dietary Fiber	8.97 g			
Fat-Total	6.74 g			
Fat-Saturated	1.03 g			
Fat-Mono	2.26 g			
Fat-Poly	1.59 g			
Cholesterol	133 mg			

Calories from protein:	35%	Poly/Sat	=	1.5:1
Calories from carbohydrates:	51%	Sod/Pot	=	0.3:1
Calories from fats:	14%	Ca/Phos	=	0.6:1
		CSI	=	7.7

Okra, Chicken, and Crab Gumbo with Rice

Serves 2

INGREDIENTS:

1/2 cup chopped onion
1/4 cup chopped green onion
*1/4 cup chopped green bell
  pepper*
1/4 cup chopped celery
1/4 cup sliced okra
1 clove garlic, minced
1 teaspoon minced fresh parsley
*2 tablespoons dry brown
  "roux"*
2 cups water

1 bay leaf
1/4 teaspoon thyme
*1/4 teaspoon freshly ground
  black pepper*
Pinch cayenne
*1 gumbo (blue) crab, cleaned
  and quartered*
*4 ounces cooked lean chicken
  breast cut into 1/2-inch cubes*
*1 cup hot cooked rice (no oil or
  salt added in cooking)*

PREPARATION:

Put the onion, green onion, bell pepper, celery, okra, garlic, and parsley in a saucepan and cook while stirring for 5 minutes.

Stir in the "roux" and slowly blend in the water.

Add the bay leaf, thyme, pepper, and cayenne and bring to a boil, then reduce to a simmer.

Add the crab and the chicken, cover the pot, and continue simmering for 30 minutes.

TO SERVE:

Spoon the Gumbo into warm soup bowls and top with 1/2 cup rice in the center of each. Serve immediately.

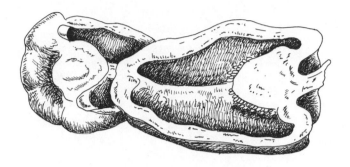

NOTE:

Since the "roux" is made before you start the Gumbo (always be sure that it is), there are no tricks to getting this right. The preparation is as simple as it sounds and as delicious as some far more complicated preparations.

VARIATIONS:

There are as many different preparations of Gumbo as there are cooks. Make your own substitutions and calculate the dietary differences by using the analyses in the Appendix. Remember, though, to keep it light.

OKRA, CHICKEN, AND CRAB GUMBO   *One serving*

Calories	300		Calcium	99.7 mg
Protein	27.6 g		Iron	3.72 mg
Carbohydrates	38.0 g		Sodium	147 mg
Dietary Fiber	2.64 g			
Fat-Total	3.51 g			
Fat-Saturated	0.884 g			
Fat-Mono	1.03 g			
Fat-Poly	0.935 g			
Cholesterol	76.1 mg			

Calories from protein:	38%	Poly/Sat	=	1.1:1
Calories from carbohydrates:	52%	Sod/Pot	=	0.3:1
Calories from fats:	11%	Ca/Phos	=	0.4:1
		CSI	=	4.7

SUGGESTED MENU: *One serving*

Shrimp Rémoulade
Okra, Chicken, and Crab Gumbo
Tomato and Green-Onion Citronette
Ambrosia

Calories	505		Calcium	396 mg
Protein	45.3 g		Iron	7.08 mg
Carbohydrates	65.9 g		Sodium	662 mg
Dietary Fiber	8.39 g			
Fat-Total	6.42 g			
Fat-Saturated	1.12 g			
Fat-Mono	2.55 g			
Fat-Poly	1.65 g			
Cholesterol	159 mg			

Calories from protein:	36%	Poly/Sat	=	1.5:1
Calories from carbohydrates:	52%	Sod/Pot	=	0.5:1
Calories from fats:	11%	Ca/Phos	=	0.8:1
		CSI	=	9.1

FISH AND SEAFOOD

Red Snapper Courtbouillon

Poached Trout with Lemon and Horseradish

Baked Breaded Bluefish
    with Mock Tartar Sauce

Matelote of Sheepshead

Shrimp Etouffée

Fillet of Trout
    with White Wine and Oyster Sauce

Grouper Fillets Amandine

Catfish Cakes

Stuffed Flounder Fillets with White Wine Sauce

Shrimp Creole

Red Snapper Courtbouillon

Serves 2

INGREDIENTS:

1 cup chopped onion
1/2 cup chopped green onion
2 cups chopped, seeded tomato
1/2 cup red wine
2 cloves garlic, minced
1/4 teaspoon thyme
1/4 teaspoon marjoram

1/4 teaspoon allspice
1/4 teaspoon freshly ground
  black pepper
1 bay leaf
Pinch cayenne
1-pound whole red snapper,
  drawn and scaled

PREPARATION:

Heat a skillet large enough to hold the fish. Dry-cook onion and green onion, stirring, until they start to color.

Add all remaining ingredients except the fish. Cover the skillet and simmer for 2 minutes.

Lay the fish in the sauce, cover the skillet, and cook at a simmer for 8 minutes. With 2 spatulas, carefully turn the fish over in the sauce, re-cover the pan, and cook for 10 minutes more, until the fish flakes apart at the touch of a fork.

TO SERVE:

Using a knife or serving spoon, lift the fillet of the top side of the fish and place it onto a warmed dinner plate. Remove and discard the head and bones of the remaining fish and place the remaining fillet onto another plate. Spoon all the sauce over the fish and serve.

NOTES:

It is interesting that the early Creoles almost exclusively used red wine in all their cookery because it survived the crossing from France better than white wines.

All the vegetables we have added will cook up to a thickness somewhere between a soup and a sauce. This is a proper Creole Courtbouillon.

VARIATION:

Almost any fish can be used here and you don't have to use the whole fish; use fillets instead if you prefer.

RED SNAPPER COURTBOUILLON
One serving

Calories	298	Calcium	124 mg
Protein	47.9 g	Iron	2.44 mg
Carbohydrates	19.6 g	Sodium	116 mg
Dietary Fiber	4.60 g		
Fat-Total	3.57 g		
Fat-Saturated	0.719 g		
Fat-Mono	0.640 g		
Fat-Poly	1.26 g		
Cholesterol	79.9 mg		

Calories from protein:	63%	Poly/Sat	=	1.8:1
Calories from carbohydrates:	26%	Sod/Pot	=	0.1:1
Calories from fats:	11%	Ca/Phos	=	0.3:1
		CSI	=	4.7

SUGGESTED MENU:

One serving

Iceberg Lettuce with Onion and Parmesan Dressing
Red Snapper Courtbouillon
Smothered Yellow Squash
Orange Flip

Calories	448		Calcium	361 mg
Protein	66.1 g		Iron	3.60 mg
Carbohydrates	38.1 g		Sodium	261 mg
Dietary Fiber	8.29 g			
Fat-Total	5.67 g			
Fat-Saturated	1.91 g			
Fat-Mono	1.13 g			
Fat-Poly	2.07 g			
Cholesterol	139 mg			

Calories from protein:	57%	Poly/Sat	=	1.1:1
Calories from carbohydrates:	33%	Sod/Pot	=	0.1:1
Calories from fats:	11%	Ca/Phos	=	0.7:1
		CSI	=	8.9

Poached Trout with Lemon and Horseradish

Serves 2

INGREDIENTS:

1 cup water
1/2 cup white wine
1/2 cup sliced onion
1 rib celery, chopped
2 bay leaves

6 whole black peppercorns
2 three-ounce trout fillets
2 teaspoons prepared
   horseradish
1 lemon, halved

PREPARATION:

Pour the water and wine into a saucepan and add the onion, celery, bay leaves, and peppercorns.

Bring the liquid to a simmer and let it simmer for 2 minutes to draw the flavors from the vegetables and seasonings.

Lay the fish in the liquid and poach for 5 minutes.

TO SERVE:

Carefully remove the fillets and place on plates. Top them with the sauce and serve each with a teaspoon of horseradish and a lemon half.

NOTE:

Don't overcook the fish. Be careful to lift the fillets out of the poaching liquor with a spatula so they don't break into pieces.

VARIATIONS:

Any fillet of fish will do in this recipe. Buy whatever looks the freshest, and if you use this recipe often vary the type of fish.

Fish steaks can also be prepared this way.

POACHED TROUT WITH LEMON AND HORSERADISH *One serving*

Calories	102		Calcium	19.5 mg
Protein	21.1 g		Iron	0.585 mg
Carbohydrates	2.99 g		Sodium	49.3 mg
Dietary Fiber	0.463 g			
Fat-Total	4.33 g			
Fat-Saturated	0.924 g			
Fat-Mono	1.91 g			
Fat-Poly	1.08 g			
Cholesterol	53.6 mg			

Calories from protein:	62%	Poly/Sat	=	1.2:1
Calories from carbohydrates:	9%	Sod/Pot	=	0.1:1
Calories from fats:	29%	Ca/Phos	=	0.1:1
		CSI	=	3.6

SUGGESTED MENU: *One serving*

Tomato Bisque
Red and White Bean Salad
Poached Trout with Lemon and Horseradish
Boiled New Potatoes
Pear Compote with Brandied Vanilla Cream

Calories	618		Calcium	273 mg
Protein	41.1 g		Iron	8.81 mg
Carbohydrates	111 g		Sodium	136 mg
Dietary Fiber	20.2 g			
Fat-Total	6.88 g			
Fat-Saturated	1.28 g			
Fat-Mono	2.29 g			
Fat-Poly	2.11 g			
Cholesterol	54.1 mg			

Calories from protein:	24%	Poly/Sat	=	1.7:1
Calories from carbohydrates:	66%	Sod/Pot	=	0.1:1
Calories from fats:	9%	Ca/Phos	=	0.4:1
		CSI	=	4.0

Baked Breaded Bluefish
with Mock Tartar Sauce

Serves 2

INGREDIENTS:

¼ cup skim milk
1 egg white
⅛ teaspoon freshly ground
   black pepper

2 four-ounce bluefish fillets
¼ cup bread crumbs
Mock Tartar Sauce (recipe
   follows)

PREPARATION:

Preheat the oven to 350 degrees.
Combine the skim milk, egg white, and pepper to make a seasoned egg-wash.
Dip the fillets into the egg-wash, then dredge them in the bread crumbs.
Lay the fillets on a nonstick baking sheet and bake for 10 minutes.

TO SERVE:

Serve the fish with the Mock Tartar Sauce.

NOTE:

For me this dish is a marvelous replacement for fried fish.

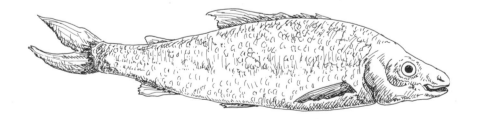

A speck of cayenne will spice up the egg wash a bit. Dried thyme, oregano, or basil will also give a boost to the bread crumbs.

Serve quartered lemons in addition to the Mock Tartar Sauce, or if you prefer, serve only the lemon.

BAKED BREADED BLUEFISH

One serving

Calories	201	Calcium	72.6 mg
Protein	27.5 g	Iron	1.17 mg
Carbohydrates	10.9 g	Sodium	193 mg
Dietary Fiber	0.522 g		
Fat-Total	6.08 g		
Fat-Saturated	1.38 g		
Fat-Mono	2.62 g		
Fat-Poly	1.46 g		
Cholesterol	68.0 mg		

Calories from protein:	53%	Poly/Sat	=	1.1:1
Calories from carbohydrates:	21%	Sod/Pot	=	0.4:1
Calories from fats:	26%	Ca/Phos	=	0.2:1
		CSI	=	4.8

Mock Tartar Sauce

Makes about ⅔ cup

INGREDIENTS:

½ cup nonfat yogurt
1 tablespoon minced sour pickle
1 tablespoon minced pitted
   green olive
1 tablespoon minced fresh
   parsley

¼ teaspoon powdered mustard
1 teaspoon fresh lemon juice
⅛ teaspoon freshly ground
   pepper

PREPARATION:

Combine all ingredients and refrigerate in a tightly covered container.

NOTES:

This sauce will keep for a week if stored as suggested.

Use this as you would regular tartar sauce with any dish. Try it as a replacement for mayonnaise on sandwiches and in salads.

VARIATION:

Use sweet pickle in place of the sour.

MOCK TARTAR SAUCE   *One serving*

Calories	10.4		Calcium	25.9 mg
Protein	0.734 g		Iron	0.121 mg
Carbohydrates	1.07 g		Sodium	112 mg
Dietary Fiber	0.195 g			
Fat-Total	0.476 g			
Fat-Saturated	0.059 g			
Fat-Mono	0.278 g			
Fat-Poly	0.026 g			
Cholesterol	0.200 mg			

Calories from protein:	26%	Poly/Sat	=	0.4:1
Calories from carbohydrates:	37%	Sod/Pot	=	2.8:1
Calories from fats:	37%	Ca/Phos	=	1.4:1
		CSI	=	0.1

SUGGESTED MENU: *One serving*

Stuffed Mushrooms
Baked Breaded Bluefish with Mock Tartar Sauce
Coleslaw
Pineapple Bread Pudding with Rum Sauce

Calories	627		Calcium	586 mg
Protein	61.1 g		Iron	4.78 mg
Carbohydrates	59.0 g		Sodium	995 mg
Dietary Fiber	5.10 g			
Fat-Total	13.4 g			
Fat-Saturated	4.76 g			
Fat-Mono	4.62 g			
Fat-Poly	2.69 g			
Cholesterol	133 mg			

Calories from protein:	41%	Poly/Sat	=	0.6:1
Calories from carbohydrates:	39%	Sod/Pot	=	0.7:1
Calories from fats:	20%	Ca/Phos	=	0.7:1
		CSI	=	11.5

Matelote of Sheepshead

Serves 2

INGREDIENTS:

½ cup chopped onion
1 tablespoon dry brown "roux"
1 cup dry red wine
2 cloves garlic, minced
1 cup sliced raw mushrooms
1 bay leaf
¼ teaspoon thyme
⅛ teaspoon ground cloves
⅛ teaspoon ground allspice

1 cup fish stock, made by simmering fish heads and bones in 1½ cups water, covered, for 10 minutes
Freshly ground black pepper to taste
2 three-ounce fillets of sheepshead, skin off
1 teaspoon chopped fresh parsley

PREPARATION:

Cook the onion for 2 minutes in a dry hot pan, stirring, until they begin to color.

Stir in the "roux," then blend in the wine a little at a time. Add all remaining ingredients except the sheepshead and parsley and bring to a boil. Reduce to a simmer, cover, and simmer for 20 minutes.

Five minutes before serving, add the sheepshead, cover, and simmer for 5 minutes more.

TO SERVE:

Serve in warm soup bowls garnished with a sprinkle of the parsley.

NOTE:

Matelote originally meant "the fisherman's wife" in French. The dish *matelote* became the fish stew that she made.

VARIATIONS:

This is a good recipe to make use of inexpensive pieces of fish like the catfish nuggets or pieces of catfish fillet often available in the fish market.

White wine can be used in place of the red.

MATELOTE OF SHEEPSHEAD   *One serving*

Calories	215	Calcium	89.8 mg
Protein	18.2 g	Iron	1.94 mg
Carbohydrates	10.9 g	Sodium	63.5 mg
Dietary Fiber	1.74 g		
Fat-Total	3.34 g		
Fat-Saturated	0.461 g		
Fat-Mono	1.14 g		
Fat-Poly	0.905 g		
Cholesterol	56.1 mg		

Calories from protein:	34%	Poly/Sat	=	2.0:1
Calories from carbohydrates:	20%	Sod/Pot	=	0.1:1
Calories from fats:	14%	Ca/Phos	=	0.3:1
Other calories (i.e. alcohol):	32%	CSI	=	3.3

SUGGESTED MENU: *One serving*

Boiled Onion Salad
Matelote of Sheepshead
Maque Choux
Pear Compote with Brandied Vanilla Cream

Calories	475	Calcium	216 mg
Protein	25.4 g	Iron	4.05 mg
Carbohydrates	68.7 g	Sodium	206 mg
Dietary Fiber	13.7 g		
Fat-Total	5.82 g		
Fat-Saturated	0.759 g		
Fat-Mono	1.94 g		
Fat-Poly	1.70 g		
Cholesterol	56.6 mg		

Calories from protein:	21%	Poly/Sat	=	2.2:1
Calories from carbohydrates:	58%	Sod/Pot	=	0.1:1
Calories from fats:	11%	Ca/Phos	=	0.5:1
Other calories (i.e. alcohol):	10%	CSI	=	3.6

Shrimp Etouffée

Serves 2

INGREDIENTS:

1 cup chopped onion
½ cup chopped green onion
¼ cup chopped celery
¼ cup chopped green bell pepper
2 tablespoons dry brown "roux"
½ cup water

3 cloves garlic, minced
¼ teaspoon thyme
⅛ teaspoon freshly ground black pepper
Pinch cayenne
6 ounces raw peeled shrimp
1½ cups hot cooked rice

PREPARATION:

Cook the onion, green onion, celery, and bell pepper, in a saucepan over high heat, stirring frequently to prevent sticking and burning, until the vegetables color slightly, about 2 minutes.

Add the "roux" and blend in the water.

Add all seasonings and simmer slowly for 20 minutes.

Just before serving, add the shrimp and cook for 2 minutes, or just until they turn pink and are good and hot.

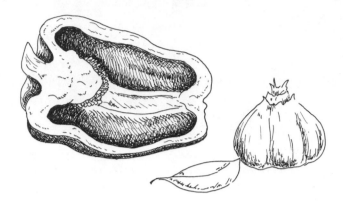

TO SERVE:

Spoon the rice into warm serving dishes or bowls and ladle the Shrimp Etouffée over.

NOTES:

Don't overcook the shrimp! They should be firm with a nice al dente texture.
Watch the liquid. You want a sort-of gravy affair, not dry. Add more water if
necessary.

VARIATIONS:

This recipe, excellent also when done with washed crayfish meat, becomes
Crayfish Etouffée, a very popular Louisiana dish.
Without the rice, this preparation served as a sauce over baked breaded fish
fillets makes a truly delicious entree.

SHRIMP ETOUFFÉE   *One serving*

Calories	320	Calcium	126 mg	
Protein	21.5 g	Iron	5.36 mg	
Carbohydrates	55.1 g	Sodium	154 mg	
Dietary Fiber	3.13 g			
Fat-Total	1.79 g			
Fat-Saturated	0.371 g			
Fat-Mono	0.313 g			
Fat-Poly	0.646 g			
Cholesterol	113 mg			

Calories from protein:	27%	Poly/Sat	=	1.7:1
Calories from carbohydrates:	68%	Sod/Pot	=	0.3:1
Calories from fats:	5%	Ca/Phos	=	0.4:1
		CSI	=	6.0

SUGGESTED MENU:

One serving

Deviled Eggs
Shrimp Etouffée
Creole Tomatoes with Basil, Garlic, and Green-Onion Dressing
Cherries Jubilee

Calories	590		Calcium	290 mg
Protein	37.2 g		Iron	7.27 mg
Carbohydrates	99.0 g		Sodium	558 mg
Dietary Fiber	7.00 g			
Fat-Total	3.74 g			
Fat-Saturated	0.946 g			
Fat-Mono	1.01 g			
Fat-Poly	1.02 g			
Cholesterol	115 mg			

Calories from protein:	26%	Poly/Sat	=	1.1:1
Calories from carbohydrates:	68%	Sod/Pot	=	0.4:1
Calories from fats:	6%	Ca/Phos	=	0.7:1
		CSI	=	6.7

Fillet of Trout with White Wine and Oyster Sauce

Serves 2

INGREDIENTS:

1 cup water
1/2 cup chopped onion
2 three-ounce fillets of trout
1 tablespoon dry blond "roux"
1/4 cup white wine
1/4 cup chopped green onion

1 clove garlic, minced
1/4 teaspoon thyme
Freshly ground black pepper to
  taste
6 raw oysters, shucked

PREPARATION:

Put the water and onion into a saucepan and simmer for 2 minutes to make a poaching liquor.

Lay the trout in the poaching liquor, cover, and poach for 5 minutes.

Carefully remove the trout to a warm plate, cover with a warm damp towel, and hold in a warm oven.

Strain the liquid from the saucepan into a measuring cup.

Make a sauce by blending 3/4 cup of the reserved poaching liquor with the "roux"; add all remaining ingredients except the oysters. Simmer for 10 minutes.

Add the oysters to the sauce and simmer for 2 minutes.

Serve the trout fillets with the White Wine and Oyster Sauce spooned over.

NOTE:

Don't overcook the fish or the oysters.

VARIATION:

Shrimp or crabmeat in place of the oysters is excellent.

TROUT WITH WHITE WINE AND OYSTER SAUCE   *One serving*

Calories	191	Calcium	48.6 mg
Protein	26.5 g	Iron	4.45 mg
Carbohydrates	6.73 g	Sodium	106 mg
Dietary Fiber	0.498 g		
Fat-Total	4.97 g		
Fat-Saturated	1.46 g		
Fat-Mono	1.35 g		
Fat-Poly	1.06 g		
Cholesterol	82.5 mg		

Calories from protein:	60%	Poly/Sat	=	0.7:1
Calories from carbohydrates:	15%	Sod/Pot	=	0.1:1
Calories from fats:	25%	Ca/Phos	=	0.2:1
		CSI	=	5.6

SUGGESTED MENU: *One serving*

Fillet of Trout with White Wine and Oyster Sauce
Celery Rémoulade
Pear Compote with Brandied Vanilla Cream

Calories	353	Calcium	182 mg
Protein	30.4 g	Iron	5.97 mg
Carbohydrates	42.0 g	Sodium	405 mg
Dietary Fiber	7.31 g		
Fat-Total	6.53 g		
Fat-Saturated	1.57 g		
Fat-Mono	2.15 g		
Fat-Poly	1.30 g		
Cholesterol	83.0 mg		

Calories from protein:	35%	Poly/Sat	=	0.8:1
Calories from carbohydrates:	48%	Sod/Pot	=	0.3:1
Calories from fats:	17%	Ca/Phos	=	0.4:1
		CSI	=	5.7

Grouper Fillets Amandine *Serves 2*

INGREDIENTS:

1 cup puréed raw onion
1 clove garlic, minced
1 cup water
¼ cup dry white wine
2-inch-piece lemon peel (yellow
    zest only)

2 bay leaves
1 teaspoon chopped fresh parsley
2 three-ounce fillets of grouper
2 tablespoons toasted almond
    slivers

PREPARATION:

Cook the onion in a saucepan over medium heat while stirring often for about 2 minutes.

Add the garlic, water, wine, lemon zest, bay leaves, and parsley.

Bring to a boil, reduce to a simmer, and continue cooking for 3 minutes to get all the flavors well developed in the liquid.

Lay the fish in the simmering liquid, cover the saucepan, and poach for about 5 minutes.

Carefully remove the cooked fillets to a warm plate, cover with a warm damp towel, and hold in a warm oven.

To make the sauce, bring the poaching liquor back to a boil and reduce by half.

TO SERVE:

Lay the fillets on warm plates and spoon the sauce over the top.
Sprinkle the almonds over all.

NOTE:

Toast the almonds on a dry baking sheet in a 350 degree oven for 3 minutes.

VARIATION:

Any fish can be used in this preparation. Any fish dish in this book can be done with whatever fish is available to you.

GROUPER FILLETS AMANDINE

One serving

Calories	179		Calcium	98.9 mg
Protein	19.3 g		Iron	0.956 mg
Carbohydrates	8.66 g		Sodium	49.4 mg
Dietary Fiber	1.95 g			
Fat-Total	5.77 g			
Fat-Saturated	0.739 g			
Fat-Mono	3.20 g			
Fat-Poly	1.56 g			
Cholesterol	42.5 mg			

Calories from protein:	43%	Poly/Sat	=	2.1:1
Calories from carbohydrates:	19%	Sod/Pot	=	0.1:1
Calories from fats:	29%	Ca/Phos	=	0.6:1
Other calories (i.e. alcohol):	8%	CSI	=	2.9

SUGGESTED MENU:

One serving

Green Salad with Creamy Creole Dressing
Grouper Fillets Amandine
Seasoned Boiled Brussels Sprouts
Rice Pudding

Calories	401		Calcium	325 mg
Protein	33.1 g		Iron	4.67 mg
Carbohydrates	53.9 g		Sodium	246 mg
Dietary Fiber	9.17 g			
Fat-Total	7.40 g			
Fat-Saturated	1.14 g			
Fat-Mono	3.65 g			
Fat-Poly	2.07 g			
Cholesterol	43.9 mg			

Calories from protein:	32%	Poly/Sat	=	1.8:1
Calories from carbohydrates:	52%	Sod/Pot	=	0.2:1
Calories from fats:	16%	Ca/Phos	=	0.8:1
		CSI	=	3.3

Catfish Cakes

Serves 2

INGREDIENTS:

1　6-ounce catfish fillet, chopped
2　slices stale bread, crushed
¼　cup water
1　tablespoon minced green
　　onion
1　teaspoon minced fresh parsley
1　egg white
1　teaspoon fresh lemon juice

½　teaspoon powdered mustard
⅛　teaspoon freshly ground
　　black pepper
1　egg white
¼　cup skim milk
¼　cup bread crumbs
1　lemon, quartered

PREPARATION:

Preheat the oven to 375 degrees.

Combine the first 9 ingredients and make 4 cakes, using your hands to pat them into patties as you would hamburgers.

Whisk the egg white with the skim milk; dip the patties into the mixture then coat them with the bread crumbs.

Bake on a lightly greased or non-stick baking sheet for 12 minutes.

TO SERVE:

Serve 2 cakes garnished with lemon quarters per person.

NOTE:

This is a delightful way to make use of any leftover cooked fish. It also gives the impression of being a very fattening dish.

VARIATIONS:

Serve this dish with the Mock Tartar Sauce (see recipe page 87).
Use crabmeat to make Crab Cakes.
Any other fish can be used.

CATFISH CAKES

One serving

Calories	194	Calcium	115 mg
Protein	22.7 g	Iron	1.38 mg
Carbohydrates	17.2 g	Sodium	274 mg
Dietary Fiber	0.796 g		
Fat-Total	4.21 g		
Fat-Saturated	0.766 g		
Fat-Mono	1.55 g		
Fat-Poly	1.03 g		
Cholesterol	56.7 mg		

Calories from protein:	46%	Poly/Sat	=	1.3:1
Calories from carbohydrates:	35%	Sod/Pot	=	0.7:1
Calories from fats:	19%	Ca/Phos	=	0.5:1
		CSI	=	3.6

SUGGESTED MENU:

One serving

Celery Rémoulade
Catfish Cakes
Eggplant Fingers
Pineapple with Port Wine

Calories	458	Calcium	306 mg
Protein	30.8 g	Iron	4.05 mg
Carbohydrates	56.9 g	Sodium	739 mg
Dietary Fiber	7.53 g		
Fat-Total	6.86 g		
Fat-Saturated	1.46 g		
Fat-Mono	2.70 g		
Fat-Poly	1.48 g		
Cholesterol	58.5 mg		

Calories from protein:	27%	Poly/Sat	=	1.0:1
Calories from carbohydrates:	50%	Sod/Pot	=	0.6:1
Calories from fats:	13%	Ca/Phos	=	0.8:1
Other calories (i.e. alcohol):	10%	CSI	=	4.4

Stuffed Flounder Fillets with White Wine Sauce

Serves 2

CRABMEAT STUFFING INGREDIENTS:

¼ cup chopped onion
¼ cup chopped green onion
2 tablespoons chopped celery
1 tablespoon minced green bell pepper
1 clove garlic, minced
1 teaspoon minced fresh parsley
⅛ teaspoon thyme
¼ cup bread crumbs
Freshly ground black pepper to taste
¼ cup water
1 egg white

2 ounces crabmeat, cartilage removed

2 three-ounce flounder fillets, skin off
2 ounces (¼ cup) dry white wine
Paprika
1 teaspoon cornstarch
1 tablespoon water
½ teaspoon fresh lemon juice
Freshly ground black pepper to taste

PREPARATION:

Cook the onion, green onion, celery, bell pepper, garlic, parsley, and thyme over medium heat, stirring, for 4 minutes, or until they begin to brown slightly.

Blend in the bread crumbs. Remove from the heat and season with pepper.

Moisten the mixture with the water and blend in the egg white.

Fold in the crabmeat.

TO ASSEMBLE:

Preheat the oven to 350 degrees.

Divide the stuffing in half and shape into balls with your hands.

Wrap a flounder fillet around each ball and secure with a toothpick, or tie around with a string to hold the fillet in place during cooking.

Set the fillets seam side up in a baking dish with the wine and sprinkle them with paprika. Cover.

Bake for 30 minutes.

Carefully transfer the fish to warm plates. Measure the cooking liquid, add enough water to it to make ½ cup and return it to the pan. Blend the cornstarch with the tablespoon water and add it to the cooking liquid. Season with the lemon juice and pepper and stir over low heat just until hot. Spoon the sauce over the fish.

NOTE:

The sauce adds a great deal to this dish, but the fish can also be baked without it.

VARIATIONS:

This dish can be prepared with a fillet from practically any fish.

Try stuffing the fillets with shrimp instead of crabmeat, or use the artificial king or snow crabmeat now available in groceries at far less the cost of the real thing. In stuffings and sauces you would hardly know the difference.

STUFFED FLOUNDER WITH WHITE WINE SAUCE   *One serving*

Calories	202	Calcium	78.1 mg
Protein	25.8 g	Iron	1.84 mg
Carbohydrates	14.2 g	Sodium	512 mg
Dietary Fiber	1.41 g		
Fat-Total	2.37 g		
Fat-Saturated	0.646 g		
Fat-Mono	0.604 g		
Fat-Poly	0.911 g		
Cholesterol	73.2 mg		

Calories from protein:	51%	Poly/Sat	=	1.4:1
Calories from carbohydrates:	28%	Sod/Pot	=	1.2:1
Calories from fats:	11%	Ca/Phos	=	0.3:1
Other calories (i.e. alcohol):	10%	CSI	=	4.3

SUGGESTED MENU: *One serving*

Pickled Mirliton Salad
Stuffed Flounder Fillet with White Wine Sauce
Stewed Okra and Tomato
Hot Apple Soufflé

Calories	355	Calcium	150 mg
Protein	31.8 g	Iron	3.25 mg
Carbohydrates	48.6 g	Sodium	571 mg
Dietary Fiber	7.58 g		
Fat-Total	3.52 g		
Fat-Saturated	0.776 g		
Fat-Mono	0.673 g		
Fat-Poly	1.15 g		
Cholesterol	73.2 mg		

Calories from protein:	36%	Poly/Sat	=	1.5:1
Calories from carbohydrates:	55%	Sod/Pot	=	0.5:1
Calories from fats:	9%	Ca/Phos	=	0.4:1
		CSI	=	4.4

Shrimp Creole   *Serves 2*

INGREDIENTS:

2/3 cup chopped onion
1/3 cup chopped green bell
   pepper
1 cup chopped peeled and
   seeded tomato
1 clove garlic, minced
1 teaspoon chopped parsley

1/2 teaspoon paprika
1/4 teaspoon dried thyme
Pinch cayenne
Freshly ground black pepper to
   taste
8 ounces peeled raw shrimp
1 cup hot cooked white rice

PREPARATION:

Cook the onion and bell pepper in a saucepan over medium heat for 2 minutes, stirring frequently to keep from sticking and to insure uniform cooking.

Add the tomato and all the herbs and seasonings.

Let the mixture come to a simmer and continue simmering for 2 minutes.

Add the shrimp and simmer only long enough for them to become pink and just cooked, about 2 minutes.

TO SERVE:

Spoon 1/2 cup of the rice onto the center of each plate and ladle the Shrimp Creole around it in a circle.

NOTES:

Fresh tomatoes, if they are very ripe, sometimes collapse in the sauce and become liquid. If this happens you may want to thicken the sauce by mixing a teaspoon of cornstarch with a tablespoon of water and then stirring it quickly into the sauce before you add the shrimp. This thickening will allow your sauce to lay better on the rice and have a seemingly richer texture.

VARIATION:

This same preparation can be made using crabmeat, lobster, scallops, chicken, or even a fillet of steak or fish.

SHRIMP CREOLE
One serving

Calories	233	Calcium	94.6 mg
Protein	19.6 g	Iron	4.22 mg
Carbohydrates	36.2 g	Sodium	147 mg
Dietary Fiber	3.06 g		
Fat-Total	1.81 g		
Fat-Saturated	0.350 g		
Fat-Mono	0.305 g		
Fat-Poly	0.671 g		
Cholesterol	113 mg		

Calories from protein:	33%	Poly/Sat	=	1.9:1
Calories from carbohydrates:	61%	Sod/Pot	=	0.3:1
Calories from fats:	7%	Ca/Phos	=	0.3:1
		CSI	=	6.0

SUGGESTED MENU:
One serving

Celery Rémoulade
Shrimp Creole with White Rice
Green Salad with Creamy Creole Dressing
Ambrosia

Calories	380	Calcium	283 mg
Protein	25.1 g	Iron	6.05 mg
Carbohydrates	64.0 g	Sodium	547 mg
Dietary Fiber	9.44 g		
Fat-Total	3.41 g		
Fat-Saturated	0.456 g		
Fat-Mono	1.33 g		
Fat-Poly	0.896 g		
Cholesterol	113 mg		

Calories from protein:	26%	Poly/Sat	=	2.0:1
Calories from carbohydrates:	66%	Sod/Pot	=	0.4:1
Calories from fats:	8%	Ca/Phos	=	0.7:1
		CSI	=	6.1

CHICKEN AND DUCK

Chicken Creole

Roast Duck with Apples and Onions

Chicken with Potatoes and Petits Pois

Charcoal-Grilled Chicken Breasts
  with Green-Grape Sauce

Baked Breaded Chicken

Chicken in Red Wine Sauce
  with Mushrooms and Pearl Onions

Spicy Roasted Chicken Breasts

Chicken Fricassee

Chicken Roasted with Garlic Cloves

Chicken Sauce Piquante

Chicken Creole

Serves 2

INGREDIENTS:

¾ cup chopped onion
½ cup chopped green bell
  pepper
1 cup chopped tomato
2 cloves garlic, minced
1 bay leaf
½ teaspoon thyme

1 tablespoon minced fresh
  parsley
⅛ teaspoon freshly ground
  black pepper
Pinch cayenne
2 three-ounce skinless boneless
  chicken breasts

PREPARATION:

In a heavy saucepan over high heat cook the onion and bell pepper, stirring regularly until they begin to color.

Add all remaining ingredients, including the chicken breasts.

Cover and simmer gently for 10 minutes.

NOTES:

Chicken Creole is generally served with hot fluffy white rice.

The tomatoes you use determine the texture of the sauce. Ones that are not quite ripe hold up better in the cooking, while very ripe ones tend to collapse and liquify.

If the sauce is too thin, blend in a mixture of a little cornstarch and water to bind it.

VARIATION:

Shrimp Creole, an equally delicious dish, is also in this collection (see recipe page 103).

CHICKEN CREOLE   *One serving*

Calories	201	Calcium	49.9 mg
Protein	25.2 g	Iron	2.61 mg
Carbohydrates	11.1 g	Sodium	70.7 mg
Dietary Fiber	3.01 g		
Fat-Total	6.23 g		
Fat-Saturated	1.65 g		
Fat-Mono	2.09 g		
Fat-Poly	1.53 g		
Cholesterol	70.5 mg		

Calories from protein:	50%	Poly/Sat	=	0.9:1
Calories from carbohydrates:	22%	Sod/Pot	=	0.1:1
Calories from fats:	28%	Ca/Phos	=	0.3:1
		CSI	=	5.2

SUGGESTED MENU: *One serving*

Red Bean Soup
Chicken Creole
White Rice
Cherries Jubilee

Calories	629	Calcium	213 mg
Protein	40.7 g	Iron	7.93 mg
Carbohydrates	91.9 g	Sodium	118 mg
Dietary Fiber	15.0 g		
Fat-Total	8.21 g		
Fat-Saturated	2.27 g		
Fat-Mono	2.53 g		
Fat-Poly	2.21 g		
Cholesterol	72.6 mg		

Calories from protein:	27%	Poly/Sat	=	1.0:1
Calories from carbohydrates:	61%	Sod/Pot	=	0.1:1
Calories from fats:	12%	Ca/Phos	=	0.4:1
		CSI	=	5.9

Roast Duck with Apples and Onions

Serves 4

INGREDIENTS:

*1 three-pound duckling, skin
    and fat removed*
*¼ teaspoon freshly ground
    black pepper*

1 stalk celery
¼ teaspoon thyme
2 apples, quartered and cored
2 onions, peeled and quartered

PREPARATION:

Preheat the oven to 350 degrees.

Rub the duck with the pepper. Put the celery and the thyme into the cavity, and stuff it with as much of the apple and onion as possible.

Put the duck in a roasting pan and surround it with the remaining apple and onion.

Cover the pan and roast for 1½ hours.

TO SERVE:

Cut the duck into quarters and serve with the defatted pan juices and the apples and onions as accompaniments.

NOTE:

Be sure to remove all the skin and fat from the duck before you begin the dish.

VARIATIONS:

Wild ducks are particularly good prepared this way. Skinless chicken breast is a delicious and simple replacement in this recipe.

ROAST DUCK WITH APPLES AND ONION   *One serving*

Calories	370		Calcium	42.4 mg
Protein	34.3 g		Iron	4.41 mg
Carbohydrates	20.8 g		Sodium	93.9 mg
Dietary Fiber	3.93 g			
Fat-Total	16.5 g			
Fat-Saturated	6.01 g			
Fat-Mono	5.29 g			
Fat-Poly	2.20 g			
Cholesterol	127 mg			

Calories from protein:	37%	Poly/Sat	=	0.4:1
Calories from carbohydrates:	23%	Sod/Pot	=	0.2:1
Calories from fats:	40%	Ca/Phos	=	0.1:1
		CSI	=	12.4

SUGGESTED MENU: *One serving*

Eggplant Fingers
Roast Duck with Apples and Onion
Red and White Bean Salad
Raisin Oat-Bran Cookies

Calories	788		Calcium	320 mg
Protein	59.8 g		Iron	11.2 mg
Carbohydrates	93.7 g		Sodium	474 mg
Dietary Fiber	16.8 g			
Fat-Total	20.2 g			
Fat-Saturated	7.04 g			
Fat-Mono	6.32 g			
Fat-Poly	3.46 g			
Cholesterol	129 mg			

Calories from protein:	30%	Poly/Sat	=	0.5:1
Calories from carbohydrates:	47%	Sod/Pot	=	0.3:1
Calories from fats:	23%	Ca/Phos	=	0.4:1
		CSI	=	13.6

Chicken with Potatoes and Petits Pois

Serves 2

INGREDIENTS:

1 cup chopped onion
1 cup diced potato, ½-inch
    cubes
1 clove garlic, minced
1 teaspoon chopped fresh parsley
2 tablespoons chopped celery
1 cup water

1 bay leaf
⅛ teaspoon thyme
Freshly ground black pepper to
    taste
1 cup petits pois
2 three-ounce skinless boneless
    chicken breasts

PREPARATION:

Heat a heavy skillet and add the onion and potato.

Stir while cooking over medium heat until they begin to color, then add remaining ingredients except the petit pois and chicken. Stir and bring to a boil.

Lay the chicken in the sauce, reduce the heat to a simmer, cover, and cook for about 12 minutes.

Uncover the pan, add the petits pois, and continue simmering until the liquid is reduced, about 5 minutes.

TO SERVE:

Lay a chicken breast on each plate and spoon the sauce over the top.

NOTE:

The potatoes and petits pois are the vegetables in this dish.

VARIATION:

Add some pearl onions at the beginning of cooking for a nice variation.

CHICKEN WITH POTATOES AND PETITS POIS

One serving

Calories	324	Calcium	67.1 mg
Protein	33.4 g	Iron	2.95 mg
Carbohydrates	37.5 g	Sodium	80.7 mg
Dietary Fiber	6.70 g		
Fat-Total	4.32 g		
Fat-Saturated	1.18 g		
Fat-Mono	1.36 g		
Fat-Poly	1.04 g		
Cholesterol	71.7 mg		

Calories from protein:	41%	Poly/Sat	=	0.9:1
Calories from carbohydrates:	47%	Sod/Pot	=	0.1:1
Calories from fats:	12%	Ca/Phos	=	0.2:1
		CSI	=	4.8

SUGGESTED MENU:

One serving

Italian Shrimp
Chicken with Potatoes and Petits Pois
Green Salad with Creamy Creole Dressing
Strawberry Bavarian Cream

Calories	562	Calcium	371 mg
Protein	59.4 g	Iron	6.54 mg
Carbohydrates	58.7 g	Sodium	393 mg
Dietary Fiber	10.3 g		
Fat-Total	6.57 g		
Fat-Saturated	1.60 g		
Fat-Mono	1.98 g		
Fat-Poly	1.68 g		
Cholesterol	186 mg		

Calories from protein:	45%	Poly/Sat	=	1.0:1
Calories from carbohydrates:	44%	Sod/Pot	=	0.2:1
Calories from fats:	11%	Ca/Phos	=	0.5:1
		CSI	=	10.9

Charcoal-Grilled Chicken Breasts with Green-Grape Sauce

Serves 2

INGREDIENTS:

2 3-ounce chicken
  breasts

¼ teaspoon freshly ground
  black pepper

SAUCE:

1 cup chopped green onion
¼ cup minced celery
1 clove garlic, minced
1 tablespoon dry blond "roux"
½ cup water
½ cup halved seedless green
  grapes

1 tablespoon sherry
1 tablespoon red currant jelly
⅛ teaspoon thyme
Freshly ground black pepper to
  taste

PREPARATION:

Preheat the charcoal grill.

MAKE THE SAUCE:

In a heavy saucepan cook the green onion with the celery and garlic over medium heat, stirring, until they have rendered their liquid.

Stir in the "roux" and cook while stirring for 1 minute more.

Add remaining sauce ingredients and simmer for 20 minutes.

Meanwhile, rub the chicken breasts with the ¼ teaspoon pepper.

Grill the chicken over charcoal for approximately 12 minutes, turning once.

TO SERVE:

Serve each person one chicken breast with the Green-Grape Sauce spooned over.

NOTE:

You can roast the chicken for 30 minutes at 350 degrees but you will not get the great charcoal-grilled taste.

VARIATION:

Skinned duck breasts would also do nicely.

GRILLED CHICKEN BREASTS WITH GRAPE SAUCE *One serving*

Calories	224	Calcium	30.0 mg
Protein	27.2 g	Iron	1.53 mg
Carbohydrates	17.7 g	Sodium	82.5 mg
Dietary Fiber	0.988 g		
Fat-Total	4.15 g		
Fat-Saturated	1.18 g		
Fat-Mono	1.33 g		
Fat-Poly	0.937 g		
Cholesterol	71.7 mg		

Calories from protein:	50%	Poly/Sat	=	0.8:1
Calories from carbohydrates:	33%	Sod/Pot	=	0.2:1
Calories from fats:	17%	Ca/Phos	=	0.2:1
		CSI	=	4.8

SUGGESTED MENU: *One serving*

Boiled Onion Salad
Charcoal-Grilled Chicken Breasts with Green-Grape Sauce
Turnips and Greens
Strawberry Bavarian Cream

Calories	334	Calcium	226 mg
Protein	36.0 g	Iron	2.79 mg
Carbohydrates	36.6 g	Sodium	268 mg
Dietary Fiber	5.75 g		
Fat-Total	5.07 g		
Fat-Saturated	1.31 g		
Fat-Mono	1.73 g		
Fat-Poly	1.15 g		
Cholesterol	72.7 mg		

Calories from protein:	43%	Poly/Sat	=	0.9:1
Calories from carbohydrates:	44%	Sod/Pot	=	0.3:1
Calories from fats:	14%	Ca/Phos	=	0.6:1
		CSI	=	5.0

Baked Breaded Chicken   *Serves 4*

INGREDIENTS:

1 three-pound chicken, skinned
1 cup bread crumbs
$1/2$ teaspoon freshly ground
   black pepper

$1/4$ teaspoon cayenne
$1/2$ cup skim milk
1 egg white

PREPARATION:

Preheat the oven to 350 degrees.
Cut the chicken into pieces.
Combine the bread crumbs, pepper, and cayenne.
Beat the skim milk with the egg white to make an egg wash.
Dip the chicken pieces into the egg wash and then into the bread crumbs.
Place the chicken on a nonstick baking sheet and bake for 30 minutes, or until nicely browned.

NOTE:

This is an excellent, healthful, and tasty replacement for fried chicken.

NOTE:

Don't want to skin the chicken? Buy skinless breasts or breast strips. They're much easier to deal with and you don't have to fight the bones in the eating. Reduce cooking time to 20 minutes.

VARIATION:

Try some dried thyme or oregano in the bread-crumb mixture for an herbal flavor.

BAKED BREADED CHICKEN   *One serving*

Calories	373	Calcium	61.1 mg
Protein	50.8 g	Iron	2.59 mg
Carbohydrates	10.1 g	Sodium	254 mg
Dietary Fiber	0.540 g		
Fat-Total	12.9 g		
Fat-Saturated	3.58 g		
Fat-Mono	4.60 g		
Fat-Poly	2.93 g		
Cholesterol	148 mg		

Calories from protein:	56%	Poly/Sat	=	0.8:1
Calories from carbohydrates:	11%	Sod/Pot	=	0.6:1
Calories from fats:	32%	Ca/Phos	=	0.2:1
		CSI	=	11.0

SUGGESTED MENU: *One serving*

Oyster and Artichoke Soup
Iceberg Lettuce with Onion and Parmesan Dressing
Baked Breaded Chicken
Rice Pudding

Calories	623	Calcium	360 mg
Protein	66.2 g	Iron	9.32 mg
Carbohydrates	53.0 g	Sodium	482 mg
Dietary Fiber	5.48 g		
Fat-Total	15.3 g		
Fat-Saturated	4.68 g		
Fat-Mono	5.04 g		
Fat-Poly	3.47 g		
Cholesterol	180 mg		

Calories from protein:	43%	Poly/Sat	=	0.7:1
Calories from carbohydrates:	34%	Sod/Pot	=	0.4:1
Calories from fats:	22%	Ca/Phos	=	0.5:1
		CSI	=	13.7

Chicken in Red Wine Sauce with Mushrooms and Pearl Onions

Serves 4

INGREDIENTS:

1 *three-pound chicken, skinned*
1/4 *teaspoon freshly ground*
    black pepper
2 *cups peeled pearl onions*
2 *cups whole small mushrooms*
1/2 *cup chopped celery*

1/2 *cup dry red wine*
1/2 *teaspoon thyme*
4 *cloves garlic, minced*
2 *tablespoons minced fresh*
    parsley

PREPARATION:

Preheat the oven to 350 degrees.
Rub the chicken with the pepper and place it in a nonstick roasting pan.
Add remaining ingredients, cover the pan, and roast for 1 hour.

TO SERVE:

Cut the chicken into pieces and serve with the onions, mushrooms, and pan liquid poured over.

NOTE:

It is a bit tricky to skin the chicken. You may prefer to have that done by your butcher.

VARIATIONS:

Use four skinned chicken breasts, two Cornish hens, or one duck in place of the chicken.

CHICKEN WITH MUSHROOMS AND ONIONS   *One serving*

Calories	382		Calcium	75.3 mg
Protein	51.4 g		Iron	3.51 mg
Carbohydrates	10.7 g		Sodium	170 mg
Dietary Fiber	2.85 g			
Fat-Total	13.0 g			
Fat-Saturated	3.54 g			
Fat-Mono	4.55 g			
Fat-Poly	3.04 g			
Cholesterol	152 mg			

Calories from protein:	56%		Poly/Sat	=	0.9:1
Calories from carbohydrates:	12%		Sod/Pot	=	0.2:1
Calories from fats:	32%		Ca/Phos	=	0.2:1
			CSI	=	11.2

SUGGESTED MENU: *One serving*

Crabmeat Ravigote
Chicken in Red Wine Sauce with Mushrooms and Pearl Onions
Seasoned Eggplant Fingers
Ambrosia

Calories	658		Calcium	311 mg
Protein	76.9 g		Iron	6.03 mg
Carbohydrates	49.3 g		Sodium	399 mg
Dietary Fiber	10.4 g			
Fat-Total	16.0 g			
Fat-Saturated	4.43 g			
Fat-Mono	5.36 g			
Fat-Poly	3.91 g			
Cholesterol	220 mg			

Calories from protein:	47%		Poly/Sat	=	0.9:1
Calories from carbohydrates:	30%		Sod/Pot	=	0.2:1
Calories from fats:	22%		Ca/Phos	=	0.4:1
			CSI	=	15.4

Spicy Roasted Chicken Breasts

Serves 2

INGREDIENTS:

1 tablespoon fresh lemon juice
¼ teaspoon freshly ground
   black pepper

Pinch cayenne
2 three-ounce chicken breasts,
   skinned

PREPARATION:

Preheat the oven to 350 degrees.

Combine the lemon juice, pepper, and cayenne and brush it over the chicken breasts.

Place the chicken in a small roasting pan and roast for 30 minutes.

NOTE:

A half teaspoon of dried basil or oregano will add their flavor to this recipe.

VARIATION:

Cook these on the charcoal grill.

SPICY ROASTED CHICKEN BREASTS   *One serving*

Calories	150	Calcium	14.6 mg
Protein	26.4 g	Iron	0.989 mg
Carbohydrates	0.864 g	Sodium	65.8 mg
Dietary Fiber	0.087 g		
Fat-Total	3.87 g		
Fat-Saturated	1.09 g		
Fat-Mono	1.32 g		
Fat-Poly	0.847 g		
Cholesterol	71.7 mg		

Calories from protein:	73%	Poly/Sat	=	0.8:1	
Calories from carbohydrates:	2%	Sod/Pot	=	0.3:1	
Calories from fats:	24%	Ca/Phos	=	0.1:1	
		CSI	=	4.7	

SUGGESTED MENU: *One serving*

Stuffed Mushrooms
Spicy Roasted Chicken Breasts
Country Rice
Green Salad with Creamy Creole Dressing
Hot Apple Soufflé

Calories	556	Calcium	206 mg
Protein	52.7 g	Iron	5.18 mg
Carbohydrates	64.0 g	Sodium	676 mg
Dietary Fiber	6.87 g		
Fat-Total	7.94 g		
Fat-Saturated	2.30 g		
Fat-Mono	2.42 g		
Fat-Poly	1.83 g		
Cholesterol	122 mg		

Calories from protein:	39%	Poly/Sat	=	0.8:1	
Calories from carbohydrates:	48%	Sod/Pot	=	0.6:1	
Calories from fats:	13%	Ca/Phos	=	0.4:1	
		CSI	=	8.4	

Chicken Fricassee

Serves 2

INGREDIENTS:

*½ chicken (about 1 pound),
    skinned and all fat cut away*
½ teaspoon paprika
*¼ teaspoon freshly ground
    black pepper*

¼ cup all-purpose flour
1 egg white
¼ cup skim milk
*Country Rice (see recipe page
    199)*

GRAVY INGREDIENTS:

¼ cup dry brown "roux"
1½ cups water
1 cup chopped onion
*½ cup chopped green
    onion*
2 cloves garlic, minced

*1 tablespoon chopped fresh
    parsley*
⅛ teaspoon ground allspice
¼ teaspoon thyme
*⅛ teaspoon freshly ground
    black pepper*

PREPARATION:

Preheat the oven to 350 degrees.

Cut the chicken into pieces.

Blend the paprika and pepper with the flour.

Beat the egg white with the milk.

Dip the chicken into the egg-white mixture and then into the seasoned flour.

Lay the chicken in a baking pan and bake for 30 minutes, or until golden brown.

While the chicken is baking, make the Country Rice.

MAKE THE FRICASSEE GRAVY:

Put the "roux" into a saucepan and blend in the water a little at a time so there are no lumps and the sauce is smooth.

Add all remaining ingredients, cover, and simmer gently for 15 to 20 minutes.

Remove the chicken from the oven and add it to the pot with the Fricassee gravy.

Let all simmer for another 15 minutes, or until the chicken is very tender and easily comes off the bones.

TO SERVE:

Spoon the Chicken Fricassee onto plates and accompany with the Country Rice.

NOTES:

The chicken is even good served just out of the oven without the Fricassee gravy. Tastes like fried!

There are few dishes that appeal to me more that a good Chicken Fricassee. This dish is one of my favorites in this book.

VARIATION:

The skinned chicken breasts you buy at the grocery, or skinless turkey breasts cut into strips both make an excellent Fricassee.

CHICKEN FRICASSEE

One serving

Calories	376		Calcium	86.4 mg
Protein	39.0 g		Iron	4.01 mg
Carbohydrates	32.6 g		Sodium	125 mg
Dietary Fiber	2.95 g			
Fat-Total	9.12 g			
Fat-Saturated	2.44 g			
Fat-Mono	3.09 g			
Fat-Poly	2.21 g			
Cholesterol	101 mg			

Calories from protein:	42%		Poly/Sat	=	0.9:1
Calories from carbohydrates:	35%		Sod/Pot	=	0.2:1
Calories from fats:	22%		Ca/Phos	=	0.3:1
			CSI	=	7.5

SUGGESTED MENU:

One serving

Green Salad with Creamy Creole Dressing
Chicken Fricassee
Country Rice
Pineapple with Port Wine

Calories	645		Calcium	193 mg
Protein	44.1 g		Iron	6.17 mg
Carbohydrates	78.8 g		Sodium	261 mg
Dietary Fiber	6.04 g			
Fat-Total	10.1 g			
Fat-Saturated	2.55 g			
Fat-Mono	3.49 g			
Fat-Poly	2.44 g			
Cholesterol	101 mg			

Calories from protein:	27%		Poly/Sat	=	1.0:1
Calories from carbohydrates:	49%		Sod/Pot	=	0.3:1
Calories from fats:	14%		Ca/Phos	=	0.5:1
Other calories (i.e. alcohol):	10%		CSI	=	7.6

Chicken Roasted
with Garlic Cloves

Serves 2

INGREDIENTS:

2 *three-ounce skinless chicken*
   breasts
¼ *teaspoon freshly ground*
   black pepper

Cloves of one whole head garlic,
peeled

PREPARATION:

Preheat the oven to 350 degrees.
Rub the chicken with the pepper.
Put the chicken and garlic in a roasting pan and roast, covered, for 30 minutes.
Serve each breast with garlic cloves on the side.

NOTE:

The garlic loses its pungent flavor when roasted and becomes mild enough to
eat piece by piece with the chicken.

VARIATIONS:

A dash of sherry or fresh lemon juice rubbed on the breasts adds a nice flavor.
Duck or Cornish hen are also delicious this way.

CHICKEN ROASTED WITH GARLIC CLOVES *One serving*

Calories	175	Calcium	46.5 mg
Protein	27.5 g	Iron	1.29 mg
Carbohydrates	6.13 g	Sodium	68.8 mg
Dietary Fiber	0.335 g		
Fat-Total	3.93 g		
Fat-Saturated	1.10 g		
Fat-Mono	1.32 g		
Fat-Poly	0.881 g		
Cholesterol	71.7 mg		

Calories from protein:	65%	Poly/Sat	=	0.8:1
Calories from carbohydrates:	14%	Sod/Pot	=	0.2:1
Calories from fats:	21%	Ca/Phos	=	0.2:1
		CSI	=	4.7

SUGGESTED MENU: *One serving*

Crayfish Cardinal
Chicken Roasted with Garlic Cloves
Steamed Spinach with Onion
Bananas Foster

Calories	507	Calcium	460 mg
Protein	49.0 g	Iron	7.63 mg
Carbohydrates	52.2 g	Sodium	372 mg
Dietary Fiber	9.89 g		
Fat-Total	7.04 g		
Fat-Saturated	2.25 g		
Fat-Mono	1.95 g		
Fat-Poly	1.53 g		
Cholesterol	108 mg		

Calories from protein:	39%	Poly/Sat	=	0.7:1
Calories from carbohydrates:	41%	Sod/Pot	=	0.2:1
Calories from fats:	13%	Ca/Phos	=	0.8:1
Other calories (i.e. alcohol):	8%	CSI	=	7.7

Chicken Sauce Piquante   *Serves 2*

INGREDIENTS:

½ cup chopped onion
2 tablespoons dry brown
   "roux"
1 cup chopped tomato
½ cup water
2 teaspoons red wine vinegar
4 cloves garlic, minced

½ teaspoon thyme
1 bay leaf
¼ teaspoon freshly ground
   black pepper
⅛ teaspoon cayenne
2 three-ounce skinless chicken
   breasts

PREPARATION:

Cook the onion in a heavy saucepan over medium heat, stirring regularly until slightly brown.

Blend in the "roux."

Add remaining ingredients except the chicken breasts, cover, and simmer for 15 minutes.

Place the chicken in the sauce, cover, and cook for 10 minutes more.

NOTE:

This dish should have both a pepper and vinegar bite to the taste; it draws its name, *piquant,* from the French meaning "pungent, tart, biting."

VARIATIONS:

Any vinegar can be used in place of the red wine vinegar.

If you cut up the breast meat into bite-size pieces, you can serve this dish as a stew over rice.

Rabbit, squirrel, and duck are all used in Sauce Piquante variations.

CHICKEN SAUCE PIQUANTE

One serving

Calories	206	Calcium	47.4 mg
Protein	27.1 g	Iron	2.38 mg
Carbohydrates	15.5 g	Sodium	65.1 mg
Dietary Fiber	2.53 g		
Fat-Total	3.99 g		
Fat-Saturated	1.03 g		
Fat-Mono	1.21 g		
Fat-Poly	0.921 g		
Cholesterol	65.0 mg		

Calories from protein:	53%	Poly/Sat	=	0.9:1
Calories from carbohydrates:	30%	Sod/Pot	=	0.1:1
Calories from fats:	17%	Ca/Phos	=	0.3:1
		CSI	=	4.3

SUGGESTED MENU:

One serving

Oyster and Artichoke Soup
Chicken Sauce Piquante
Country Rice
Cauliflower with Dill Pickle Salad
Cherries Jubilee

Calories	577	Calcium	276 mg
Protein	40.6 g	Iron	9.60 mg
Carbohydrates	85.8 g	Sodium	205 mg
Dietary Fiber	9.26 g		
Fat-Total	6.65 g		
Fat-Saturated	1.96 g		
Fat-Mono	1.72 g		
Fat-Poly	1.68 g		
Cholesterol	95.4 mg		

Calories from protein:	29%	Poly/Sat	=	0.9:1
Calories from carbohydrates:	61%	Sod/Pot	=	0.1:1
Calories from fats:	11%	Ca/Phos	=	0.6:1
		CSI	=	6.8

MEAT

Bouilli (Boiled Beef)

Daube Glacé

Grillades and Grits

Tripe Creole

Braised Pork Tenderloin

Fillet Marchand de Vin

Bouilli (Boiled Beef)

Serves 2

INGREDIENTS:

1 rib celery
1 sprig fresh parsley
4 whole black peppercorns
1 cup sliced onion
1 clove garlic, crushed
1 bay leaf

1/4 teaspoon thyme
Water
8 ounces lean beef roast
2 tablespoons prepared
    horseradish

PREPARATION:

Tie the celery, parsley, and peppercorns in cheesecloth. Add them with the next four ingredients to a saucepan with enough water to later cover the meat.

Bring to a boil and boil for 5 minutes to get all the flavors into the cooking liquid.

Add the meat and simmer, covered, for 2 hours, or until it is very tender and can be broken apart with a fork.

TO SERVE:

Cut the bouilli in half and place on 2 dinner plates. Accompany each serving with a tablespoon of horseradish.

NOTE:

Bouilli, which means "boiled beef," is often served in 2 courses. First the bouillon that has evolved when the beef was boiled (make sure to remove the cheesecloth bag), then the meat as a separate course.

VARIATIONS:

Traditionally this dish was done with brisket, but we have opted for a lean and less fatty cut. Do not use other high-fat cuts such as chuck or rib; flank, round, rump, or blade would be appropriate. The cut can be tough because it is going to cook for a long time until it is tender.

Add some carrots to the water for more of a vegetable taste.

BOUILLI (BOILED BEEF)   *One serving*

Calories	206	Calcium	7.54 mg
Protein	33.7 g	Iron	2.30 mg
Carbohydrates	0.467 g	Sodium	74.0 mg
Dietary Fiber	0.045 g		
Fat-Total	7.57 g		
Fat-Saturated	2.87 g		
Fat-Mono	3.18 g		
Fat-Poly	0.308 g		
Cholesterol	78.6 mg		

Calories from protein:	66%	Poly/Sat	=	0.1:1
Calories from carbohydrates:	1%	Sod/Pot	=	0.2:1
Calories from fats:	33%	Ca/Phos	=	0.0:1
		CSI	=	6.8

SUGGESTED MENU: *One serving*

Celery-Stuffed Artichoke Hearts
Bouilli (Boiled Beef)
Smothered Yellow Squash
Rice Pudding

Calories	440	Calcium	203 mg
Protein	43.8 g	Iron	6.45 mg
Carbohydrates	51.2 g	Sodium	243 mg
Dietary Fiber	8.38 g		
Fat-Total	8.56 g		
Fat-Saturated	3.20 g		
Fat-Mono	3.30 g		
Fat-Poly	0.629 g		
Cholesterol	79.6 mg		

Calories from protein:	38%	Poly/Sat	=	0.2:1
Calories from carbohydrates:	45%	Sod/Pot	=	0.2:1
Calories from fats:	17%	Ca/Phos	=	0.4:1
		CSI	=	7.2

Daube Glacé

Serves 2

INGREDIENTS:

8 ounces lean round steak
1 cup sliced carrot
1 cup chopped onion
¼ cup chopped celery
2 cloves garlic, minced
1 tablespoon minced fresh
   parsley
¼ teaspoon thyme

2 bay leaves
¼ teaspoon ground allspice
⅛ teaspoon freshly ground
   black pepper
¼ cup sherry
3 cups water
1-ounce packet unflavored
   gelatin

PREPARATION:

Put the meat, vegetables, and remaining ingredients in a saucepan.

Simmer covered over very low heat for about 3 hours, or until the meat is tender enough to break apart easily with a fork.

Break the meat into pieces and return to the saucepan. Pour everything into a small loaf pan or soup bowl, cover tightly, and place in the refrigerator to set.

When the Daube has set, dip the bottom of the mold in hot water to loosen it from its container. Turn out onto a plate.

TO SERVE:

Carefully slice the Daube Glacé.

NOTES:

The liquid may simmer down during this long cooking. Add some water if there is not enough liquid to come level with the top of the cooked ingredients in the loaf pan.

The word *daube* means "to stew." A Daube Glacé is an "iced," or chilled, stew.

VARIATION:

You might want to use 4 whole allspice instead of the ground and 4 whole cloves wrapped together in cheesecloth to get more of a spice taste. Remember to remove and discard these after cooking and before refrigerating the Daube Glacé.

DAUBE GLACÉ   *One serving*

Calories	279		Calcium	56.2 mg
Protein	38.0 g		Iron	3.30 mg
Carbohydrates	12.0 g		Sodium	116 mg
Dietary Fiber	3.50 g			
Fat-Total	7.91 g			
Fat-Saturated	2.94 g			
Fat-Mono	3.22 g			
Fat-Poly	0.446 g			
Cholesterol	78.6 mg			

Calories from protein:	56%	Poly/Sat	=	0.2:1
Calories from carbohydrates:	18%	Sod/Pot	=	0.2:1
Calories from fats:	26%	Ca/Phos	=	0.2:1
		CSI	=	6.9

SUGGESTED MENU: *One serving*

Red Bean Soup
Creole Tomatoes with Basil, Garlic, and Green-Onion Dressing
Daube Glacé
Pineapple with Port Wine

Calories	606		Calcium	188 mg
Protein	51.1 g		Iron	8.26 mg
Carbohydrates	64.8 g		Sodium	165 mg
Dietary Fiber	17.8 g			
Fat-Total	9.23 g			
Fat-Saturated	3.11 g			
Fat-Mono	3.38 g			
Fat-Poly	1.09 g			
Cholesterol	78.8 mg			

Calories from protein:	34%	Poly/Sat	=	0.4:1
Calories from carbohydrates:	43%	Sod/Pot	=	0.1:1
Calories from fats:	14%	Ca/Phos	=	0.3:1
Other calories (i.e. alcohol):	10%	CSI	=	7.1

Grillades and Grits

Serves 2

INGREDIENTS:

*6 ounces lean veal or beef round
    steak*
½ cup chopped onion
*¼ cup chopped green bell
    pepper*
½ cup chopped peeled tomato
1 tablespoon dry brown "roux"
2 cloves garlic, minced

*1 tablespoon minced fresh
    parsley*
1 bay leaf
1 cup water
*Freshly ground black pepper to
    taste*
1 cup hot cooked grits

PREPARATION:

Pound the meat to tenderize it and cut it into 2-by-3-inch pieces.

Heat a wide heavy skillet over high heat and lightly sear the meat for 30 seconds on each side.

Add the onion and bell pepper and cook 5 minutes, or until the onion begins to brown.

Add remaining ingredients, cover, and simmer gently for 1 hour, or until the meat is very tender and the ingredients have become a rich gravy.

Serve the Grillades and the gravy with ½ cup grits per portion.

NOTES:

The steak may not take as long as an hour to become tender. Test as you simmer.

Add more water or some beef stock if the gravy becomes too thick.

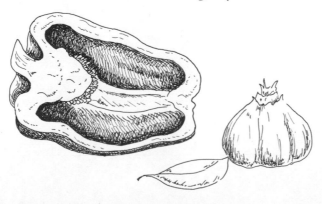

VARIATIONS:

Many cooks make grillades without the tomatoes. I prefer the taste that the tomatoes give to the sauce.

The Grillades can be served with rice instead of grits.

GRILLADES AND GRITS
One serving

Calories	279	Calcium	27.0 mg	
Protein	30.0 g	Iron	4.34 mg	
Carbohydrates	25.3 g	Sodium	50.4 mg	
Dietary Fiber	2.17 g			
Fat-Total	9.28 g			
Fat-Saturated	2.99 g			
Fat-Mono	3.81 g			
Fat-Poly	0.612 g			
Cholesterol	81.7 mg			

Calories from protein:	39%	Poly/Sat	=	0.2:1
Calories from carbohydrates:	33%	Sod/Pot	=	0.1:1
Calories from fats:	27%	Ca/Phos	=	0.1:1
		CSI	=	7.1

SUGGESTED MENU:
One serving

Brandy Milk Punch
Grillades and Grits
Vinegared Cucumber and Mustard-Seed Salad
Stewed Okra and Tomato
Pineapple Bread Pudding with Rum Sauce.

Calories	619	Calcium	548 mg
Protein	48.8 g	Iron	6.87 mg
Carbohydrates	75.1 g	Sodium	484 mg
Dietary Fiber	7.61 g		
Fat-Total	14.5 g		
Fat-Saturated	5.51 g		
Fat-Mono	5.49 g		
Fat-Poly	1.23 g		
Cholesterol	97.3 mg		

Calories from protein:	31%	Poly/Sat	=	0.2:1
Calories from carbohydrates:	48%	Sod/Pot	=	0.3:1
Calories from fats:	21%	Ca/Phos	=	0.8:1
		CSI	=	10.4

Tripe Creole

Serves 2

INGREDIENTS:

4 cloves
6 whole black peppercorns
1 teaspoon white vinegar
2 cups water
8 ounces raw beef tripe
3/4 cup chopped onion
1/2 cup minced green bell
    pepper
1/4 cup minced celery
1 tablespoon minced fresh
    parsley

1 cup chopped peeled tomato
2 cloves garlic, minced
1/4 teaspoon thyme
1/4 teaspoon ground allspice
2 bay leaves
1 tablespoon tomato paste
1/4 cup red wine
Freshly ground black pepper to
    taste

PREPARATION:

Add the cloves, peppercorns, and vinegar to the water and bring to a boil.

Add the tripe and simmer for 2 hours, or until it is very tender.

Drain the tripe, cut it into bite-size pieces, and set aside. Discard cooking liquid.

In a heavy saucepan cook the onion and bell pepper, stirring, for 2 minutes, then add all remaining ingredients including the tripe.

Simmer for 20 minutes.

TO SERVE:

Spoon the Tripe Creole into warm soup bowls and serve.

NOTES:

Tripe is not as popular in the United States as it once was, although in countries such as France it remains an extremely popular dish.

Tripe has a distinctive taste that is quite delicious.

VARIATIONS:

You may want to add 2 teaspoons of dry brown "roux" to thicken the sauce and to give it a deep smoky taste.

Brandy in place of the wine is quite delicious.

TRIPE CREOLE   *One serving*

Calories	113	Calcium	115 mg
Protein	12.2 g	Iron	2.79 mg
Carbohydrates	14.6 g	Sodium	68.7 mg
Dietary Fiber	3.43 g		
Fat-Total	1.77 g		
Fat-Saturated	0.697 g		
Fat-Mono	0.466 g		
Fat-Poly	0.270 g		
Cholesterol	44.9 mg		

Calories from protein:	40%	Poly/Sat	=	0.4:1
Calories from carbohydrates:	47%	Sod/Pot	=	0.1:1
Calories from fats:	13%	Ca/Phos	=	1.1:1
		CSI	=	2.9

SUGGESTED MENU: *One serving*

Red Bean Soup
Tripe Creole
Boiled New Potatoes
Green Salad with Creamy Creole Dressing
Strawberry Bavarian Cream

Calories	451	Calcium	403 mg
Protein	34.3 g	Iron	8.80 mg
Carbohydrates	76.7 g	Sodium	273 mg
Dietary Fiber	18.3 g		
Fat-Total	3.06 g		
Fat-Saturated	0.913 g		
Fat-Mono	0.889 g		
Fat-Poly	0.682 g		
Cholesterol	46.3 mg		

Calories from protein:	29%	Poly/Sat	=	0.7:1
Calories from carbohydrates:	65%	Sod/Pot	=	0.1:1
Calories from fats:	6%	Ca/Phos	=	0.8:1
		CSI	=	3.2

Braised Pork Tenderloin

Serves 2

INGREDIENTS:

6 ounces lean pork tenderloin
1/2 cup chopped onion
1/4 cup chopped green onion
1/4 cup chopped green bell pepper
2 tablespoons chopped celery

2 cloves garlic, minced
1 teaspoon minced fresh parsley
1/4 teaspoon thyme
1/4 teaspoon freshly ground black pepper

PREPARATION:

Preheat the oven to 375 degrees. Lay the pork in a small baking pan.

Combine all the vegetables and seasonings and spoon them on and around the meat in the pan. Cover.

Bake for 45 minutes.

Slice the tenderloin and serve it with the cooking vegetables as garnish.

NOTE:

This is an unusually light way to use lean pork.

VARIATIONS:

Pork is also delicious baked with a chopped apple, an onion, and 2 cloves of garlic.

BRAISED PORK TENDERLOIN   *One serving*

Calories	223	Calcium	35.9 mg
Protein	28.3 g	Iron	1.74 mg
Carbohydrates	5.88 g	Sodium	75.5 mg
Dietary Fiber	1.39 g		
Fat-Total	9.13 g		
Fat-Saturated	3.11 g		
Fat-Mono	4.04 g		
Fat-Poly	1.17 g		
Cholesterol	83.9 mg		

Calories from protein:	52%	Poly/Sat	=	0.4:1
Calories from carbohydrates:	11%	Sod/Pot	=	0.1:1
Calories from fats:	38%	Ca/Phos	=	0.2:1
		CSI	=	7.3

SUGGESTED MENU: *One serving*

Oyster and Crab Casserole
Braised Pork Tenderloin
Cauliflower with Dill Pickle Salad
Pear Compote with Brandied Vanilla Cream

Calories	500	Calcium	255 mg
Protein	44.7 g	Iron	7.67 mg
Carbohydrates	51.0 g	Sodium	386 mg
Dietary Fiber	9.26 g		
Fat-Total	12.1 g		
Fat-Saturated	3.99 g		
Fat-Mono	4.64 g		
Fat-Poly	1.97 g		
Cholesterol	136 mg		

Calories from protein:	36%	Poly/Sat	=	0.5:1
Calories from carbohydrates:	42%	Sod/Pot	=	0.3:1
Calories from fats:	22%	Ca/Phos	=	0.5:1
		CSI	=	10.8

Fillet Marchand de Vin   *Serves 2*

INGREDIENTS FOR THE SAUCE:

(Makes 1 1/2 cups, 6 servings.)
1/2 cup pureed raw onion
2 tablespoons crushed garlic
1 cup pureed mushrooms
1/2 cup pureed tomato pulp, no skin or seeds
2 tablespoons minced celery
1 tablespoon minced fresh parsley
2 teaspoons dry brown "roux"

1 tablespoon tomato paste
1/4 cup red wine
1/2 cup unsalted beef stock
1 bay leaf
1/4 teaspoon thyme
1/8 teaspoon freshly ground black pepper

2 three-ounce lean beef fillets

PREPARATION:

Combine all the sauce ingredients in a saucepan, cover, and simmer gently for 20 minutes.

Grill or broil the beef fillets to your liking.

Serve the meat with the sauce spooned over or on the side.

NOTE:

This sauce can be divided into small quantities and frozen for future use.

VARIATIONS:

The *Marchand de Vin,* or "wine merchant sauce" can also be used with lean veal, pork, or chicken.

FILLET MARCHAND DE VIN   *One serving*

Calories	193		Calcium	20.3 mg
Protein	25.2 g		Iron	2.90 mg
Carbohydrates	4.71 g		Sodium	61.3 mg
Dietary Fiber	0.930 g			
Fat-Total	7.00 g			
Fat-Saturated	2.50 g			
Fat-Mono	2.94 g			
Fat-Poly	0.362 g			
Cholesterol	70.0 mg			

Calories from protein:	55%	Poly/Sat	=	0.1:1
Calories from carbohydrates:	10%	Sod/Pot	=	0.1:1
Calories from fats:	34%	Ca/Phos	=	0.1:1
		CSI	=	6.0

SUGGESTED MENU: *One serving*

Creole Chicken Soup
Fillet Marchand de Vin
Leeks Vinaigrette
Boiled New Potatoes
Strawberry Bavarian Cream

Calories	564		Calcium	225 mg
Protein	62.9 g		Iron	7.79 mg
Carbohydrates	48.7 g		Sodium	228 mg
Dietary Fiber	9.18 g			
Fat-Total	16.1 g			
Fat-Saturated	4.88 g			
Fat-Mono	6.12 g			
Fat-Poly	2.18 g			
Cholesterol	159 mg			

Calories from protein:	43%	Poly/Sat	=	0.4:1
Calories from carbohydrates:	33%	Sod/Pot	=	0.1:1
Calories from fats:	24%	Ca/Phos	=	0.4:1
		CSI	=	12.9

SPECIALTIES

Red Beans and Rice

Jambalaya

Stuffed Green Bell Peppers

Mirliton Stuffed with Shrimp

Eggplant Stuffed with
  Crabmeat and Turkey Ham

Corn Oat-Bran Bread

Red Beans and Rice

Serves 2

INGREDIENTS:

½ cup dried red kidney beans
2 cups water
½ cup chopped onion
¼ cup chopped green bell
  pepper
¼ cup chopped green onion
1 bay leaf
¼ teaspoon thyme

1 clove garlic, minced
⅛ teaspoon freshly ground
  black pepper
3 ounces turkey ham, cut into
  ½-inch cubes
1 cup hot cooked white rice, no
  salt or fat added

PREPARATION:

Put all the ingredients except the rice in a saucepan and simmer covered for 1½ hours, or until the beans are tender and the sauce is thick.

TO SERVE:

Spoon ½ cup of rice onto each plate and ladle the Red Beans and Turkey Ham over or around the rice.

NOTES:

You may want to add the turkey ham during the last 30 minutes of cooking so it doesn't become so tender that it falls apart.

If you want fairly firm beans but a thick gravy at the same time, mash ½ cup of the cooked beans and stir them back into the pot. This will thicken the remaining liquid.

VARIATIONS:

The turkey ham is not a necessary ingredient. The beans themselves are very tasty and with the other seasonings can hold their own.

Serve chopped onion, white or green, as a garnish to sprinkle on the beans.

Hot Sauce and pickled hot peppers are also customary accompaniments.

RED BEANS AND RICE   *One serving*

Calories	335	Calcium	89.9 mg
Protein	21.0 g	Iron	6.45 mg
Carbohydrates	55.0 g	Sodium	419 mg
Dietary Fiber	11.5 g		
Fat-Total	3.05 g		
Fat-Saturated	0.830 g		
Fat-Mono	0.670 g		
Fat-Poly	1.03 g		
Cholesterol	23.9 mg		

Calories from protein:	25%	Poly/Sat	=	1.2:1
Calories from carbohydrates:	66%	Sod/Pot	=	0.5:1
Calories from fats:	8%	Ca/Phos	=	0.3:1
		CSI	=	2.0

SUGGESTED MENU: *One serving*

Oyster and Artichoke Soup
Red Beans and Rice
Pickled Mirliton Salad
Stewed Okra and Tomatoes
Pineapple Bread Pudding with Rum Sauce

Calories	667	Calcium	541 mg
Protein	41.7 g	Iron	13.5 mg
Carbohydrates	103 g	Sodium	783 mg
Dietary Fiber	18.5 g		
Fat-Total	8.98 g		
Fat-Saturated	3.49 g		
Fat-Mono	2.10 g		
Fat-Poly	1.97 g		
Cholesterol	65.8 mg		

Calories from protein:	25%	Poly/Sat	=	0.6:1
Calories from carbohydrates:	62%	Sod/Pot	=	0.4:1
Calories from fats:	12%	Ca/Phos	=	0.7:1
		CSI	=	6.8

Jambalaya

Serves 2

INGREDIENTS:

½ cup chopped onion
¼ cup chopped green bell
  pepper
½ cup chopped tomato
2 cloves garlic, minced
1 bay leaf
¼ teaspoon thyme
2 teaspoons minced fresh
  parsley

⅛ teaspoon freshly ground
  black pepper
Pinch cayenne
1 cup chicken stock made
  without salt or fat (see recipe
  page 30)
½ cup uncooked rice
2 ounces cubed lean chicken,
  cooked or raw

PREPARATION:

Heat a saucepan and add the onion and bell pepper. Using a wooden spoon, stir them over medium heat until they begin to color while you scrape the sides and bottom of the pan to be sure that nothing sticks and burns.

Add the tomato, garlic, herbs, and seasonings and stir together.

Add the stock and bring to a boil.

Add the rice and chicken and bring to a simmer. Cover and simmer gently for 20 minutes, then uncover and let the Jambalaya dry out a bit.

Fluff up the Jambalaya with a fork and serve.

NOTES:

Different rices will vary this dish. Experiment. It is not necessary that each grain be separate. Jambalaya, by the nature of its cooking process, may be somewhat sticky and perhaps the better dish for it.

VARIATION:

Jambalaya can be made with shrimp, lean turkey sausage, smoked chicken, or smoked turkey. Just remember to keep it light.

JAMBALAYA
One serving

Calories	250	Calcium	35.2 mg
Protein	12.4 g	Iron	2.45 mg
Carbohydrates	43.5 g	Sodium	32.3 mg
Dietary Fiber	2.16 g		
Fat-Total	2.58 g		
Fat-Saturated	0.674 g		
Fat-Mono	0.838 g		
Fat-Poly	0.669 g		
Cholesterol	25.3 mg		

Calories from protein:	20%	Poly/Sat	=	1.0:1
Calories from carbohydrates:	70%	Sod/Pot	=	0.1:1
Calories from fats:	9%	Ca/Phos	=	0.3:1
		CSI	=	1.9

SUGGESTED MENU:
One serving

Crab and Corn Bisque
Jambalaya
Leeks Vinaigrette
Hot Apple Soufflé

Calories	525	Calcium	131 mg
Protein	32.3 g	Iron	5.38 mg
Carbohydrates	94.6 g	Sodium	152 mg
Dietary Fiber	13.1 g		
Fat-Total	5.03 g		
Fat-Saturated	1.08 g		
Fat-Mono	1.37 g		
Fat-Poly	1.70 g		
Cholesterol	69.1 mg		

Calories from protein:	23%	Poly/Sat	=	1.6:1
Calories from carbohydrates:	68%	Sod/Pot	=	0.1:1
Calories from fats:	8%	Ca/Phos	=	0.3:1
		CSI	=	4.5

Stuffed Green Bell Peppers   *Serves 2*

INGREDIENTS:

1 cup chopped onion	*1 cup water*
1/2 cup chopped green onion	*1/8 teaspoon freshly ground*
1/4 cup minced celery	*black pepper*
2 cloves garlic, minced	*1/3 cup uncooked white rice*
1 cup ground lean turkey	*2 green bell peppers*

PREPARATION:

Heat a heavy skillet and add the onion, green onion, and celery. Cook over medium heat while stirring regularly with a wooden spoon to be sure that nothing sticks to the pan.

When the onions begin to color, add the garlic and turkey. Cook, stirring, for 1 minute more.

Add the water and ground pepper. Bring to a boil and add the rice. Cover and simmer for 20 minutes.

Preheat the oven to 375 degrees.

Cut the tops off the bell peppers and remove the stems and seeds. Stuff the shells with the rice mixture.

Bake for 25 minutes, or until the bell pepper shells are tender.

NOTES:

Keep the stuffing mixture moving in the skillet. Remember that you are cooking with no fat and otherwise the ingredients can stick to the pan. Use a wooden spoon or spatula and just keep scraping the ingredients from around the sides and bottom. If your bell peppers are small and you have leftover stuffing, try it with any stuffable vegetable; tomatoes are great!

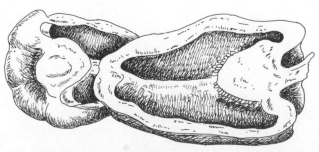

VARIATIONS:

You can get a decidedly firmer texture by adding ½ cup bread crumbs to the mixture after you've removed it from the heat. Then when slightly cooled, blend in an egg white to bind the stuffing during the baking.

Chicken or lean veal or beef could be substituted for the turkey. Shrimp or crabmeat also make excellent stuffing.

STUFFED GREEN BELL PEPPERS   *One serving*

Calories	288		Calcium	77.8 mg
Protein	24.9 g		Iron	4.01 mg
Carbohydrates	37.4 g		Sodium	72.9 mg
Dietary Fiber	3.61 g			
Fat-Total	4.21 g			
Fat-Saturated	1.28 g			
Fat-Mono	0.819 g			
Fat-Poly	1.34 g			
Cholesterol	53.5 mg			

Calories from protein:	35%	Poly/Sat	=	1.0:1
Calories from carbohydrates:	52%	Sod/Pot	=	0.1:1
Calories from fats:	13%	Ca/Phos	=	0.3:1
		CSI	=	4.0

SUGGESTED MENU: *One serving*

Stuffed Green Bell Peppers
Banana Baked with Sherry
Green Salad with Creamy Creole Dressing
Strawberry Bavarian Cream

Calories	442		Calcium	279 mg
Protein	34.3 g		Iron	4.98 mg
Carbohydrates	62.5 g		Sodium	244 mg
Dietary Fiber	7.20 g			
Fat-Total	5.20 g			
Fat-Saturated	1.50 g			
Fat-Mono	1.22 g			
Fat-Poly	1.51 g			
Cholesterol	54.9 mg			

Calories from protein:	32%	Poly/Sat	=	1.0:1
Calories from carbohydrates:	58%	Sod/Pot	=	0.2:1
Calories from fats:	11%	Ca/Phos	=	0.7:1
		CSI	=	4.3

Mirliton (Chayote or Vegetable Pear) Stuffed with Shrimp

Serves 2

INGREDIENTS:

1 medium mirliton
Water
1/2 cup chopped onion
1 clove garlic, minced
1 teaspoon minced fresh parsley
1/8 teaspoon thyme

1/8 teaspoon freshly ground
  black pepper
Pinch cayenne
4 ounces small peeled, deveined
  shrimp
1/4 cup bread crumbs

PREPARATION:

Put the mirliton in a pot with enough water to cover and bring to a boil.

Simmer covered for 45 minutes to 1 hour, or until the mirliton is tender enough to be easily pierced with the blade of a small sharp knife. Remove from the water and set aside to cool. Discard the water.

When cool enough to handle, cut the mirliton in half lengthwise and discard the seed. Scrape out the meat, making a shell of the skin about 1/4-inch thick. Chop the meat and set it aside with the shells.

Heat a heavy skillet and add the onion. Stir with a wooden spoon while cooking over high heat until lightly colored.

Add the garlic and cook it with the onions for 1 minute.

Add the mirliton meat, the parsley, thyme, pepper, and cayenne. Cook while stirring occasionally to be sure that all is cooking evenly and nothing is sticking to the bottom or sides of the skillet. Continue cooking for 2 minutes.

Add the shrimp to the mixture and stir. Reduce the heat to medium and cover the skillet for 1 minute to cook the shrimp.

Stir in the bread crumbs and continue heating for another minute, then remove from heat.

Preheat the oven to 375 degrees.

Let the stuffing mixture cool slightly and spoon it into the mirliton shells. Place them in a baking pan.

Bake for 20 minutes.

NOTE:

This dish can be served as an appetizer, an entree, or even as a side course with another dish.

VARIATIONS:

You can add an egg white to the mixture before you stuff it into the shells to bind the filling better. I have done this with some other stuffings in this collection but it is not necessary here.

Use crabmeat in place of the shrimp.

MIRLITON STUFFED WITH SHRIMP   *One serving*

Calories	151		Calcium	95.4 mg
Protein	14.0 g		Iron	2.47 mg
Carbohydrates	21.6 g		Sodium	190 mg
Dietary Fiber	2.21 g			
Fat-Total	1.98 g			
Fat-Saturated	0.376 g			
Fat-Mono	0.361 g			
Fat-Poly	0.442 g			
Cholesterol	76.0 mg			

Calories from protein:	35%	Poly/Sat	=	1.2:1
Calories from carbohydrates:	54%	Sod/Pot	=	0.4:1
Calories from fats:	11%	Ca/Phos	=	0.5:1
		CSI	=	4.2

SUGGESTED MENU: *One serving*

Creole Fish Stew
Mirliton Stuffed with Shrimp
Celery Rémoulade
Orange Flip

Calories	409		Calcium	394 mg
Protein	38.7 g		Iron	5.87 mg
Carbohydrates	55.2 g		Sodium	596 mg
Dietary Fiber	8.97 g			
Fat-Total	6.74 g			
Fat-Saturated	1.03 g			
Fat-Mono	2.26 g			
Fat-Poly	1.59 g			
Cholesterol	133 mg			

Calories from protein:	35%	Poly/Sat	=	1.5:1
Calories from carbohydrates:	51%	Sod/Pot	=	0.3:1
Calories from fats:	14%	Ca/Phos	=	0.6:1
		CSI	=	7.7

Eggplant Stuffed with Crabmeat and Turkey Ham   *Serves 2*

INGREDIENTS:

1 medium eggplant
Water
1 cup chopped onion
1 cup chopped green onion
1/2 cup chopped green bell
*   pepper*
1/2 cup chopped celery
1/2 cup crabmeat, cartilage
*   removed*

4 ounces turkey ham, cut into
*   1/4-inch cubes*
2 cloves garlic, minced
1 tablespoon minced fresh
*   parsley*
1 bay leaf
1/4 teaspoon thyme
1/4 teaspoon freshly ground
*   black pepper*

PREPARATION:

Cut the eggplant in half lengthwise and put it in a saucepan with enough water to cover. Bring to a boil and cook for approximately 20 minutes, or until the eggplant is soft to the touch.

Carefully remove the eggplant from the water and set aside to drain and cool. Preheat the oven to 375 degrees.

When cool enough to handle, scrape the meat from the inside of the eggplant halves with a spoon, leaving about 1/4 inch meat on the shells. Be very cautious that you don't tear the skins, which become the shells for stuffing. Set aside.

Heat a heavy skillet over medium heat and add the onion, green onion, bell pepper, and celery. Cook while stirring until they begin to color.

Add the eggplant meat and all remaining ingredients. Cook while stirring for 2 minutes more.

Spoon the mixture into the eggplant shells and place them in a baking pan. Bake for 15 minutes.

NOTE:

This dish makes a wonderful meal with nothing more than a salad and a light dessert.

VARIATIONS:

Shrimp can be used in place of the crab.
Omit the turkey ham if you like.

STUFFED EGGPLANT
One serving

Calories	190	Calcium	106 mg
Protein	21.2 g	Iron	4.33 mg
Carbohydrates	21.0 g	Sodium	600 mg
Dietary Fiber	7.87 g		
Fat-Total	4.15 g		
Fat-Saturated	1.16 g		
Fat-Mono	0.941 g		
Fat-Poly	1.24 g		
Cholesterol	57.8 mg		

Calories from protein:	41%	Poly/Sat	=	1.1:1
Calories from carbohydrates:	41%	Sod/Pot	=	0.6:1
Calories from fats:	18%	Ca/Phos	=	0.4:1
		CSI	=	4.1

SUGGESTED MENU:
One serving

Oyster and Artichoke Soup
Stuffed Eggplant
Seasoned Boiled Brussels Sprouts
Raisin Oat-Bran Cookies

Calories	459	Calcium	320 mg
Protein	41.8 g	Iron	12.3 mg
Carbohydrates	68.1 g	Sodium	883 mg
Dietary Fiber	17.9 g		
Fat-Total	7.46 g		
Fat-Saturated	1.98 g		
Fat-Mono	1.60 g		
Fat-Poly	2.59 g		
Cholesterol	86.6 mg		

Calories from protein:	33%	Poly/Sat	=	1.3:1
Calories from carbohydrates:	54%	Sod/Pot	=	0.4:1
Calories from fats:	13%	Ca/Phos	=	0.5:1
		CSI	=	6.3

Corn Oat-Bran Bread

Serves 4

INGREDIENTS:

½ cup yellow cornmeal
½ cup oat bran
½ cup skim milk
¼ cup chopped onion
¼ cup chopped green bell pepper

1 egg white
1 teaspoon baking powder
⅛ teaspoon ground allspice
⅛ teaspoon freshly ground black
  pepper

PREPARATION:

Preheat the oven to 350 degrees.
Blend all ingredients and pour into a small (8×4-inch) nonstick loaf pan.
Bake for 35 minutes, or until a knife inserted in the center of the bread comes out clean.

NOTE:

The oat bran makes this a most healthful and enjoyable accompaniment to any meal.

VARIATIONS:

Using ½ cup fresh corn kernels in place of the onion and bell pepper is a tasty alternative.
The addition of ¼ teaspoon cayenne will add a nice bit of spice to this bread.

CORN OAT-BRAN BREAD   *One serving*

Calories	123		Calcium	63.1 mg
Protein	5.05 g		Iron	1.32 mg
Carbohydrates	9.95 g		Sodium	112 mg
Dietary Fiber	1.41 g			
Fat-Total	0.962 g			
Fat-Saturated	0.189 g			
Fat-Mono	0.296 g			
Fat-Poly	0.402 g			
Cholesterol	0.500 mg			

Calories from protein:	16%	Poly/Sat	=	2.1:1
Calories from carbohydrates:	32%	Sod/Pot	=	0.7:1
Calories from fats:	7%	Ca/Phos	=	0.5:1
Other calories (i.e. alcohol):	44%	CSI	=	0.2

SALADS

Red and White Bean Salad

Creole Tomatoes with Basil, Garlic, and
    Green-Onion Dressing

Artichokes and Aioli

Coleslaw

Cauliflower Salad with Dill Pickle

Iceberg Lettuce with Onion and Parmesan Dressing

Boiled Onion Salad

Celery Rémoulade

Vinegared Cucumber and Mustard-Seed Salad

Pickled Mirliton Salad

Green Salad with Creamy Creole Dressing

Celery-Stuffed Artichoke-Heart Salad

Tomato and Green-Onion Salad Citronette

Red and White Bean Salad   *Serves 2*

INGREDIENTS:

$^1/_4$ *cup dried red beans*
$^1/_4$ *cup dried white beans*
$^1/_2$ *cup chopped onion*
1 clove garlic, minced

$^1/_4$ *teaspoon thyme*
$^1/_8$ *teaspoon freshly ground
   black pepper*
2 cups water

DRESSING INGREDIENTS:

2 tablespoons vinegar
$^1/_4$ *teaspoon powdered mustard*

$^1/_8$ *teaspoon freshly ground
   black pepper*

1 cup chopped romaine lettuce
*2 tablespoons chopped green
   onion*

2 tablespoons chopped celery

PREPARATION:

Place the beans, the onion, garlic, thyme, pepper, and water in a pot and bring to a rolling boil. Turn down to a simmer and cook covered for 1 $^1/_2$ hours, or until the beans are tender but not mushy.

Drain the beans, discarding the liquid, and refrigerate them in a covered container for 2 to 3 hours.

MAKE THE SALAD:

Combine the dressing ingredients and set aside.
Combine the lettuce, green onion, and celery with the chilled beans.
Toss the bean mixture with the dressing and serve.

NOTES:

Soaking the beans in warm water for an hour or so before you begin to cook them will plump them up a bit and prevent the skin from breaking.

VARIATION:

You don't need both red and white beans here to make a good salad. Either one will do alone, as would black beans, a combination of the three, or any other colorful beans.

RED AND WHITE BEAN SALAD   *One serving*

Calories	181	Calcium	98.4 mg
Protein	11.5 g	Iron	4.47 mg
Carbohydrates	32.8 g	Sodium	30.8 mg
Dietary Fiber	7.46 g		
Fat-Total	0.842 g		
Fat-Saturated	0.115 g		
Fat-Mono	0.103 g		
Fat-Poly	0.477 g		
Cholesterol	0 mg		

Calories from protein:	25%	Poly/Sat	=	4.2:1
Calories from carbohydrates:	71%	Sod/Pot	=	0.0:1
Calories from fats:	4%	Ca/Phos	=	0.4:1
		CSI	=	0.1

SUGGESTED MENU: *One serving*

Seasoned Eggplant Fingers
Roast Duck with Apples and Onion
Red and White Bean Salad
Raisin Oat-Bran Cookies

Calories	788	Calcium	320 mg
Protein	59.8 g	Iron	11.2 mg
Carbohydrates	93.7 g	Sodium	474 mg
Dietary Fiber	16.8 g		
Fat-Total	20.2 g		
Fat-Saturated	7.04 g		
Fat-Mono	6.32 g		
Fat-Poly	3.46 g		
Cholesterol	129 mg		

Calories from protein:	30%	Poly/Sat	=	0.5:1
Calories from carbohydrates:	47%	Sod/Pot	=	0.3:1
Calories from fats:	23%	Ca/Phos	=	0.4:1
		CSI	=	13.6

Creole Tomatoes with Basil, Garlic, and Green-Onion Dressing

Serves 2

INGREDIENTS:

2 small Creole tomatoes
Coarsely ground fresh black
  pepper

¼ cup Basil, Garlic, and
  Green-Onion Dressing (recipe
  follows)

PREPARATION:

Slice the tomatoes and lay them out attractively in circles on chilled salad plates.
Sprinkle with the pepper.
Spoon a dollop of the dressing on each tomato slice.

NOTE:

Our Creole tomatoes are considered by many to be the finest tomatoes in the world. Unfortunately, like many other great fresh produce they are available for only short periods of the year and then in limited quantity. Just choose the best ripe, meaty tomatoes when Creole tomatoes are unavailable.

Basil, Garlic, and Green-Onion Dressing

Serves 2 (Makes about ¼ cup)

INGREDIENTS:

1 teaspoon minced fresh basil
1 clove garlic, minced

2 tablespoons chopped green
  onion
2 tablespoons nonfat yogurt
1 tablespoon cider vinegar

PREPARATION:

Combine all ingredients, cover tightly, and refrigerate until chilled.

NOTES:

Dressing can be kept for a week in a tightly covered jar in the refrigerator. This dressing is pungent, so be cautious.

VARIATIONS:

Add more garlic for the garlic lovers.
A teaspoon of Parmesan cheese adds to the Italian flavor of this dressing.

TOMATOES WITH BASIL, GARLIC, AND GREEN ONION *One serving*

Calories	37.8	Calcium	52.4 mg
Protein	2.17 g	Iron	0.966 mg
Carbohydrates	7.99 g	Sodium	21.6 mg
Dietary Fiber	2.27 g		
Fat-Total	0.319 g		
Fat-Saturated	0.057 g		
Fat-Mono	0.048 g		
Fat-Poly	0.116 g		
Cholesterol	0.250 mg		

Calories from protein:	20%	Poly/Sat	=	2.0:1
Calories from carbohydrates:	73%	Sod/Pot	=	0.1:1
Calories from fats:	7%	Ca/Phos	=	0.9:1
		CSI	=	0.1

SUGGESTED MENU: *One serving*

Red Bean Soup
Creole Tomatoes with Basil, Garlic, and Green-Onion Dressing
Daube Glacé
Pineapple with Port Wine

Calories	606	Calcium	188 mg
Protein	51.1 g	Iron	8.26 mg
Carbohydrates	64.8 g	Sodium	165 mg
Dietary Fiber	17.8 g		
Fat-Total	9.23 g		
Fat-Saturated	3.11 g		
Fat-Mono	3.38 g		
Fat-Poly	1.09 g		
Cholesterol	78.8 mg		

Calories from protein:	34%	Poly/Sat	=	0.4:1
Calories from carbohydrates:	43%	Sod/Pot	=	0.1:1
Calories from fats:	14%	Ca/Phos	=	0.3:1
Other calories (i.e. alcohol):	10%	CSI	=	7.1

Artichokes and Aioli (Garlic Dressing)

Serves 2

INGREDIENTS:

water   *2 medium artichokes*

AIOLI INGREDIENTS:

1/2 cup nonfat yogurt   *1/2 teaspoon powdered mustard*
3 cloves garlic, crushed   *1/4 teaspoon freshly ground*
1 teaspoon fresh lemon juice   *black pepper*

PREPARATION:

Put enough water in a pot to cover the artichokes and bring it to a boil. Add the artichokes and simmer gently, covered, for 40 minutes, or until the leaves are easily removed from the choke and the meat is tender. Refrigerate the artichokes.

Make the Aioli by combining the yogurt with the garlic, lemon juice, mustard, and pepper.

Serve the artichokes with small bowls of the Aioli for dipping.

NOTE:

This is a very tangy recipe. Be sure that you serve it to garlic lovers.

VARIATIONS:

Instead of the powdered mustard you could use two teaspoons of Creole mustard to give the Aioli an even more New Orleans taste.

The Aioli can be used as a dip for other cooked and raw vegetables such as broccoli, cauliflower, carrots, celery, or mushrooms, or served as a sauce with cold poached fish or chicken.

ARTICHOKES AND AIOLI   *One serving*

Calories	93.7		Calcium	171 mg
Protein	6.40 g		Iron	1.85 mg
Carbohydrates	18.7 g		Sodium	139 mg
Dietary Fiber	4.08 g			
Fat-Total	0.402 g			
Fat-Saturated	0.123 g			
Fat-Mono	0.090 g			
Fat-Poly	0.107 g			
Cholesterol	1.00 mg			

Calories from protein:	25%	Poly/Sat	=	0.9:1
Calories from carbohydrates:	72%	Sod/Pot	=	0.3:1
Calories from fats:	3%	Ca/Phos	=	1.0:1
		CSI	=	0.2

SUGGESTED MENU: *One serving*

Crab and Corn Bisque
Braised Pork Tenderloin
Artichokes and Aioli
Bananas Foster

Calories	663		Calcium	412 mg
Protein	55.1 g		Iron	5.40 mg
Carbohydrates	73.5 g		Sodium	323 mg
Dietary Fiber	12.0 g			
Fat-Total	12.7 g			
Fat-Saturated	4.34 g			
Fat-Mono	4.92 g			
Fat-Poly	2.18 g			
Cholesterol	133 mg			

Calories from protein:	35%	Poly/Sat	=	0.5:1
Calories from carbohydrates:	47%	Sod/Pot	=	0.2:1
Calories from fats:	18%	Ca/Phos	=	0.5:1
		CSI	=	11.0

Coleslaw

Serves 2

INGREDIENTS:

1/2 cup nonfat yogurt
1 small sweet pickle, minced
2 tablespoons minced green
  onion
1 teaspoon fresh lemon juice

1/8 teaspoon freshly ground
  black pepper
1 cup shredded cabbage
1/3 cup shredded carrot

PREPARATION:

In a bowl, combine the yogurt, pickle, green onion, lemon juice, and pepper.

Fold in the cabbage and carrot, being sure that the yogurt mixture is evenly distributed and all the cabbage and carrot is well coated.

Chill before serving.

NOTE:

Sometimes you can find pre-shredded bags of cabbage-and-carrot mixture in the grocery. This makes the Coleslaw quite simple to prepare.

VARIATIONS:

This coleslaw without the pickle is fine. Experiment with pineapple or apple.

COLESLAW   *One serving*

Calories	59.1		Calcium	137 mg
Protein	3.97 g		Iron	0.530 mg
Carbohydrates	11.2 g		Sodium	109 mg
Dietary Fiber	1.41 g			
Fat-Total	0.230 g			
Fat-Saturated	0.088 g			
Fat-Mono	0.036 g			
Fat-Poly	0.061 g			
Cholesterol	1.00 mg			

Calories from protein:	25%	Poly/Sat	=	0.7:1
Calories from carbohydrates:	71%	Sod/Pot	=	0.3:1
Calories from fats:	3%	Ca/Phos	=	1.3:1
		CSI	=	0.1

SUGGESTED MENU: *One serving*

Stuffed Mushrooms
Baked Breaded Bluefish
Coleslaw
Pineapple Bread Pudding with Rum Sauce

Calories	627		Calcium	586 mg
Protein	61.1 g		Iron	4.78 mg
Carbohydrates	59.0 g		Sodium	995 mg
Dietary Fiber	5.10 g			
Fat-Total	13.4 g			
Fat-Saturated	4.76 g			
Fat-Mono	4.62 g			
Fat-Poly	2.69 g			
Cholesterol	133 mg			

Calories from protein:	41%	Poly/Sat	=	0.6:1
Calories from carbohydrates:	39%	Sod/Pot	=	0.7:1
Calories from fats:	20%	Ca/Phos	=	0.7:1
		CSI	=	11.5

Cauliflower Salad
with Dill Pickle

Serves 2

INGREDIENTS:

    1 bay leaf
    1/8 teaspoon cayenne

    3 cups water, or enough to cover
      the cauliflower
    1 1/2 cups cauliflower florets

VINAIGRETTE INGREDIENTS:

    4 tablespoons red wine vinegar
    1/4 teaspoon powdered mustard

    1/8 teaspoon freshly ground
      black pepper

    2 tablespoons chopped dill
      pickle

PREPARATION:

Add the bay leaf and cayenne to the water in a saucepan and bring to a boil. Boil for 1 minute to bring out the flavors of the seasonings.

Drop the cauliflower into the boiling water and blanch for 1 minute. Remove the florets from the water and refrigerate them, covered, for 2 hours.

Combine the vinegar, mustard, and pepper to make the Vinaigrette. Cover and set aside.

TO SERVE:

Arrange the cauliflower florets attractively on chilled salad plates and spoon on the Vinaigrette.

Top each salad with a tablespoon of pickle.

NOTE:

Don't overcook the cauliflower florets. This is not a raw salad but the vegetable should still be firm and fairly crisp.

VARIATIONS:

Broccoli and carrots both make good alternatives in this salad in place of the cauliflower.

Use capers instead of the chopped dill pickle.

Try adding ¼ cup nonfat yogurt to the dressing to relax the tartness of the vinegar and to give the dressing both body and additional flavor.

CAULIFLOWER SALAD WITH DILL PICKLE   *One serving*

Calories	23.5		Calcium	27.6 mg
Protein	1.64 g		Iron	0.814 mg
Carbohydrates	5.90 g		Sodium	181 mg
Dietary Fiber	2.13 g			
Fat-Total	0.190 g			
Fat-Saturated	0.029 g			
Fat-Mono	0.037 g			
Fat-Poly	0.074 g			
Cholesterol	0 mg			

Calories from protein:	21%	Poly/Sat	=	2.6:1
Calories from carbohydrates:	74%	Sod/Pot	=	0.6:1
Calories from fats:	5%	Ca/Phos	=	0.7:1
		CSI	=	0.0

SUGGESTED MENU: *One serving*

Baked Oyster and Crabmeat Casserole
Braised Pork Tenderloin
Cauliflower Salad with Dill Pickle
Pear Compote with Brandied Vanilla Cream

Calories	500		Calcium	255 mg
Protein	44.7 g		Iron	7.67 mg
Carbohydrates	51.0 g		Sodium	386 mg
Dietary Fiber	9.26 g			
Fat-Total	12.1 g			
Fat-Saturated	3.99 g			
Fat-Mono	4.64 g			
Fat-Poly	1.97 g			
Cholesterol	136 mg			

Calories from protein:	36%	Poly/Sat	=	0.5:1
Calories from carbohydrates:	42%	Sod/Pot	=	0.3:1
Calories from fats:	22%	Ca/Phos	=	0.5:1
		CSI	=	10.8

Iceberg Lettuce with Onion and Parmesan Dressing

Serves 2

INGREDIENTS:

½ cup thinly sliced onion
¼ cup nonfat yogurt
1 tablespoon grated Parmesan cheese
1 teaspoon fresh lemon juice

⅛ teaspoon freshly ground black pepper
2 one-inch-thick cross-slices of iceberg lettuce

PREPARATION:

Make the dressing by combining the onion, yogurt, Parmesan, lemon juice, and pepper.

Make the salad by putting one slice of lettuce on each salad plate without breaking it up, and top it with the Onion and Parmesan Dressing.

NOTE:

This is a very delicious and tasty salad that could easily stand alone as a light lunch.

VARIATIONS:

Grated Romano cheese does equally as well as the Parmesan.
You can use chopped lettuce instead of the slices.

ICEBERG LETTUCE WITH ONION AND PARMESAN   *One serving*

Calories	49.1	Calcium	113 mg
Protein	3.74 g	Iron	0.517 mg
Carbohydrates	6.67 g	Sodium	74.7 mg
Dietary Fiber	1.46 g		
Fat-Total	1.03 g		
Fat-Saturated	0.550 g		
Fat-Mono	0.258 g		
Fat-Poly	0.120 g		
Cholesterol	2.46 mg		

Calories from protein:	29%	Poly/Sat	=	0.2:1
Calories from carbohydrates:	52%	Sod/Pot	=	0.3:1
Calories from fats:	18%	Ca/Phos	=	1.3:1
		CSI	=	0.7

SUGGESTED MENU: *One serving*

Oyster and Artichoke Soup
Iceberg Lettuce with Onion and Parmesan Dressing
Baked Breaded Chicken
Rice Pudding

Calories	623	Calcium	360 mg
Protein	66.2 g	Iron	9.32 mg
Carbohydrates	53.0 g	Sodium	482 mg
Dietary Fiber	5.48 g		
Fat-Total	15.3 g		
Fat-Saturated	4.68 g		
Fat-Mono	5.04 g		
Fat-Poly	3.47 g		
Cholesterol	180 mg		

Calories from protein:	43%	Poly/Sat	=	0.7:1
Calories from carbohydrates:	34%	Sod/Pot	=	0.4:1
Calories from fats:	22%	Ca/Phos	=	0.5:1
		CSI	=	13.7

Boiled Onion Salad

Serves 2

INGREDIENTS:

4 whole cloves
4 whole allspice, optional
2 bay leaves
2 cloves garlic, crushed
1 tablespoon cider vinegar
½ teaspoon dried thyme leaves

¼ teaspoon cayenne
1 quart water
2 whole medium red onions
   (3 ounces each), peeled
¼ cup Creole Vinaigrette
   (recipe follows)

PREPARATION:

Add all seasoning ingredients to the water and bring to a boil.

Boil for 2 minutes to bring out the flavors of the seasonings, then add the onions. Boil them for 10 minutes, until they are tender and easily pierced with a fork.

Remove the onions from the water. Drain, cover, and refrigerate until chilled.

TO ASSEMBLE:

Cut into the onions from the top almost all the way through at ½-inch intervals. Repeat the cuts crosswise to create a checkerboard pattern.

Place the onions on chilled salad plates and fold them out on all sides to create a flower-like effect.

TO SERVE:

Spoon the Creole Vinaigrette over the onions and serve.

NOTE:

Any onion can be used in this preparation but I prefer red ones for their sweetness and color.

VARIATION:

Enhance the flower look by placing the Boiled Onions on lettuce leaves and sprinkling them with a chopped hard-boiled egg-white.

Creole Vinaigrette

Serves 2 (Makes ¼ cup)

INGREDIENTS:

1 tablespoon Creole mustard
1 tablespoon minced celery

1 tablespoon white vinegar
1 tablespoon water

PREPARATION:

Combine all ingredients, cover tightly, and refrigerate.

NOTE:

This dressing will keep indefinitely in the refrigerator.

Variation:

One tablespoon fresh lemon juice in place of the vinegar will make this dressing a variation of Creole Citronette (*citron* is French for "lemon") and is a refreshing change.

BOILED ONION SALAD
One serving

Calories	36.1	Calcium	29.8 mg
Protein	1.40 g	Iron	0.533 mg
Carbohydrates	7.30 g	Sodium	103 mg
Dietary Fiber	1.35 g		
Fat-Total	0.569 g		
Fat-Saturated	0.040 g		
Fat-Mono	0.345 g		
Fat-Poly	0.090 g		
Cholesterol	0 mg		

Calories from protein:	14%	Poly/Sat	=	2.3:1
Calories from carbohydrates:	73%	Sod/Pot	=	0.6:1
Calories from fats:	13%	Ca/Phos	=	0.9:1
		CSI	=	0.0

SUGGESTED MENU:
One serving

Boiled Onion Salad
Braised Pork Tenderloin
Banana Baked with Sherry
Hot Apple Soufflé

Calories	349	Calcium	74.4 mg
Protein	31.0 g	Iron	2.59 mg
Carbohydrates	31.3 g	Sodium	189 mg
Dietary Fiber	4.73 g		
Fat-Total	10.0 g		
Fat-Saturated	3.27 g		
Fat-Mono	4.41 g		
Fat-Poly	1.33 g		
Cholesterol	83.9 mg		

Calories from protein:	36%	Poly/Sat	=	0.4:1
Calories from carbohydrates:	37%	Sod/Pot	=	0.2:1
Calories from fats:	27%	Ca/Phos	=	0.3:1
		CSI	=	7.5

Celery Rémoulade

Serves 2

INGREDIENTS:

2 tablespoons Creole mustard
2 tablespoons chopped green
  onion
1 tablespoon water
1 teaspoon minced fresh parsley

1 teaspoon fresh lemon juice
1 ½ cups sliced celery, cut
  crosswise into ¼– to ½–inch
  pieces
2 leaves Romaine lettuce

PREPARATION:

In a bowl combine the mustard, green onion, water, parsley, and lemon juice.
Fold in the celery, being sure that all of the pieces are well coated with the
mustard mixture.

TO SERVE:

Place the lettuce leaves on chilled salad plates and spoon the Celery Rémoulade onto them.

NOTES:

You may prefer the inner ribs of the celery stalks, which are more delicate.
I find the celery leaves are sometimes bitter—not unpleasantly, however . . .
something like endive. You may want to remove them. Personally, I like the bitter
taste but would caution against serving to guests who may not.
If you use large outside ribs of celery, you might scrape off the strings.

VARIATIONS:

Endive, raw vegetables such as cauliflower or broccoli, or crispy apples all
make good salads with this dressing.
Be adventuresome! Make something special with a combination of the vegetables and/or fruit that you like the most.
Chop a hard-boiled egg-white and sprinkle it over the Celery Rémoulade to
add taste, texture, and color contrast.

CELERY RÉMOULADE

One serving

Calories	30.2		Calcium	54.5 mg
Protein	1.63 g		Iron	1.01 mg
Carbohydrates	5.12 g		Sodium	276 mg
Dietary Fiber	1.94 g			
Fat-Total	0.830 g			
Fat-Saturated	0.037 g			
Fat-Mono	0.649 g			
Fat-Poly	0.075 g			
Cholesterol	0 mg			

Calories from protein:	19%	Poly/Sat	=	2.0:1	
Calories from carbohydrates:	59%	Sod/Pot	=	0.8:1	
Calories from fats:	22%	Ca/Phos	=	1.3:1	
		CSI	=	0.0	

SUGGESTED MENU:

One serving

Creole Fish Stew
Mirliton Stuffed with Shrimp
Celery Rémoulade
Orange Flip

Calories	409		Calcium	394 mg
Protein	38.7 g		Iron	5.87 mg
Carbohydrates	55.2 g		Sodium	596 mg
Dietary Fiber	8.97 g			
Fat-Total	6.74 g			
Fat-Saturated	1.03 g			
Fat-Mono	2.26 g			
Fat-Poly	1.59 g			
Cholesterol	133 mg			

Calories from protein:	35%	Poly/Sat	=	1.5:1	
Calories from carbohydrates:	51%	Sod/Pot	=	0.3:1	
Calories from fats:	14%	Ca/Phos	=	0.6:1	
		CSI	=	7.7	

Vinegared Cucumber and Mustard-Seed Salad

Serves 2

INGREDIENTS:

1 medium cucumber
¼ cup cider vinegar

1 tablespoon brown whole
   mustard seeds
¼ teaspoon freshly ground
   black pepper

PREPARATION:

Peel the cucumber and cut it in half lengthwise. Use a teaspoon to remove the seeds and cut the halves crosswise into ¼-inch slices. The result will be crescent-shaped cucumber morsels.

In a salad bowl combine the vinegar, mustard seeds, and pepper.

Add the cucumber slices and toss.

Cover and refrigerate until ready to serve.

NOTE:

The flavor of the mustard seeds develops more fully if the salad is allowed to chill for an hour or so.

VARIATIONS:

A teaspoon of any chopped fresh herb such as basil or mint is a delightful addition.

Use fresh lemon juice in place of the vinegar for a different taste.

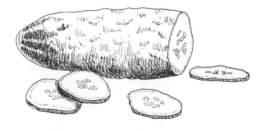

CUCUMBER AND MUSTARD-SEED SALAD   *One serving*

Calories	29.3	Calcium	29.9 mg
Protein	1.20 g	Iron	0.790 mg
Carbohydrates	6.74 g	Sodium	101 mg
Dietary Fiber	1.80 g		
Fat-Total	0.543 g		
Fat-Saturated	0.053 g		
Fat-Mono	0.319 g		
Fat-Poly	0.080 g		
Cholesterol	0 mg		

Calories from protein:	13%	Poly/Sat	=	1.5:1
Calories from carbohydrates:	74%	Sod/Pot	=	0.4:1
Calories from fats:	13%	Ca/Phos	=	0.9:1
		CSI	=	0.1

SUGGESTED MENU: *One serving*

Brandy Milk Punch
Grillades and Grits
Vinegared Cucumber and Mustard-Seed Salad
Stewed Okra and Tomato
Pineapple Bread Pudding with Rum Sauce

Calories	619	Calcium	548 mg
Protein	48.8 g	Iron	6.87 mg
Carbohydrates	75.1 g	Sodium	484 mg
Dietary Fiber	7.61 g		
Fat-Total	14.5 g		
Fat-Saturated	5.51 g		
Fat-Mono	5.49 g		
Fat-Poly	1.23 g		
Cholesterol	97.3 mg		

Calories from protein:	31%	Poly/Sat	=	0.2:1
Calories from carbohydrates:	48%	Sod/Pot	=	0.3:1
Calories from fats:	21%	Ca/Phos	=	0.8:1
		CSI	=	10.4

Pickled Mirliton Salad   *Serves 2*

INGREDIENTS:

1 mirliton (vegetable pear or
   chayote)
2 cups water
1/2 cup vinegar
6 whole allspice
6 whole black peppercorns
1 teaspoon whole mustard seeds

2 cloves garlic, mashed
2 bay leaves

2 tablespoons vinegar
Freshly ground black pepper to
   taste

PREPARATION:

Peel the mirliton, cut it in half lengthwise, and discard the seed. Cut the halves lengthwise into 1/2-inch strips.

Bring the water to a boil with the next 6 ingredients and let boil for 2 minutes to gain the flavors of the seasoning ingredients.

Add the mirliton strips and boil them for 5 minutes, or until they are just cooked but still crisp to the bite.

Remove them from the water and refrigerate until chilled.

TO SERVE:

Serve sprinkled with the vinegar and pepper.

NOTE:

You don't want to overcook the mirliton. It should not be soft; it should remain crisp.

VARIATIONS:

Try the mirliton with Creole Vinaigrette (see recipe page 174) in place of the vinegar and pepper.

Use the Aioli recipe (see page 165) as a dip with the mirliton slices.

PICKLED MIRLITON SALAD   *One serving*

Calories	22.7		Calcium	13.2 mg
Protein	0.555 g		Iron	0.351 mg
Carbohydrates	5.39 g		Sodium	0.782 mg
Dietary Fiber	0.529 g			
Fat-Total	0.418 g			
Fat-Saturated	0.004 g			
Fat-Mono	0.004 g			
Fat-Poly	0.004 g			
Cholesterol	0 mg			

Calories from protein:	8%	Poly/Sat	=	1.2:1
Calories from carbohydrates:	78%	Sod/Pot	=	0.0:1
Calories from fats:	14%	Ca/Phos	=	0.5:1
		CSI	=	0.0

SUGGESTED MENU: *One serving*

Oyster and Artichoke Soup
Red Beans and Rice
Pickled Mirliton Salad
Stewed Okra and Tomato
Pineapple Bread Pudding with Rum Sauce

Calories	667		Calcium	541 mg
Protein	41.7 g		Iron	13.5 mg
Carbohydrates	103 g		Sodium	783 mg
Dietary Fiber	18.5 g			
Fat-Total	8.98 g			
Fat-Saturated	3.49 g			
Fat-Mono	2.10 g			
Fat-Poly	1.97 g			
Cholesterol	65.8 mg			

Calories from protein:	25%	Poly/Sat	=	0.6:1
Calories from carbohydrates:	62%	Sod/Pot	=	0.4:1
Calories from fats:	12%	Ca/Phos	=	0.7:1
		CSI	=	6.8

Green Salad with Creamy Creole Dressing

Serves 2

INGREDIENTS:

¹/₂ cup torn watercress
¹/₂ cup torn Belgian endive
¹/₂ cup torn Romaine lettuce

¹/₂ cup torn Bibb lettuce
¹/₄ cup Creamy Creole Dressing
  (recipe follows)

PREPARATION:

Combine all the salad greens and toss with the Creamy Creole Dressing. Serve on cold salad plates.

NOTE:

Be sure all the greens are well washed, drained, and patted dry before you tear them into bite-size pieces.

VARIATIONS:

If any of these greens are not available simply substitute something else like spinach or Boston lettuce.

The Creole Vinaigrette (see recipe page 174) is a good alternate to this creamy version.

Creamy Creole Dressing

Serves 2 (Makes approximately ¹/₄ cup)

INGREDIENTS:

3 tablespoons nonfat yogurt
1 tablespoon Creole mustard

1 teaspoon vinegar

PREPARATION:

Combine the ingredients and refrigerate in a tightly covered jar.

NOTE:

This dressing is very simple to make and you may want to make a larger quantity to keep in the refrigerator. Remember though that it does contain nonfat yogurt and shouldn't be kept for over a week.

VARIATION:

An eighth teaspoon of freshly ground black pepper adds a nice bite, and a tablespoon of minced green onions gives the recipe another texture and taste.

GREEN SALAD WITH CREAMY CREOLE DRESSING   *One serving*

Calories	25.1		Calcium	75.3 mg
Protein	2.34 g		Iron	0.506 mg
Carbohydrates	3.47 g		Sodium	122 mg
Dietary Fiber	0.824 g			
Fat-Total	0.476 g			
Fat-Saturated	0.042 g			
Fat-Mono	0.326 g			
Fat-Poly	0.048 g			
Cholesterol	0.375 mg			

Calories from protein:	34%	Poly/Sat	=	1.1:1
Calories from carbohydrates:	50%	Sod/Pot	=	0.6:1
Calories from fats:	16%	Ca/Phos	=	1.3:1
		CSI	=	0.1

SUGGESTED MENU: *One serving*

Stuffed Mushrooms
Spicy Roasted Chicken Breasts
Country Rice
Green Salad with Creamy Creole Dressing
Hot Apple Soufflé

Calories	556		Calcium	206 mg
Protein	52.7 g		Iron	5.18 mg
Carbohydrates	64.0 g		Sodium	676 mg
Dietary Fiber	6.87 g			
Fat-Total	7.94 g			
Fat-Saturated	2.30 g			
Fat-Mono	2.42 g			
Fat-Poly	1.83 g			
Cholesterol	122 mg			

Calories from protein:	39%	Poly/Sat	=	0.8:1
Calories from carbohydrates:	48%	Sod/Pot	=	0.6:1
Calories from fats:	13%	Ca/Phos	=	0.4:1
		CSI	=	8.4

Celery-Stuffed Artichoke-Heart Salad

Serves 2

INGREDIENTS:

2 cold cooked artichokes (see
   recipe page 165)
½ cup minced celery
2 tablespoons minced green
   onion

2 tablespoons red wine vinegar
1 tablespoon minced fresh
   parsley
¼ teaspoon freshly ground
   black pepper

PREPARATION:

Remove and clean the hearts of the artichokes and set aside.

Scrape the meat from the leaves and combine with the remaining ingredients except the artichoke hearts.

Halve the mixture and form each half into a ball.

Place a ball on each artichoke heart.

Serve on chilled salad plates.

NOTE:

This is an excellent salad that could make a nice light lunch.

Variation:

A tablespoon of chopped pimiento adds flavor and color.

CELERY ARTICHOKE SALAD

One serving

Calories	62.5		Calcium	66.2 mg
Protein	3.14 g		Iron	2.16 mg
Carbohydrates	15.0 g		Sodium	107 mg
Dietary Fiber	4.78 g			
Fat-Total	0.262 g			
Fat-Saturated	0.063 g			
Fat-Mono	0.018 g			
Fat-Poly	0.114 g			
Cholesterol	0 mg			

Calories from protein:	17%	Poly/Sat	=	1.8:1
Calories from carbohydrates:	80%	Sod/Pot	=	0.2:1
Calories from fats:	3%	Ca/Phos	=	0.8:1
		CSI	=	0.1

SUGGESTED MENU:

One serving

Celery-Stuffed Artichoke-Heart Salad
Bouilli (Boiled Beef)
Smothered Yellow Squash
Rice Pudding

Calories	440		Calcium	203 mg
Protein	43.8 g		Iron	6.45 mg
Carbohydrates	51.2 g		Sodium	243 mg
Dietary Fiber	8.38 g			
Fat-Total	8.56 g			
Fat-Saturated	3.20 g			
Fat-Mono	3.30 g			
Fat-Poly	0.629 g			
Cholesterol	79.6 mg			

Calories from protein:	38%	Poly/Sat	=	0.2:1
Calories from carbohydrates:	45%	Sod/Pot	=	0.2:1
Calories from fats:	17%	Ca/Phos	=	0.4:1
		CSI	=	7.2

Tomato and Green-Onion Salad Citronette

Serves 2

INGREDIENTS:

2 tablespoons fresh lemon juice
1 tablespoon water
¼ teaspoon powdered mustard
⅛ teaspoon freshly ground

black pepper
⅛ teaspoon thyme
1 large tomato, cut into 6 slices
¼ cup chopped green onion

PREPARATION:

In a bowl combine the lemon juice, water, mustard, pepper, and thyme to make the Citronette Dressing. Set aside.

Arrange 3 tomato slices on each plate and sprinkle with the green onions.

Pour on the Citronette dressing and serve.

NOTE:

Citronette comes from the French *citron,* meaning lemon; *vinaigrette* comes from the French *vinaigre* for vinegar.

VARIATION:

Try lime juice in place of the lemon for a very summery taste.

TOMATO AND GREEN-ONION SALAD CITRONETTE *One serving*

Calories	20.1		Calcium	15.9 mg
Protein	0.873 g		Iron	0.697 mg
Carbohydrates	4.87 g		Sodium	13.9 mg
Dietary Fiber	1.42 g			
Fat-Total	0.231 g			
Fat-Saturated	0.032 g			
Fat-Mono	0.052 g			
Fat-Poly	0.076 g			
Cholesterol	0 mg			

Calories from protein:	14%	Poly/Sat	=	2.4:1
Calories from carbohydrates:	78%	Sod/Pot	=	0.1:1
Calories from fats:	8%	Ca/Phos	=	0.8:1
		CSI	=	0.0

SUGGESTED MENU: *One serving*

Shrimp Rémoulade
Okra, Chicken, and Crab Gumbo
Tomato and Green-Onion Salad Citronette
Ambrosia

Calories	505		Calcium	396 mg
Protein	45.3 g		Iron	7.08 mg
Carbohydrates	65.9 g		Sodium	662 mg
Dietary Fiber	8.39 g			
Fat-Total	6.42 g			
Fat-Saturated	1.12 g			
Fat-Mono	2.55 g			
Fat-Poly	1.65 g			
Cholesterol	159 mg			

Calories from protein:	36%	Poly/Sat	=	1.5:1
Calories from carbohydrates:	52%	Sod/Pot	=	0.5:1
Calories from fats:	11%	Ca/Phos	=	0.8:1
		CSI	=	9.1

VEGETABLES

Stewed Okra and Tomatoes

Seasoned Eggplant Fingers

Boiled New Potatoes

Smothered Yellow Squash

Country Rice

Leeks Vinaigrette

Turnips and Greens

Steamed Spinach with Onion

Steamed Cabbage with Turkey Ham

Banana Baked with Sherry

Seasoned Boiled Brussels Sprouts

Maque Choux

Stewed Okra and Tomatoes *Serves 2*

INGREDIENTS:

1 cup sliced okra
1/2 cup chopped onion
1 tomato, cut into eighths
1/4 cup water
1 clove garlic, minced

1 teaspoon white vinegar
1/8 teaspoon dried thyme
1 bay leaf
Freshly ground black pepper to taste

PREPARATION:

Heat the okra and onion in a skillet, stirring frequently until they become limp.

Add remaining ingredients, cover, and simmer until almost all the liquid has evaporated.

NOTE:

The vinegar not only gives this vegetable dish a nice bite but it also cuts the thickening quality of the okra.

VARIATION:

Fresh corn kernels are sometimes used in place of the tomato.

STEWED OKRA AND TOMATOES   *One serving*

Calories	41.9	Calcium	45.8 mg
Protein	1.92 g	Iron	0.785 mg
Carbohydrates	9.36 g	Sodium	8.12 mg
Dietary Fiber	2.57 g		
Fat-Total	0.321 g		
Fat-Saturated	0.059 g		
Fat-Mono	0.047 g		
Fat-Poly	0.119 g		
Cholesterol	0 mg		

Calories from protein:	16%	Poly/Sat	=	2.0:1
Calories from carbohydrates:	78%	Sod/Pot	=	0.0:1
Calories from fats:	6%	Ca/Phos	=	0.9:1
		CSI	=	0.1

SUGGESTED MENU: *One serving*

Brandy Milk Punch
Grillades and Grits
Vinegared Cucumber and Mustard-Seed Salad
Stewed Okra and Tomatoes
Pineapple Bread Pudding with Rum Sauce

Calories	619	Calcium	548 mg
Protein	48.8 g	Iron	6.87 mg
Carbohydrates	75.1 g	Sodium	484 mg
Dietary Fiber	7.61 g		
Fat-Total	14.5 g		
Fat-Saturated	5.51 g		
Fat-Mono	5.49 g		
Fat-Poly	1.23 g		
Cholesterol	97.3 mg		

Calories from protein:	31%	Poly/Sat	=	0.2:1
Calories from carbohydrates:	48%	Sod/Pot	=	0.3:1
Calories from fats:	21%	Ca/Phos	=	0.8:1
		CSI	=	10.4

Seasoned Eggplant Fingers

Serves 2

INGREDIENTS:

1 small eggplant
1 egg white
1/4 cup skim milk
1/2 cup bread crumbs
2 teaspoons grated Parmesan
  cheese

1/4 teaspoon thyme
1/4 teaspoon oregano
1/4 teaspoon freshly ground
  black pepper

PREPARATION:

Preheat the oven to 375 degrees.

Skin the eggplant and cut it into strips the size of your finger.

In one bowl beat the egg white with the milk.

In another bowl mix the bread crumbs with the cheese and seasonings.

Dip the eggplant fingers into the egg-white mixture then into the seasoned bread crumbs, being sure that they are well coated with each.

Place on a nonstick baking sheet and bake for 10 to 15 minutes, or until golden.

Serve immediately.

VARIATIONS:

Mushrooms, broccoli, and cauliflower can all be prepared in this fashion.

Serve with lemon quarters to give additional zip to the Seasoned Eggplant Fingers.

If you really like tart tastes, try this with slices of dill pickles in place of the eggplant.

SEASONED EGGPLANT FINGERS   *One serving*

Calories	105		Calcium	123 mg
Protein	6.07 g		Iron	1.23 mg
Carbohydrates	17.4 g		Sodium	179 mg
Dietary Fiber	3.31 g			
Fat-Total	1.46 g			
Fat-Saturated	0.630 g			
Fat-Mono	0.462 g			
Fat-Poly	0.249 g			
Cholesterol	1.81 mg			

Calories from protein:	23%	Poly/Sat	=	0.4:1
Calories from carbohydrates:	65%	Sod/Pot	=	0.6:1
Calories from fats:	12%	Ca/Phos	=	1.3:1
		CSI	=	0.7

SUGGESTED MENU: *One serving*

Seasoned Eggplant Fingers
Roast Duck with Apples and Onion
Red and White Bean Salad
Raisin Oat-Bran Cookies

Calories	788		Calcium	320 mg
Protein	59.8 g		Iron	11.2 mg
Carbohydrates	93.7 g		Sodium	474 mg
Dietary Fiber	16.8 g			
Fat-Total	20.2 g			
Fat-Saturated	7.04 g			
Fat-Mono	6.32 g			
Fat-Poly	3.46 g			
Cholesterol	129 mg			

Calories from protein:	30%	Poly/Sat	=	0.5:1
Calories from carbohydrates:	47%	Sod/Pot	=	0.3:1
Calories from fats:	23%	Ca/Phos	=	0.4:1
		CSI	=	13.6

Boiled New Potatoes

Serves 2

INGREDIENTS:

2 cups water
4 whole black peppercorns
1 bay leaf

6 new potatoes
1 teaspoon chopped fresh parsley

PREPARATION:

Bring the water to a boil with the peppercorns and bay leaf.

Wash the potatoes but do not peel them.

Drop the potatoes into the water and boil gently for 20 minutes, or until they can easily be pierced with a fork.

Drain and serve sprinkled with the parsley.

NOTE:

If you don't care for the skins (which I hold as the best part of the potato), then remove them after boiling.

VARIATIONS:

New potatoes are delicious boiled in water that has been seasoned with a tablespoon of pickling spice.

Chives can replace the parsley and nonfat yogurt can be used as a sauce for the potatoes.

BOILED NEW POTATOES   *One serving*

Calories	92.8	Calcium	9.23 mg
Protein	1.97 g	Iron	1.20 mg
Carbohydrates	21.5 g	Sodium	6.99 mg
Dietary Fiber	1.68 g		
Fat-Total	0.086 g		
Fat-Saturated	0.022 g		
Fat-Mono	0.002 g		
Fat-Poly	0.038 g		
Cholesterol	0 mg		

Calories from protein:	8%	Poly/Sat	=	1.7:1
Calories from carbohydrates:	91%	Sod/Pot	=	0.0:1
Calories from fats:	1%	Ca/Phos	=	0.2:1
		CSI	=	0.0

SUGGESTED MENU: *One serving*

Creole Chicken Soup
Fillet Marchand de Vin
Leeks Vinaigrette
Boiled New Potatoes
Strawberry Bavarian Cream

Calories	564	Calcium	225 mg
Protein	62.9 g	Iron	7.79 mg
Carbohydrates	48.7 g	Sodium	228 mg
Dietary Fiber	9.18 g		
Fat-Total	16.1 g		
Fat-Saturated	4.88 g		
Fat-Mono	6.12 g		
Fat-Poly	2.18 g		
Cholesterol	159 mg		

Calories from protein:	43%	Poly/Sat	=	0.4:1
Calories from carbohydrates:	33%	Sod/Pot	=	0.1:1
Calories from fats:	24%	Ca/Phos	=	0.4:1
		CSI	=	12.9

Smothered Yellow Squash

Serves 2

INGREDIENTS:

1 ½ *cups sliced yellow squash*
½ *cup chopped onion*
½ *cup water*
1 *clove garlic, minced*

⅛ *teaspoon chili powder*
Freshly ground black pepper to taste

PREPARATION:

Put all ingredients in a small saucepan, cover, and simmer for 15 to 20 minutes, or until the squash is very tender.

NOTE:

At the end of the cooking you may want to let the squash simmer uncovered for a few minutes to reduce some of the excess liquid.

VARIATIONS:

Tomatoes, okra, and corn can all be cooked this same way.
Sprinkle 1 teaspoon chopped parsley over the Smothered Yellow Squash to add a different touch.

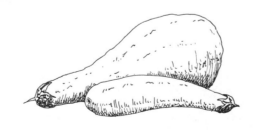

SMOTHERED YELLOW SQUASH   *One serving*

Calories	34.2	Calcium	34.1 mg
Protein	1.50 g	Iron	0.661 mg
Carbohydrates	7.45 g	Sodium	4.14 mg
Dietary Fiber	2.31 g		
Fat-Total	0.370 g		
Fat-Saturated	0.073 g		
Fat-Mono	0.038 g		
Fat-Poly	0.154 g		
Cholesterol	0 mg		

Calories from protein:	15%	Poly/Sat	=	2.1:1
Calories from carbohydrates:	76%	Sod/Pot	=	0.0:1
Calories from fats:	9%	Ca/Phos	=	0.7:1
		CSI	=	0.1

SUGGESTED MENU: *One serving*

Celery-Stuffed Artichoke-Heart Salad
Bouilli (Boiled Beef)
Smothered Yellow Squash
Rice Pudding

Calories	440	Calcium	203 mg
Protein	43.8 g	Iron	6.45 mg
Carbohydrates	51.2 g	Sodium	243 mg
Dietary Fiber	8.38 g		
Fat-Total	8.56 g		
Fat-Saturated	3.20 g		
Fat-Mono	3.30 g		
Fat-Poly	0.629 g		
Cholesterol	79.6 mg		

Calories from protein:	38%	Poly/Sat	=	0.2:1
Calories from carbohydrates:	45%	Sod/Pot	=	0.2:1
Calories from fats:	17%	Ca/Phos	=	0.4:1
		CSI	=	7.2

Country Rice

Serves 2

INGREDIENTS:

$^1/_2$ cup chicken stock made
  without salt or fat (see recipe
  page 30)
$^1/_3$ cup chopped green onion

Pinch freshly ground black
  pepper
$^1/_3$ cup uncooked white rice

PREPARATION:

Bring the stock to a boil with the green onion and pepper.
Add the rice, turn down to a simmer, cover, and cook for 20 minutes.

NOTE:

If you want drier rice, remove the cover at 20 minutes and heat just a minute
or so longer.

VARIATIONS:

Rice made with fish stock (see recipe page 89) can be served with fish, beef-
stock rice with beef.
If you begin adding more vegetables you will end up with a Jambalaya instead
of a side course of Country Rice.

COUNTRY RICE   *One serving*

Calories	115		Calcium	18.7 mg
Protein	2.34 g		Iron	1.22 mg
Carbohydrates	25.5 g		Sodium	3.93 mg
Dietary Fiber	0.783 g			
Fat-Total	0.147 g			
Fat-Saturated	0.037 g			
Fat-Mono	0.036 g			
Fat-Poly	0.055 g			
Cholesterol	0 mg			

Calories from protein:	8%	Poly/Sat	=	1.5:1
Calories from carbohydrates:	91%	Sod/Pot	=	0.1:1
Calories from fats:	1%	Ca/Phos	=	0.5:1
		CSI	=	0.0

SUGGESTED MENU: *One serving*

Stuffed Mushrooms
Spicy Roasted Chicken Breasts
Country Rice
Green Salad with Creamy Creole Dressing
Hot Apple Soufflé

Calories	556		Calcium	206 mg
Protein	52.7 g		Iron	5.18 mg
Carbohydrates	64.0 g		Sodium	676 mg
Dietary Fiber	6.87 g			
Fat-Total	7.94 g			
Fat-Saturated	2.30 g			
Fat-Mono	2.42 g			
Fat-Poly	1.83 g			
Cholesterol	122 mg			

Calories from protein:	39%	Poly/Sat	=	0.8:1
Calories from carbohydrates:	48%	Sod/Pot	=	0.6:1
Calories from fats:	13%	Ca/Phos	=	0.4:1
		CSI	=	8.4

Leeks Vinaigrette

Serves 2

INGREDIENTS:

Water
1 bay leaf

4 whole black peppercorns
2 leeks, well cleaned

VINAIGRETTE INGREDIENTS:

2 tablespoons vinegar
1 teaspoon chopped fresh parsley
1/4 teaspoon powdered mustard

1/8 teaspoon freshly ground
  black pepper

PREPARATION:

Pour enough water in a saucepan to later cover the leeks and add the bay leaf and peppercorns.

Bring the water to a boil and add the leeks. Reduce to a simmer and poach them for 5 minutes, or until tender.

Remove the leeks from the water. Drain, cover, and refrigerate.

MAKE THE VINAIGRETTE:

Combine the vinegar, parsley, mustard, and pepper.

TO SERVE:

Cut the leeks in half lengthwise and lay them on chilled salad plates.
Spoon the Vinaigrette over the leeks and serve.

NOTE:

As leeks vary considerably in size, so does the cooking time. A small leek takes about 5 minutes to cook, a large one about 7 minutes.

VARIATION:

Serve the Leeks Vinaigrette warm and it becomes a vegetable course rather than a salad. This is actually the way that I like it the best.

LEEKS VINAIGRETTE   *One serving*

Calories	28.9	Calcium	27.8 mg
Protein	0.735 g	Iron	1.08 mg
Carbohydrates	7.46 g	Sodium	17.0 mg
Dietary Fiber	2.83 g		
Fat-Total	0.201 g		
Fat-Saturated	0.023 g		
Fat-Mono	0.030 g		
Fat-Poly	0.096 g		
Cholesterol	0 mg		

Calories from protein:	8%	Poly/Sat	=	4.1:1
Calories from carbohydrates:	86%	Sod/Pot	=	0.2:1
Calories from fats:	5%	Ca/Phos	=	1.7:1
		CSI	=	0.0

SUGGESTED MENU: *One serving*

Crab and Corn Bisque
Jambalaya
Leeks Vinaigrette
Hot Apple Soufflé

Calories	525	Calcium	131 mg
Protein	32.3 g	Iron	5.38 mg
Carbohydrates	94.6 g	Sodium	152 mg
Dietary Fiber	13.1 g		
Fat-Total	5.03 g		
Fat-Saturated	1.08 g		
Fat-Mono	1.37 g		
Fat-Poly	1.70 g		
Cholesterol	69.1 mg		

Calories from protein:	23%	Poly/Sat	=	1.6:1
Calories from carbohydrates:	68%	Sod/Pot	=	0.1:1
Calories from fats:	8%	Ca/Phos	=	0.3:1
		CSI	=	4.5

Turnips and Greens

Serves 2

INGREDIENTS:

2 medium turnips with their
   tops
1/2 cup water
1/4 cup chopped green onion

1 clove garlic, minced
1/8 teaspoon freshly ground
   black pepper

PREPARATION:

Cut the tops off the turnips and carefully wash both the greens and the turnips.
Chop the greens and set them aside.
Peel the turnips and cut them into 1/2-inch cubes.
Put the cubes in a saucepan with the water, green onion, garlic, and pepper.
Simmer for 10 minutes, or until the turnip is almost tender.
Add the turnip tops, cover, and simmer for another 10 minutes, or until they
are tender.

TO SERVE:

Spoon onto dinner plates with your entree.

NOTE:

Turnips have an unusual and marvelous tangy taste.

VARIATION:

The green onion and garlic are not absolutely necessary since the turnips themselves have such a robust flavor.

TURNIPS AND GREENS
One serving

Calories	18.7	Calcium	47.4 mg
Protein	0.890 g	Iron	0.538 mg
Carbohydrates	4.64 g	Sodium	35.0 mg
Dietary Fiber	2.09 g		
Fat-Total	0.110 g		
Fat-Saturated	0.019 g		
Fat-Mono	0.009 g		
Fat-Poly	0.051 g		
Cholesterol	0 mg		

Calories from protein:	15%	Poly/Sat	=	2.7:1
Calories from carbohydrates:	80%	Sod/Pot	=	0.2:1
Calories from fats:	4%	Ca/Phos	=	2.2:1
		CSI	=	0.0

SUGGESTED MENU:
One serving

Crabmeat Ravigote
Jambalaya
Red and White Bean Salad
Turnips and Greens
Raisin Oat-Bran Cookies

Calories	660	Calcium	292 mg
Protein	50.6 g	Iron	9.49 mg
Carbohydrates	106 g	Sodium	316 mg
Dietary Fiber	14.4 g		
Fat-Total	6.11 g		
Fat-Saturated	1.32 g		
Fat-Mono	1.71 g		
Fat-Poly	2.25 g		
Cholesterol	91.5 mg		

Calories from protein:	30%	Poly/Sat	=	1.7:1
Calories from carbohydrates:	62%	Sod/Pot	=	0.2:1
Calories from fats:	8%	Ca/Phos	=	0.4:1
		CSI	=	5.9

Steamed Spinach with Onion *Serves 2*

INGREDIENTS:

1 cup chopped onion
1 clove garlic, minced
10 ounces fresh spinach, washed
 and stemmed

Freshly ground black pepper to
 taste

PREPARATION:

Put the onion and garlic in a heavy saucepan and cook over high heat while stirring for 1 to 2 minutes, or until they begin to color.

Add the spinach and pepper. Cover the pan tightly and cook for a few more minutes, or until the spinach has collapsed and rendered its liquid.

NOTES:

This recipe is so simple and delicious that it should be used often as the vegetable dish. It is very important to use good quality fresh spinach. The best spinach has its loose leaves tied together rather than being prepackaged.

There is nothing worse than grit in your spinach. Wash the spinach thoroughly! Fill a large bowl with water and wash the spinach in it. Lift the spinach out of the bowl so the sand and dirt will fall to the bottom and discard the water. Rinse the bowl well and repeat several times.

VARIATION:

Spinach without the onions and garlic is delicious. The taste is marvelous and seems to give me an energy boost.

STEAMED SPINACH WITH ONION   *One serving*

Calories	60.4		Calcium	163 mg
Protein	5.09 g		Iron	4.17 mg
Carbohydrates	11.3 g		Sodium	113 mg
Dietary Fiber	6.98 g			
Fat-Total	0.712 g			
Fat-Saturated	0.115 g			
Fat-Mono	0.045 g			
Fat-Poly	0.293 g			
Cholesterol	0 mg			

Calories from protein:	28%	Poly/Sat	=	2.5:1
Calories from carbohydrates:	63%	Sod/Pot	=	0.1:1
Calories from fats:	9%	Ca/Phos	=	1.7:1
		CSI	=	0.1

SUGGESTED MENU: *One serving*

Crayfish Cardinal
Chicken Roasted with Garlic Cloves
Steamed Spinach with Onion
Bananas Foster

Calories	507		Calcium	460 mg
Protein	49.0 g		Iron	7.63 mg
Carbohydrates	52.2 g		Sodium	372 mg
Dietary Fiber	9.89 g			
Fat-Total	7.04 g			
Fat-Saturated	2.25 g			
Fat-Mono	1.95 g			
Fat-Poly	1.53 g			
Cholesterol	108 mg			

Calories from protein:	39%	Poly/Sat	=	0.7:1
Calories from carbohydrates:	41%	Sod/Pot	=	0.2:1
Calories from fats:	13%	Ca/Phos	=	0.8:1
Other calories (i.e. alcohol):	8%	CSI	=	7.7

Steamed Cabbage
with Turkey Ham

Serves 2

INGREDIENTS:

1/2 small head cabbage
Water
2 ounces turkey ham, cut into
  1/2-inch cubes

1/2 cup chopped onion
1/8 teaspoon freshly ground
  black pepper

PREPARATION:

Wash the cabbage and cut it into quarters.

Place the cabbage in a pot with enough water to give you a 1/2-inch depth in the bottom of the pot. Add the remaining ingredients and cover.

Bring the water to a boil and steam the cabbage for 10 minutes, or until tender.

Serve with the cooking liquor and turkey ham.

NOTE:

The degree to which you steam the cabbage is up to you. If you like your cabbage still slightly crisp don't steam it as long.

VARIATION:

There is sodium in the turkey ham. If you want to avoid it don't use the ham; the cabbage is still quite good without it.

STEAMED CABBAGE WITH TURKEY HAM   *One serving*

Calories	69.6	Calcium	52.0 mg
Protein	6.88 g	Iron	1.45 mg
Carbohydrates	8.00 g	Sodium	288 mg
Dietary Fiber	2.31 g		
Fat-Total	1.75 g		
Fat-Saturated	0.511 g		
Fat-Mono	0.402 g		
Fat-Poly	0.489 g		
Cholesterol	15.9 mg		

Calories from protein:	37%	Poly/Sat	=	1.0:1
Calories from carbohydrates:	43%	Sod/Pot	=	0.8:1
Calories from fats:	21%	Ca/Phos	=	0.5:1
		CSI	=	1.3

SUGGESTED MENU: *One serving*

Deviled Eggs
Braised Pork Tenderloin
Steamed Cabbage with Turkey Ham
Bananas Foster

Calories	557	Calcium	263 mg
Protein	50.6 g	Iron	4.05 mg
Carbohydrates	46.4 g	Sodium	773 mg
Dietary Fiber	5.61 g		
Fat-Total	12.6 g		
Fat-Saturated	4.43 g		
Fat-Mono	5.07 g		
Fat-Poly	1.77 g		
Cholesterol	104 mg		

Calories from protein:	36%	Poly/Sat	=	0.4:1
Calories from carbohydrates:	33%	Sod/Pot	=	0.5:1
Calories from fats:	20%	Ca/Phos	=	0.5:1
Other calories (i.e. alcohol):	10%	CSI	=	9.7

Banana Baked with Sherry

Serves 2

INGREDIENTS:

1 large firm banana
2 tablespoons medium dry sherry

⅛ teaspoon ground
    cinnamon

PREPARATION:

Preheat the oven to 375 degrees.

Slice the banana in half lengthwise and then again crosswise and lay the 4 pieces in a baking dish.

Pour the sherry over the banana and sprinkle with the cinnamon.

Bake for 15 minutes.

TO SERVE:

Spoon the banana slices onto plates and pour the pan liquids over them.

NOTE:

If you use a banana that is too ripe it will cook up too soft and will be difficult to serve.

VARIATION:

The addition of a dash of nutmeg or a sprinkle of artificial sweetener on the cooked bananas makes them even sweeter.

BANANA BAKED WITH SHERRY   *One serving*

Calories	73.9		Calcium	6.45 mg
Protein	0.630 g		Iron	0.268 mg
Carbohydrates	14.7 g		Sodium	1.66 mg
Dietary Fiber	1.45 g			
Fat-Total	0.278 g			
Fat-Saturated	0.106 g			
Fat-Mono	0.024 g			
Fat-Poly	0.051 g			
Cholesterol	0 mg			

Calories from protein:	3%	Poly/Sat	=	0.5:1
Calories from carbohydrates:	79%	Sod/Pot	=	0.0:1
Calories from fats:	3%	Ca/Phos	=	0.5:1
Other calories (i.e. alcohol):	14%	CSI	=	0.1

SUGGESTED MENU: *One serving*

Boiled Onion Salad
Braised Pork Tenderloin
Banana Baked with Sherry
Hot Apple Soufflé

Calories	349		Calcium	74.4 mg
Protein	31.0 g		Iron	2.59 mg
Carbohydrates	31.3 g		Sodium	189 mg
Dietary Fiber	4.73 g			
Fat-Total	10.0 g			
Fat-Saturated	3.27 g			
Fat-Mono	4.41 g			
Fat-Poly	1.33 g			
Cholesterol	83.9 mg			

Calories from protein:	36%	Poly/Sat	=	0.4:1
Calories from carbohydrates:	37%	Sod/Pot	=	0.2:1
Calories from fats:	27%	Ca/Phos	=	0.3:1
		CSI	=	7.5

Seasoned Boiled Brussels Sprouts

Serves 2

INGREDIENTS:

6 *whole black peppercorns*   *¼ teaspoon cayenne*
4 *whole cloves*   *¼ teaspoon thyme*
4 *whole allspice*   *1 quart water*
2 *bay leaves*   *1½ cups brussels sprouts*

PREPARATION:

Tie the peppercorns, cloves, and allspice in cheesecloth. Add all spices and seasonings to the water and bring to a boil. Let the water boil for 2 minutes to draw the flavors from the seasonings.

Add the brussels sprouts and boil for 10 minutes, or until they are tender.

Drain the sprouts and serve.

NOTES:

Be sure not to overcook the sprouts.

This seasoning combination is not unlike that used for boiling seafood; you might recognize the taste.

VARIATIONS:

Cauliflower, carrots, or broccoli do well prepared this way.

Boiling vegetables with different herbs or spices will add more of a variety of flavors to the same foods.

SEASONED BOILED BRUSSELS SPROUTS   *One serving*

Calories	45.0		Calcium	42.0 mg
Protein	4.48 g		Iron	1.41 mg
Carbohydrates	10.1 g		Sodium	12.7 mg
Dietary Fiber	3.86 g			
Fat-Total	0.597 g			
Fat-Saturated	0.123 g			
Fat-Mono	0.046 g			
Fat-Poly	0.304 g			
Cholesterol	0 mg			

Calories from protein:	28%	Poly/Sat	=	2.5:1
Calories from carbohydrates:	63%	Sod/Pot	=	0.0:1
Calories from fats:	8%	Ca/Phos	=	0.6:1
		CSI	=	0.1

SUGGESTED MENU: *One serving*

Green Salad with Creamy Creole Dressing
Grouper Fillets Amandine
Seasoned Boiled Brussels Sprouts
Rice Pudding

Calories	401		Calcium	325 mg
Protein	33.1 g		Iron	4.67 mg
Carbohydrates	53.9 g		Sodium	246 mg
Dietary Fiber	9.17 g			
Fat-Total	7.40 g			
Fat-Saturated	1.14 g			
Fat-Mono	3.65 g			
Fat-Poly	2.07 g			
Cholesterol	43.9 mg			

Calories from protein:	32%	Poly/Sat	=	1.8:1
Calories from carbohydrates:	52%	Sod/Pot	=	0.2:1
Calories from fats:	16%	Ca/Phos	=	0.8:1
		CSI	=	3.3

Maque Choux

Serves 2

INGREDIENTS:

½ *cup chopped onion*
¼ *cup chopped green bell*
  pepper
1 *cup corn kernels*
½ *cup chopped tomato*

¼ *cup water*
1 *bay leaf*
⅛ *teaspoon thyme*
⅛ *teaspoon freshly ground*
  black pepper

PREPARATION:

Put the onion and bell pepper in a heavy saucepan and cook over medium heat while stirring for 2 minutes.

Add the corn and continue cooking, stirring occasionally, for 2 more minutes.

Add the tomato, water, and the seasonings.

Simmer uncovered for 10 minutes, or until most of the liquid is evaporated.

VARIATIONS:

The addition of 1 or 2 minced cloves of garlic adds considerably to the taste of this Maque Choux.

A dash of cayenne is nice, too.

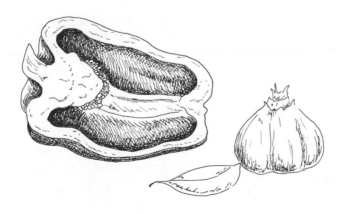

MAQUE CHOUX

One serving

Calories	91.8	Calcium	17.6 mg
Protein	3.48 g	Iron	1.07 mg
Carbohydrates	20.3 g	Sodium	16.9 mg
Dietary Fiber	5.70 g		
Fat-Total	1.18 g		
Fat-Saturated	0.184 g		
Fat-Mono	0.302 g		
Fat-Poly	0.543 g		
Cholesterol	0 mg		

Calories from protein:	13%	Poly/Sat	=	3.0:1
Calories from carbohydrates:	77%	Sod/Pot	=	0.0:1
Calories from fats:	10%	Ca/Phos	=	0.2:1
		CSI	=	0.2

SUGGESTED MENU:

One serving

Boiled Onion Salad
Matelote of Sheepshead
Maque Choux
Pear Compote with Brandied Vanilla Cream

Calories	475	Calcium	216 mg
Protein	25.4 g	Iron	4.05 mg
Carbohydrates	68.7 g	Sodium	206 mg
Dietary Fiber	13.7 g		
Fat-Total	5.82 g		
Fat-Saturated	0.759 g		
Fat-Mono	1.94 g		
Fat-Poly	1.70 g		
Cholesterol	56.6 mg		

Calories from protein:	21%	Poly/Sat	=	2.2:1
Calories from carbohydrates:	58%	Sod/Pot	=	0.1:1
Calories from fats:	11%	Ca/Phos	=	0.5:1
Other calories (i.e. alcohol):	10%	CSI	=	3.6

DESSERTS

Rice Pudding

Cherries Jubilee

Orange Flip

Ambrosia

Hot Apple Soufflé

Strawberry Bavarian Cream

Pineapple with Port Wine

Pear Compote
    with Brandied Vanilla Cream

Raisin Oat-Bran Cookies

Bananas Foster

Pineapple Bread Pudding
    with Rum Sauce

Rice Pudding

Serves 2

INGREDIENTS:

1 egg white
1/2 cup skim milk
2/3 cup cooked rice (cooked with no salt or fat)
1/4 teaspoon ground cinnamon
1/4 teaspoon ground nutmeg
1/4 teaspoon ground allspice
1/4 teaspoon vanilla extract
2 tablespoons raisins
Artificial sweetener equivalent of 2 teaspoons sugar

PREPARATION:

Preheat the oven to 325 degrees.
Beat the egg white with the skim milk.
Blend in all remaining ingredients.
Bake for 20 minutes, or until a knife inserted in the center of the pudding comes out clean.
Serve hot or cold.

NOTES:

This is an excellent way to use up that leftover rice.
Be sure the sweetener you use does not contain aspartame, which looses its sweetening power when heated for several minutes.

VARIATIONS:

The addition of 2 teaspoons of cocoa powder is a nice variation.

The raisins are not necessary but add a lovely natural sweetness and flavor to the pudding.

RICE PUDDING

One serving

Calories	137	Calcium	95.0 mg
Protein	5.49 g	Iron	1.33 mg
Carbohydrates	28.3 g	Sodium	58.0 mg
Dietary Fiber	1.25 g		
Fat-Total	0.362 g		
Fat-Saturated	0.192 g		
Fat-Mono	0.064 g		
Fat-Poly	0.053 g		
Cholesterol	1.00 mg		

Calories from protein:	16%	Poly/Sat	=	0.3:1
Calories from carbohydrates:	82%	Sod/Pot	=	0.3:1
Calories from fats:	2%	Ca/Phos	=	1.0:1
		CSI	=	0.2

SUGGESTED MENU:

One serving

Green Salad with Creamy Creole Dressing
Grouper Fillets Amandine
Seasoned Boiled Brussels Sprouts
Rice Pudding

Calories	401	Calcium	325 mg
Protein	33.1 g	Iron	4.67 mg
Carbohydrates	53.9 g	Sodium	246 mg
Dietary Fiber	9.17 g		
Fat-Total	7.40 g		
Fat-Saturated	1.14 g		
Fat-Mono	3.65 g		
Fat-Poly	2.07 g		
Cholesterol	43.9 mg		

Calories from protein:	32%	Poly/Sat	=	1.8:1
Calories from carbohydrates:	52%	Sod/Pot	=	0.2:1
Calories from fats:	16%	Ca/Phos	=	0.8:1
		CSI	=	3.3

Cherries Jubilee

Serves 2

INGREDIENTS:

8 ounces frozen vanilla low-fat
  yogurt

¼ cup brandy
1 cup pitted fresh cherries

PREPARATION:

Scoop 4 ounces of yogurt into each dessert bowl and place the bowls in the freezer.

Put the brandy and cherries in a saucepan, warm them slightly over low heat, then remove from the heat.

Avert your face and very carefully light the brandy with a long match. Swirl the cherries in the flaming brandy until the flame goes out.

TO SERVE:

Remove the bowls from the freezer and spoon the hot brandied cherries over the yogurt. Serve immediately.

NOTE:

Don't heat the brandy too long before igniting or the alcohol will evaporate and it will not light. Be careful when you light it!

VARIATION:

Jubilee can be made with fresh strawberries or other berries, or even diced peaches or nectarines. Be sure the fruit is ripe and sweet.

CHERRIES JUBILEE   *One serving*

Calories	193		Calcium	158 mg
Protein	5.07 g		Iron	0.354 mg
Carbohydrates	34.2 g		Sodium	57.7 mg
Dietary Fiber	1.10 g			
Fat-Total	1.76 g			
Fat-Saturated	0.846 g			
Fat-Mono	0.479 g			
Fat-Poly	0.244 g			
Cholesterol	4.27 mg			

Calories from protein:	11%		Poly/Sat	=	0.3:1
Calories from carbohydrates:	71%		Sod/Pot	=	0.2:1
Calories from fats:	8%		Ca/Phos	=	1.2:1
Other calories (i.e. alcohol):	10%		CSI	=	1.1

SUGGESTED MENU: *One serving*

Deviled Eggs
Shrimp Etouffée
Creole Tomatoes with Basil, Garlic, and Green-Onion Dressing
Cherries Jubilee

Calories	590		Calcium	290 mg
Protein	37.2 g		Iron	7.27 mg
Carbohydrates	99.0 g		Sodium	558 mg
Dietary Fiber	7.00 g			
Fat-Total	3.74 g			
Fat-Saturated	0.946 g			
Fat-Mono	1.01 g			
Fat-Poly	1.02 g			
Cholesterol	115 mg			

Calories from protein:	26%		Poly/Sat	=	1.1:1
Calories from carbohydrates:	68%		Sod/Pot	=	0.4:1
Calories from fats:	6%		Ca/Phos	=	0.7:1
			CSI	=	6.7

Orange Flip

Serves 2

INGREDIENTS:

4 ounces fresh orange juice
½ cup plain nonfat yogurt
Artificial sweetener equivalent
   of 2 teaspoons sugar

½ teaspoon vanilla extract
1 cup crushed ice
Grated nutmeg

PREPARATION:

Combine the orange juice, yogurt, sweetener, and vanilla in a blender at low speed.

Add the ice and blend at high speed until all is well combined and there are no large bits of ice.

Pour into tumblers and top with a dash of nutmeg.

NOTE:

This delicious drink is something like an orange milkshake.

VARIATION:

Try this recipe with ½ cup crushed strawberries in place of the orange juice.

ORANGE FLIP   *One serving*

Calories	59.9		Calcium	122 mg
Protein	3.69 g		Iron	0.183 mg
Carbohydrates	10.8 g		Sodium	47.3 mg
Dietary Fiber	0.251 g			
Fat-Total	0.253 g			
Fat-Saturated	0.100 g			
Fat-Mono	0.053 g			
Fat-Poly	0.028 g			
Cholesterol	1.00 mg			

Calories from protein:	24%	Poly/Sat	=	0.3:1
Calories from carbohydrates:	72%	Sod/Pot	=	0.2:1
Calories from fats:	4%	Ca/Phos	=	1.2:1
		CSI	=	0.2

SUGGESTED MENU: *One serving*

Creole Fish Stew
Mirliton Stuffed with Shrimp
Celery Rémoulade
Orange Flip

Calories	409		Calcium	394 mg
Protein	38.7 g		Iron	5.87 mg
Carbohydrates	55.2 g		Sodium	596 mg
Dietary Fiber	8.97 g			
Fat-Total	6.74 g			
Fat-Saturated	1.03 g			
Fat-Mono	2.26 g			
Fat-Poly	1.59 g			
Cholesterol	133 mg			

Calories from protein:	35%	Poly/Sat	=	1.5:1
Calories from carbohydrates:	51%	Sod/Pot	=	0.3:1
Calories from fats:	14%	Ca/Phos	=	0.6:1
		CSI	=	7.7

Ambrosia

Serves 2

INGREDIENTS:

2 small navel oranges, chilled   2 tablespoons cream sherry
½ cup sliced strawberries

PREPARATION:

Peel and seed the oranges, breaking the meat into the natural sections.

Slice the sections in half lengthwise over a bowl to catch any juice that may be rendered during the process.

TO ASSEMBLE:

Place a layer of orange slices, cut side up, in the bottoms of dessert bowls; add any reserved juice.

Cover with a layer of half the strawberries.

Add another layer of orange slices and then top with the remaining strawberries.

Pour a tablespoon of cream sherry over each dessert.

NOTES:

This dish is traditionally made with grated coconut instead of strawberries, but coconut was eliminated here because it is very high in saturated fat. It is just as delicious with strawberries!

It is most important that the fruit be ripe and sweet. If not, you may want to use some artificial sweetener to enhance it.

VARIATION:

The sherry is not necessary and can be eliminated or replaced with some preferred liqueur or flavored syrup. Ambrosia is quite delightful and refreshing without any sherry, liqueur, or syrup at all.

AMBROSIA
One serving

Calories	92.2		Calcium	58.4 mg
Protein	1.49 g		Iron	0.315 mg
Carbohydrates	19.2 g		Sodium	1.63 mg
Dietary Fiber	3.62 g			
Fat-Total	0.297 g			
Fat-Saturated	0.027 g			
Fat-Mono	0.049 g			
Fat-Poly	0.102 g			
Cholesterol	0 mg			

Calories from protein:	6%	Poly/Sat	=	3.7:1
Calories from carbohydrates:	83%	Sod/Pot	=	0.0:1
Calories from fats:	3%	Ca/Phos	=	2.2:1
Other calories (i.e. alcohol):	7%	CSI	=	0.0

SUGGESTED MENU:
One serving

Shrimp Rémoulade
Okra, Chicken, and Crab Gumbo
Tomato and Green-Onion Citronette
Ambrosia

Calories	505		Calcium	396 mg
Protein	45.3 g		Iron	7.08 mg
Carbohydrates	65.9 g		Sodium	662 mg
Dietary Fiber	8.39 g			
Fat-Total	6.42 g			
Fat-Saturated	1.12 g			
Fat-Mono	2.55 g			
Fat-Poly	1.65 g			
Cholesterol	159 mg			

Calories from protein:	36%	Poly/Sat	=	1.5:1
Calories from carbohydrates:	52%	Sod/Pot	=	0.5:1
Calories from fats:	11%	Ca/Phos	=	0.8:1
		CSI	=	9.1

Hot Apple Soufflé

Serves 2

INGREDIENTS:

2 medium apples, peeled and
  cored
¼ teaspoon ground cinnamon
½ cup water

1 teaspoon vanilla extract
2 egg whites, room temperature
⅛ teaspoon cream of tartar

PREPARATION:

Chop the apples and stew them over medium heat with the cinnamon and water in a small covered saucepan about 15 minutes, until the pieces are soft enough to be stirred into a purée with a fork or wooden spoon.

Remove from the heat and let cool.

Stir in the vanilla.

Preheat the oven to 400 degrees.

In a mixing bowl whip the egg whites with the cream of tartar until soft peaks form.

Fold the puree into the whites, being very careful not to work the mixture too much as it will lose some of its lightness.

Spoon the mixture into 4-ounce soufflé molds and bake for 12 to 15 minutes, or until the Soufflés are puffed and golden.

Serve immediately!

NOTE:

This will be the most healthful soufflé you've probably ever had, although maybe not the fluffiest. Considering its simplicity, it is extremely tasty.

VARIATIONS:

Any fruit could be substituted as long as you chop it up and stew it. This tenderizes the fruit, eliminates the excess liquid, and concentrates the flavor and sweetness. You will notice that I have not relied on the use of artificial sweeteners in this recipe because if the fruit is sweet enough when you begin, the sweetness of the concentrated fruit will be adequate.

HOT APPLE SOUFFLÉ   *One serving*

Calories	88.9	Calcium	12.5 mg
Protein	3.55 g	Iron	0.278 mg
Carbohydrates	19.7 g	Sodium	50.1 mg
Dietary Fiber	3.07 g		
Fat-Total	0.410 g		
Fat-Saturated	0.067 g		
Fat-Mono	0.018 g		
Fat-Poly	0.117 g		
Cholesterol	0 mg		

Calories from protein:	15%	Poly/Sat	=	1.8:1
Calories from carbohydrates:	81%	Sod/Pot	=	0.3:1
Calories from fats:	4%	Ca/Phos	=	0.9:1
		CSI	=	0.1

SUGGESTED MENU: *One serving*

Crab and Corn Bisque
Jambalaya
Leeks Vinaigrette
Hot Apple Soufflé

Calories	525	Calcium	131 mg
Protein	32.3 g	Iron	5.38 mg
Carbohydrates	94.6 g	Sodium	152 mg
Dietary Fiber	13.1 g		
Fat-Total	5.03 g		
Fat-Saturated	1.08 g		
Fat-Mono	1.37 g		
Fat-Poly	1.70 g		
Cholesterol	69.1 mg		

Calories from protein:	23%	Poly/Sat	=	1.6:1
Calories from carbohydrates:	68%	Sod/Pot	=	0.1:1
Calories from fats:	8%	Ca/Phos	=	0.3:1
		CSI	=	4.5

Strawberry Bavarian Cream   *Serves 2*

INGREDIENTS:

*¹/₂ cup puréed fresh sweet
    strawberries*
¹/₂ cup plain nonfat yogurt
¹/₂ teaspoon vanilla extract

*Artificial sweetener equivalent
    of 2 teaspoons sugar, optional*
1 ounce packet unflavored gelatin
¹/₄ cup boiling water

PREPARATION:

Fold the strawberries into the yogurt.

Add the vanilla and the sweetener, if you are using it.

Dissolve the gelatin in the water and then fold it into the strawberry-yogurt mixture, being sure that all is well distributed.

Spoon the Strawberry Bavarian Cream into dessert cups, cover with plastic wrap, and refrigerate for 1 hour, or until set.

Serve in the cups or unmolded onto dessert plates.

NOTES:

If the strawberries are sweet enough they will not require any additional sweetener. If you've used molds, release the Strawberry Bavarian Cream after it has set by dipping the molds almost to the top in hot water for 5 seconds. Place the dessert plates on top of the mold, turn them over together, and shake them gently until the dessert drops onto the plate.

VARIATION:

I do this dessert with ripe sweet cantaloupe or raspberries. Almost any fruit purée, provided it is sweet enough, should yield a delicious variation of this recipe. There is one exception, however, and that is pineapple: the acids in pineapple actually break down the gelatin and make it impossible for it to set.

STRAWBERRY BAVARIAN CREAM   *One serving*

Calories	55.5	Calcium	119 mg
Protein	6.48 g	Iron	0.194 mg
Carbohydrates	6.97 g	Sodium	47.6 mg
Dietary Fiber	1.32 g		
Fat-Total	0.239 g		
Fat-Saturated	0.073 g		
Fat-Mono	0.047 g		
Fat-Poly	0.072 g		
Cholesterol	1.00 mg		

Calories from protein:	46%	Poly/Sat	=	1.0:1
Calories from carbohydrates:	50%	Sod/Pot	=	0.2:1
Calories from fats:	4%	Ca/Phos	=	1.3:1
		CSI	=	0.1

SUGGESTED MENU: *One serving*

Creole Chicken Soup
Fillet Marchand de Vin
Leeks Vinaigrette
Boiled New Potatoes
Strawberry Bavarian Cream

Calories	564	Calcium	225 mg
Protein	62.9 g	Iron	7.79 mg
Carbohydrates	48.7 g	Sodium	228 mg
Dietary Fiber	9.18 g		
Fat-Total	16.1 g		
Fat-Saturated	4.88 g		
Fat-Mono	6.12 g		
Fat-Poly	2.18 g		
Cholesterol	159 mg		

Calories from protein:	43%	Poly/Sat	=	0.4:1
Calories from carbohydrates:	33%	Sod/Pot	=	0.1:1
Calories from fats:	24%	Ca/Phos	=	0.4:1
		CSI	=	12.9

Pineapple with Port Wine

Serves 2

INGREDIENTS:

6 ounces pared ripe pineapple,
   cut into 4 slices

4 ounces ruby port wine
1 cup crushed ice

PREPARATION:

Put the pineapple in a bowl and cover with the port. Cover tightly and refrigerate for 2 hours.

TO SERVE:

Divide the pineapple slices between dessert bowls and top each serving with crushed ice.

Pour the port marinade over the ice and serve.

NOTES:

If the pineapple is not sweet enough you may want to add some artificial sweetener.

The port should be "ruby" and will have its own sweetness.

VARIATIONS:

A Madeira could be used in place of the port.

Other fruits could be used but the fresh pineapple has an unusually refreshing quality about it.

PINEAPPLE WITH PORT WINE   *One serving*

Calories	129	Calcium	13.1 mg
Protein	0.443 g	Iron	0.434 mg
Carbohydrates	17.2 g	Sodium	9.69 mg
Dietary Fiber	1.48 g		
Fat-Total	0.362 g		
Fat-Saturated	0.027 g		
Fat-Mono	0.041 g		
Fat-Poly	0.124 g		
Cholesterol	0 mg		

Calories from protein:	1%	Poly/Sat	=	4.5:1
Calories from carbohydrates:	54%	Sod/Pot	=	0.1:1
Calories from fats:	3%	Ca/Phos	=	1.2:1
Other calories (i.e. alcohol):	43%	CSI	=	0.0

SUGGESTED MENU: *One serving*

Red Bean Soup
Creole Tomatoes with Basil, Garlic, and Green-Onion Dressing
Daube Glacé
Pineapple with Port Wine

Calories	606	Calcium	188 mg
Protein	51.1 g	Iron	8.26 mg
Carbohydrates	64.8 g	Sodium	165 mg
Dietary Fiber	17.8 g		
Fat-Total	9.23 g		
Fat-Saturated	3.11 g		
Fat-Mono	3.38 g		
Fat-Poly	1.09 g		
Cholesterol	78.8 mg		

Calories from protein:	34%	Poly/Sat	=	0.4:1
Calories from carbohydrates:	43%	Sod/Pot	=	0.1:1
Calories from fats:	14%	Ca/Phos	=	0.3:1
Other calories (i.e. alcohol):	10%	CSI	=	7.1

Pear Compote with Brandied Vanilla Cream

Serves 2

PEAR COMPOTE INGREDIENTS:

2 ripe Bartlett pears, peeled, cored, and chopped

1/2 cup water

1/2 teaspoon fresh lemon juice

1/8 teaspoon ground cinnamon

1/8 teaspoon ground allspice

BRANDIED VANILLA CREAM INGREDIENTS:

1/4 cup plain nonfat yogurt

Artificial sweetener equivalent of 2 teaspoons sugar

1 tablespoon brandy

1/2 teaspoon vanilla extract

PREPARATION:

Stew the pears in a saucepan with the water, lemon juice, cinnamon, and allspice until it is soft enough to mash when you stir it with a fork or wooden spoon and has a texture like applesauce.

Remove from the heat and refrigerate for two hours.

MAKE THE VANILLA CREAM:

Combine the yogurt with the sweetener, brandy, and vanilla.

TO ASSEMBLE:

Spoon the Pear Compote into small dessert cups and top with the Vanilla Cream.

NOTE:

This is a version of an old and popular Creole dessert.

VARIATION:

Use pear brandy in place of the regular.

PEAR COMPOTE WITH BRANDIED VANILLA CREAM *One serving*

Calories	132	Calcium	78.8 mg
Protein	2.29 g	Iron	0.507 mg
Carbohydrates	30.2 g	Sodium	23.0 mg
Dietary Fiber	4.87 g		
Fat-Total	0.730 g		
Fat-Saturated	0.074 g		
Fat-Mono	0.155 g		
Fat-Poly	0.162 g		
Cholesterol	0.500 mg		

Calories from protein:	7%	Poly/Sat	=	2.2:1
Calories from carbohydrates:	88%	Sod/Pot	=	0.1:1
Calories from fats:	5%	Ca/Phos	=	1.3:1
		CSI	=	0.1

SUGGESTED MENU: *One serving*

Boiled Onion Salad
Matelote of Sheepshead
Maque Choux
Pear Compote with Brandied Vanilla Cream

Calories	475	Calcium	216 mg
Protein	25.4 g	Iron	4.05 mg
Carbohydrates	68.7 g	Sodium	206 mg
Dietary Fiber	13.7 g		
Fat-Total	5.82 g		
Fat-Saturated	0.759 g		
Fat-Mono	1.94 g		
Fat-Poly	1.70 g		
Cholesterol	56.6 mg		

Calories from protein:	21%	Poly/Sat	=	2.2:1
Calories from carbohydrates:	58%	Sod/Pot	=	0.1:1
Calories from fats:	11%	Ca/Phos	=	0.5:1
Other calories (i.e. alcohol):	10%	CSI	=	3.6

Raisin Oat-Bran Cookies

Serves 2 (Makes about 10 small cookies)

INGREDIENTS:

¹/₄ cup rolled oats
¹/₄ cup oat bran
¹/₄ teaspoon baking soda
2 tablespoons raisins

Artificial sweetener equivalent of 4 teaspoons sugar
¹/₄ cup skim milk
2 egg whites
1 teaspoon vanilla extract

PREPARATION:

Preheat the oven to 350 degrees.

Combine the oats, oat bran, baking soda, raisins, and sweetener.

Beat the skim milk with the egg whites and vanilla and work it into the dry ingredients to make a dough.

Drop the dough by the teaspoonful onto a non-stick baking sheet.

Bake for 10 minutes, or until the edges of the cookies begin to brown. Transfer to a plate to cool.

NOTE:

The healthful aspects of the oat bran makes this treat one you may want to have around all the time for snacks.

VARIATIONS:

Other dried fruits such as dates or apricots could be chopped and used instead of the raisins.

Be sure your sweetener does not contain aspartame, which loses its sweetness during cooking.

RAISIN OAT-BRAN COOKIES   *One serving*

Calories	132		Calcium	56.7 mg
Protein	7.94 g		Iron	1.06 mg
Carbohydrates	22.7 g		Sodium	170 mg
Dietary Fiber	2.07 g			
Fat-Total	1.37 g			
Fat-Saturated	0.284 g			
Fat-Mono	0.466 g			
Fat-Poly	0.534 g			
Cholesterol	0.500 mg			

Calories from protein:	24%	Poly/Sat	=	1.9:1
Calories from carbohydrates:	67%	Sod/Pot	=	0.7:1
Calories from fats:	9%	Ca/Phos	=	0.4:1
		CSI	=	0.3

SUGGESTED MENU: *One serving*

Seasoned Eggplant Fingers
Roast Duck with Apples and Onion
Red and White Bean Salad
Raisin Oat-Bran Cookies

Calories	788		Calcium	320 mg
Protein	59.8 g		Iron	11.2 mg
Carbohydrates	93.7 g		Sodium	474 mg
Dietary Fiber	16.8 g			
Fat-Total	20.2 g			
Fat-Saturated	7.04 g			
Fat-Mono	6.32 g			
Fat-Poly	3.46 g			
Cholesterol	129 mg			

Calories from protein:	30%	Poly/Sat	=	0.5:1
Calories from carbohydrates:	47%	Sod/Pot	=	0.3:1
Calories from fats:	23%	Ca/Phos	=	0.4:1
		CSI	=	13.6

Bananas Foster

Serves 2

INGREDIENTS:

1 banana (4 ounces without skin), sliced lengthwise then crosswise

2 ounces (4 tablespoons) dark rum

2 three-ounce scoops frozen vanilla low-fat yogurt

PREPARATION:

Heat the banana and the rum in a pan.

Remove from the heat, avert your face, and carefully light the rum with a long match. Tilt the pan from side to side until the flame goes out. This will cook out the alcohol and strong alcohol taste.

TO SERVE:

Place the yogurt in dessert bowls and spoon the bananas and rum over the top.

NOTES:

You must heat the rum first or it will be difficult to flambé.

Be sure that the banana is not too ripe or the slices will dissolve during the flaming process.

VARIATION:

Slices of peaches, apples, or pineapple are delicious alternatives in this dessert.

BANANAS FOSTER

One serving

Calories	189		Calcium	149 mg
Protein	4.78 g		Iron	0.245 mg
Carbohydrates	25.0 g		Sodium	56.7 mg
Dietary Fiber	1.41 g			
Fat-Total	1.33 g			
Fat-Saturated	0.794 g			
Fat-Mono	0.313 g			
Fat-Poly	0.084 g			
Cholesterol	4.27 mg			

Calories from protein:	10%	Poly/Sat	=	0.1:1
Calories from carbohydrates:	53%	Sod/Pot	=	0.1:1
Calories from fats:	6%	Ca/Phos	=	1.2:1
Other calories (i.e. alcohol):	30%	CSI	=	1.0

SUGGESTED MENU:

One serving

Crab and Corn Bisque
Braised Pork Tenderloin
Artichokes and Aioli
Bananas Foster

Calories	663		Calcium	412 mg
Protein	55.1 g		Iron	5.40 mg
Carbohydrates	73.5 g		Sodium	323 mg
Dietary Fiber	12.0 g			
Fat-Total	12.7 g			
Fat-Saturated	4.34 g			
Fat-Mono	4.92 g			
Fat-Poly	2.18 g			
Cholesterol	133 mg			

Calories from protein:	35%	Poly/Sat	=	0.5:1
Calories from carbohydrates:	47%	Sod/Pot	=	0.2:1
Calories from fats:	18%	Ca/Phos	=	0.5:1
		CSI	=	11.0

Pineapple Bread Pudding
with Rum Sauce

Serves 2

INGREDIENTS:

1 egg white
1 cup skim milk
Artificial sweetener equivalent of
  2 teaspoons sugar
1/4 teaspoon ground cinnamon

1 cup stale French bread broken
  into 1/2-inch pieces
1/2 cup chopped ripe pineapple
1/2 teaspoon vanilla extract
1 tablespoon raisins

RUM SAUCE INGREDIENTS:

1/4 cup skim milk
1/2 teaspoon cornstarch
1 tablespoon dark rum

Artificial sweetener equivalent
  of 2 teaspoons sugar

PREPARATION:

Preheat the oven to 350 degrees.

Beat the egg white with the skim milk, sweetener, and cinnamon.

Add the bread to the liquid mixture to soak for 1 minute.

Add the remaining ingredients except the sauce and pour into a small baking
dish.

Bake for 30 minutes, or until a knife inserted into the center comes out clean.

MAKE THE RUM SAUCE:

Blend the cornstarch with the skim milk. Heat, stirring, until it thickens.
Add the rum and sweetener.

TO SERVE:

Spoon the hot bread pudding onto dessert plates and top with the Rum Sauce.

NOTES:

This is probably the most frequently served dessert in New Orleans restaurants. Delicious in its many variations, it also makes use of unused, stale French
bread.

Use an artificial sweetener which does not contain aspartame, which loses its sweetening power in cooking.

VARIATION:

Use apple or peach or other fruits. The ripeness and sweetness of the fruits is important to the taste of this dessert, so be sure you start with fruit at its peak of flavor.

BREAD PUDDING WITH RUM SAUCE   *One serving*

Calories	163	Calcium	219 mg
Protein	8.85 g	Iron	0.960 mg
Carbohydrates	25.7 g	Sodium	206 mg
Dietary Fiber	1.46 g		
Fat-Total	1.15 g		
Fat-Saturated	0.347 g		
Fat-Mono	0.314 g		
Fat-Poly	0.303 g		
Cholesterol	2.50 mg		

Calories from protein:	22%	Poly/Sat	=	0.9:1
Calories from carbohydrates:	63%	Sod/Pot	=	0.6:1
Calories from fats:	6%	Ca/Phos	=	1.2:1
Other calories (i.e. alcohol):	9%	CSI	=	0.5

SUGGESTED MENU: *One serving*

Brandy Milk Punch
Grillades and Grits
Vinegared Cucumber Salad and Mustard-Seed Salad
Stewed Okra and Tomatoes
Pineapple Bread Pudding with Rum Sauce

Calories	619	Calcium	548 mg
Protein	48.8 g	Iron	6.87 mg
Carbohydrates	75.1 g	Sodium	484 mg
Dietary Fiber	7.61 g		
Fat-Total	14.5 g		
Fat-Saturated	5.51 g		
Fat-Mono	5.49 g		
Fat-Poly	1.23 g		
Cholesterol	97.3 mg		

Calories from protein:	31%	Poly/Sat	=	0.2:1
Calories from carbohydrates:	48%	Sod/Pot	=	0.3:1
Calories from fats:	21%	Ca/Phos	=	0.8:1
		CSI	=	10.4

APPENDIX

Recommended Dietary Allowances

Individual Analyses
of Principal Ingredients

RECOMMENDED DIETARY ALLOWANCES (RDA)

	AGE (YEARS)	WEIGHT (KG)	WEIGHT (LBS)	HEIGHT (CM)	HEIGHT (IN)	PROTEIN (G)	VITAMIN A (RE)	VITAMIN D (µG)	VITAMIN E (MG)	VITAMIN C (MG)	THIAMIN (MG)	RIBOFLAVIN (MG)	NIACIN (MG EQUIV.)	VITAMIN B6 (MG)	FOLACIN (µG)	VITAMIN B12 (µG)	CALCIUM (MG)	PHOSPHORUS (MG)	MAGNESIUM (MG)	IRON (MG)	ZINC (MG)	IODINE (µG)
Infants	0.0-0.5	6	13	60	24	kg × 2.2	420	10	3	35	0.3	0.4	6	0.3	30	0.5	360	240	50	10	3	40
	0.5-1.0	9	20	71	28	kg × 2.0	400	10	4	35	0.5	0.6	8	0.6	45	1.5	540	360	70	15	5	50
Children	1-3	13	29	90	35	23	400	10	5	45	0.7	0.8	9	0.9	100	2.0	800	800	150	15	10	70
	4-6	20	44	112	44	30	500	10	6	45	0.9	1.0	11	1.3	200	2.5	800	800	200	10	10	90
	7-10	28	62	132	52	34	700	10	7	45	1.2	1.4	16	1.6	300	3.0	800	800	250	10	10	120
Males	11-14	45	99	157	62	45	1,000	10	8	50	1.4	1.6	18	1.8	400	3.0	1,200	1,200	350	18	15	150
	15-18	66	145	176	69	56	1,000	10	10	60	1.4	1.7	18	2.0	400	3.0	1,200	1,200	400	18	15	150
	19-22	70	154	177	70	56	1,000	7.5	10	60	1.5	1.7	19	2.2	400	3.0	800	800	350	10	15	150
	23-50	70	154	178	70	56	1,000	5	10	60	1.4	1.6	18	2.2	400	3.0	800	800	350	10	15	150
	51+	70	154	178	70	56	1,000	5	10	60	1.2	1.4	16	2.2	400	3.0	800	800	350	10	15	150
Females	11-14	46	101	157	62	46	800	10	8	50	1.1	1.3	15	1.8	400	3.0	1,200	1,200	300	18	15	150
	15-18	55	120	163	64	46	800	10	8	60	1.1	1.3	14	2.0	400	3.0	1,200	1,200	300	18	15	150
	19-22	55	120	163	64	44	800	7.5	8	60	1.1	1.3	14	2.0	400	3.0	800	800	300	18	15	150
	23-50	55	120	163	64	44	800	5	8	60	1.0	1.2	13	2.0	400	3.0	800	800	300	18	15	150
	51+	55	120	163	64	44	800	5	8	60	1.0	1.2	13	2.0	400	3.0	800	800	300	10	15	150
Pregnant						+30	+200	+5	+2	+20	+0.4	+0.3	+2	+0.6	+400	+1.0	+400	+400	+150	b	+5	+25
Lactating						+20	+400	+5	+3	+40	+0.5	+0.5	+5	+0.5	+100	+1.0	+400	+400	+150	b	+10	+50

Source: Recommended Dietary Allowances, 9th Edition, 1980, The National Academy of Sciences, Washington, D.C.

RECOMMENDED DIETARY ALLOWANCES (RDA)

	Age (Years)	Vitamins		
		Vitamin K (μg)	Biotin (μg)	Panto-thenic Acid (mg)
Infants	0.5–0.5	12	35	2
	0.5–1	10–20	50	3
Children and Adolescents	1–3	15–30	65	3
	4–6	20–40	85	3–4
	7–10	30–60	120	4–5
	11+	50–100	100–200	4–7
Adults		70–140	100–200	4–7

	Age (Years)	Trace Elements[b]					
		Copper (mg)	Man-ganese (mg)	Fluoride (mg)	Chromium (mg)	Selenium (mg)	Molyb-denum (mg)
Infants	0–0.5	0.5–0.7	0.5–0.7	0.1–0.5	0.01–0.04	0.01–0.04	0.03–0.06
	0.5–1	0.7–1.0	0.7–1.0	0.2–1.0	0.02–0.06	0.02–0.06	0.04–0.08
Children and Adolescents	1–3	1.0–1.5	1.0–1.5	0.5–1.5	0.02–0.08	0.02–0.08	0.05–0.1
	4–6	1.5–2.0	1.5–2.0	1.0–2.5	0.03–0.12	0.03–0.12	0.06–0.15
	7–10	2.0–2.5	2.0–3.0	1.5–2.5	0.05–0.2	0.05–0.2	0.10–0.3
	11+	2.0–3.0	2.5–5.0	1.5–2.5	0.05–0.2	0.05–0.2	0.15–0.5
Adults		2.0–3.0	2.5–5.0	1.5–4.0	0.05–0.2	0.05–0.2	0.15–0.5

	Age (Years)	Electrolytes		
		Sodium (mg)	Potassium (mg)	Chloride (mg)
Infants	0–0.5	115–350	350–925	275–700
	0.5–1	250–750	425–1275	400–1200
Children and Adolescents	1–3	325–975	550–1650	500–1500
	4–6	450–1350	775–2325	700–2100
	7–10	600–1800	1000–3000	925–2775
	11+	900–2700	1525–4575	1400–4200
Adults		1100–3300	1875–5625	1700–5100

Source: The Recommended Dietary Allowances, 9th Edition, 1980 National Academy of Sciences, Washington, D.C.

Alcohol: gin, rum, vodka, whiskey,
   80, 86, 90 proof
Almonds
Apple
Artichoke
Banana
Beans: red kidney, white Great Northerns
Beef: round steak, rump roast
Bluefish
Bran, oat
Brandy
Bread: French, dry crumbs
Brussels sprouts
Cabbage
Carrot
Catfish
Celery
Cheese: Parmesan
Cherry
Chicken: light meat, dark meat
Corn kernels
Cornmeal
Cornstarch
Crab
Crayfish
Cream of tartar
Egg white
Eggplant
Flounder/sole
Flour
Garlic
Gelatin, unflavored
Grape
Horseradish, prepared
Leek
Lemon juice, fresh

Lettuce: iceberg, Romaine
Milk, skim
Mirliton (chayote, vegetable pear)
Mushroom
Mustard, prepared
Oats, rolled
Okra
Onion: green, white
Orange
Oysters: Eastern, Pacific
Pear
Peas
Pepper: black, green bell
Pineapple
Pork, lean loin
Potato
Raisins
Rice
"Roux," blond or brown
Shrimp
Spinach
Squab
Squash
Strawberries
Thyme
Tomato
Tripe, beef
Trout
Turkey: ground, ham
Turnips, turnip greens
Vinegar, cider
Watercress
Wine: red, white, champagne, sherry
Yogurt: nonfat milk, flavored;
   vanilla/coffee

Alcohol: gin, rum, vodka, whiskey 80 proof   *1 ounce*

Weight: 28.0 grams (0.988 oz.)   Water weight: 17.9 g

Calories	63.5	Pyridoxine-B6	0 mg
Protein	0 g	Cobalamin-B12	0 mcg
Carbohydrates	0.030 g	Folacin	0 mcg
Dietary Fiber	0 g	Pantothenic	0 mg
Fat-Total	0 g	Vitamin C	0 mg
Fat-Saturated	0 g	Vitamin E	0 mg
Fat-Mono	0 g	Calcium	0 mg
Fat-Poly	0 g	Copper	0.016 mg
Cholesterol	0 mg	Iron	0.010 mg
Vit A-Carotene	0 re	Magnesium	0 mg
Vit A-Preformed	0 re	Phosphorus	0 mg
Vitamin A-Total	0 re	Potassium	1.00 mg
Thiamin-B1	0 mg	Selenium	0 mcg
Riboflavin-B2	0 mg	Sodium	0 mg
Niacin-B3	0 mg	Zinc	0 mg

Calories from protein:	0 %	Poly/Sat = 0.0:1
Calories from carbohydrates:	0 %	Sod/Pot = 0.0:1
Calories from fats:	0 %	Ca/Phos = 0.0:1
Calories from alcohol:	100 %	

Alcohol: gin, rum, vodka, whiskey 86 proof   *1 ounce*

Weight: 28.0 grams (0.988 oz.)   Water weight: 17.9 g

Calories	70.0	Pyridoxine-B6	0 mg
Protein	0 g	Cobalamin-B12	0 mcg
Carbohydrates	0.030 g	Folacin	0 mcg
Dietary Fiber	0 g	Pantothenic	0 mg
Fat-Total	0 g	Vitamin C	0 mg
Fat-Saturated	0 g	Vitamin E	0 mg
Fat-Mono	0 g	Calcium	0 mg
Fat-Poly	0 g	Copper	0.006 mg
Cholesterol	0 mg	Iron	0.011 mg
Vit A-Carotene	0 re	Magnesium	0 mg
Vit A-Preformed	0 re	Phosphorus	1.15 mg
Vitamin A-Total	0 re	Potassium	0.550 mg
Thiamin-B1	0.002 mg	Selenium	0 mcg
Riboflavin-B2	0.001 mg	Sodium	0.300 mg
Niacin-B3	0.003 mg	Zinc	0.011 mg

Calories from protein:	0 %	Poly/Sat = 0.0:1
Calories from carbohydrates:	0 %	Sod/Pot = 0.5:1
Calories from fats:	0 %	Ca/Phos = 0.0:1
Calories from alcohol:	100 %	

Alcohol: gin, rum, vodka, whiskey 90 proof   *1 ounce*

Weight: 28.0 grams (0.988 oz.)   Water weight: 17.4 g

Calories	73.5	Pyridoxine-B6	0 mg
Protein	0 g	Cobalamin-B12	0 mcg
Carbohydrates	0.006 g	Folacin	0 mcg
Dietary Fiber	0 g	Pantothenic	0 mg
Fat-Total	0 g	Vitamin C	0 mg
Fat-Saturated	0 g	Vitamin E	0 mg
Fat-Mono	0 g	Calcium	0 mg
Fat-Poly	0 g	Copper	0.015 mg
Cholesterol	0 mg	Iron	0.009 mg
Vit A-Carotene	0 re	Magnesium	0 mg
Vit A-Preformed	0 re	Phosphorus	0 mg
Vitamin A-Total	0 re	Potassium	0.850 mg
Thiamin-B1	0 mg	Selenium	0 mcg
Riboflavin-B2	0 mg	Sodium	0 mg
Niacin-B3	0 mg	Zinc	0 mg

Calories from protein:	0 %	Poly/Sat = 0.0:1	
Calories from carbohydrates:	0 %	Sod/Pot = 0.0:1	
Calories from fats:	0 %	Ca/Phos = 0.0:1	
Calories from alcohol:	100 %		

Almonds   *1 tablespoon sliced*

Weight: 5.88 grams (0.207 oz.)   Water weight: 0.260 g

Calories	34.6	Pyridoxine-B6	0.007 mg
Protein	1.17 g	Cobalamin-B12	0 mcg
Carbohydrates	1.20 g	Folacin	3.45 mcg
Dietary Fiber	0.439 g	Pantothenic	0.028 mg
Fat-Total	3.07 g	Vitamin C	0.035 mg
Fat-Saturated	0.291 g	Vitamin E	1.25 mg
Fat-Mono	1.99 g	Calcium	15.6 mg
Fat-Poly	0.644 g	Copper	0.055 mg
Cholesterol	0 mg	Iron	0.215 mg
Vit A-Carotene	0 re	Magnesium	17.4 mg
Vit A-Preformed	0 re	Phosphorus	30.6 mg
Vitamin A-Total	0 re	Potassium	43.0 mg
Thiamin-B1	0.012 mg	Selenium	0.235 mcg
Riboflavin-B2	0.046 mg	Sodium	0.625 mg
Niacin-B3	0.020 mg	Zinc	0.172 mg

Calories from protein:	13 %	Poly/Sat = 2.2:1	
Calories from carbohydrates:	13 %	Sod/Pot = 0.0:1	
Calories from fats:	74 %	Ca/Phos = 0.5:1	
		CSI = 0.3	

Apple, 1 with peel   *2.75 in diameter*

Weight: 138 grams (4.87 oz.)   Water weight: 116 g

Calories	80.0	Pyridoxine-B6	0.066 mg
Protein	0.270 g	Cobalamin-B12	0 mcg
Carbohydrates	21.0 g	Folacin	3.90 mcg
Dietary Fiber	3.87 g	Pantothenic	0.084 mg
Fat-Total	0.490 g	Vitamin C	7.80 mg
Fat-Saturated	0.100 g	Vitamin E	0.655 mg
Fat-Mono	0.021 g	Calcium	10.0 mg
Fat-Poly	0.145 g	Copper	0.057 mg
Cholesterol	0 mg	Iron	0.250 mg
Vit A-Carotene	7.40 re	Magnesium	6.00 mg
Vit A-Preformed	0 re	Phosphorus	10.0 mg
Vitamin A-Total	7.40 re	Potassium	159 mg
Thiamin-B1	0.023 mg	Selenium	0.500 mcg
Riboflavin-B2	0.019 mg	Sodium	1.00 mg
Niacin-B3	0.106 mg	Zinc	0.050 mg

Calories from protein:	1 %	Poly/Sat = 1.5:1	
Calories from carbohydrates:	94 %	Sod/Pot = 0.0:1	
Calories from fats:	5 %	Ca/Phos = 1.0:1	
		CSI = 0.1	

Artichoke   *1 cooked*

Weight: 120 grams (4.23 oz.)   Water weight: 104 g

Calories	53.0	Pyridoxine-B6	0.104 mg
Protein	2.76 g	Cobalamin-B12	0 mcg
Carbohydrates	12.4 g	Folacin	53.4 mcg
Dietary Fiber	3.96 g	Pantothenic	0.240 mg
Fat-Total	0.204 g	Vitamin C	8.90 mg
Fat-Saturated	0.048 g	Vitamin E	0.018 mg
Fat-Mono	0.006 g	Calcium	47.0 mg
Fat-Poly	0.086 g	Copper	0.073 mg
Cholesterol	0 mg	Iron	1.62 mg
Vit A-Carotene	17.2 re	Magnesium	47.0 mg
Vit A-Preformed	0 re	Phosphorus	72.0 mg
Vitamin A-Total	17.2 re	Potassium	316 mg
Thiamin-B1	0.068 mg	Selenium	0 mcg
Riboflavin-B2	0.059 mg	Sodium	79.0 mg
Niacin-B3	0.709 mg	Zinc	0.432 mg

Calories from protein:	18 %	Poly/Sat = 1.8:1	
Calories from carbohydrates:	79 %	Sod/Pot = 0.3:1	
Calories from fats:	3 %	Ca/Phos = 0.7:1	
		CSI = 0.0	

Banana

1 (peeled weight)

Weight: 114 grams (4.02 oz.)   Water weight: 84.7 g

Calories	105	Pyridoxine-B6	0.659 mg
Protein	1.18 g	Cobalamin-B12	0 mcg
Carbohydrates	26.7 g	Folacin	24.0 mcg
Dietary Fiber	2.83 g	Pantothenic	0.296 mg
Fat-Total	0.547 g	Vitamin C	10.3 mg
Fat-Saturated	0.211 g	Vitamin E	0.274 mg
Fat-Mono	0.047 g	Calcium	7.00 mg
Fat-Poly	0.101 g	Copper	0.119 mg
Cholesterol	0 mg	Iron	0.353 mg
Vit A-Carotene	9.20 re	Magnesium	32.4 mg
Vit A-Preformed	0 re	Phosphorus	22.0 mg
Vitamin A-Total	9.20 re	Potassium	451 mg
Thiamin-B1	0.051 mg	Selenium	1.14 mcg
Riboflavin-B2	0.114 mg	Sodium	1.00 mg
Niacin-B3	0.616 mg	Zinc	0.190 mg

Calories from protein:	4 %	Poly/Sat = 0.5:1	
Calories from carbohydrates:	92 %	Sod/Pot = 0.0:1	
Calories from fats:	4 %	Ca/Phos = 0.3:1	
		CSI = 0.2	

Beans, red kidney

½ cup cooked

Weight: 92.5 grams (3.26 oz.)   Water weight: 62.9 g

Calories	113	Pyridoxine-B6	0.059 mg
Protein	7.55 g	Cobalamin-B12	0 mcg
Carbohydrates	20.5 g	Folacin	57.5 mcg
Dietary Fiber	7.50 g	Pantothenic	0.205 mg
Fat-Total	0.465 g	Vitamin C	0.005 mg
Fat-Saturated	0.053 g	Vitamin E	0.575 mg
Fat-Mono	0.053 g	Calcium	26.5 mg
Fat-Poly	0.320 g	Copper	0.273 mg
Cholesterol	0 mg	Iron	3.33 mg
Vit A-Carotene	0.500 re	Magnesium	41.0 mg
Vit A-Preformed	0 re	Phosphorus	118 mg
Vitamin A-Total	0.500 re	Potassium	355 mg
Thiamin-B1	0.101 mg	Selenium	0.175 mcg
Riboflavin-B2	0.053 mg	Sodium	2.00 mg
Niacin-B3	0.680 mg	Zinc	1.01 mg

Calories from protein:	26 %	Poly/Sat = 6.0:1	
Calories from carbohydrates:	71 %	Sod/Pot = 0.0:1	
Calories from fats:	4 %	Ca/Phos = 0.2:1	
		CSI = 0.1	

Beans, white Great Northerns   *½ cup cooked*

Weight: 90.0 grams (3.17 oz.)   Water weight: 62.1 g

Calories	105	Pyridoxine-B6	0.199 mg
Protein	7.00 g	Cobalamin-B12	0 mcg
Carbohydrates	19.1 g	Folacin	37.0 mcg
Dietary Fiber	5.95 g	Pantothenic	0.277 mg
Fat-Total	0.550 g	Vitamin C	0 mg
Fat-Saturated	0.070 g	Vitamin E	0.975 mg
Fat-Mono	0.070 g	Calcium	45.0 mg
Fat-Poly	0.320 g	Copper	0.279 mg
Cholesterol	0 mg	Iron	2.45 mg
Vit A-Carotene	0 re	Magnesium	38.0 mg
Vit A-Preformed	0 re	Phosphorus	133 mg
Vitamin A-Total	0 re	Potassium	374 mg
Thiamin-B1	0.125 mg	Selenium	1.88 mcg
Riboflavin-B2	0.065 mg	Sodium	6.50 mg
Niacin-B3	0.650 mg	Zinc	0.860 mg

Calories from protein:	26 %	Poly/Sat = 4.6:1	
Calories from carbohydrates:	70 %	Sod/Pot = 0.0:1	
Calories from fats:	5 %	Ca/Phos = 0.3:1	
		CSI = 0.1	

Beef, round steak, lean only   *3 ounces*

Weight: 85.0 grams (3.00 oz.)   Water weight: 48.5 g

Calories	161	Pyridoxine-B6	0.350 mg
Protein	26.6 g	Cobalamin-B12	2.84 mcg
Carbohydrates	0 g	Folacin	4.00 mcg
Dietary Fiber	0 g	Pantothenic	0.719 mg
Fat-Total	8.72 g	Vitamin C	0 mg
Fat-Saturated	2.94 g	Vitamin E	0.388 mg
Fat-Mono	3.71 g	Calcium	4.30 mg
Fat-Poly	0.327 g	Copper	0.153 mg
Cholesterol	81.7 mg	Iron	2.70 mg
Vit A-Carotene	0 re	Magnesium	24.7 mg
Vit A-Preformed	1.00 re	Phosphorus	231 mg
Vitamin A-Total	1.00 re	Potassium	261 mg
Thiamin-B1	0.070 mg	Selenium	27.5 mcg
Riboflavin-B2	0.200 mg	Sodium	44.0 mg
Niacin-B3	3.27 mg	Zinc	4.58 mg

Calories from protein:	58 %	Poly/Sat = 0.1:1	
Calories from carbohydrates:	0 %	Sod/Pot = 0.2:1	
Calories from fats:	42 %	Ca/Phos = 0.0:1	
		CSI = 7.1	

Beef, rump roast, lean only   *3 ounces*

Weight: 85.0 grams (3.00 oz.)   Water weight: 53.6 g

Calories	153	Pyridoxine-B6	0.280 mg
Protein	25.2 g	Cobalamin-B12	2.84 mcg
Carbohydrates	0 g	Folacin	4.00 mcg
Dietary Fiber	0 g	Pantothenic	0.719 mg
Fat-Total	5.67 g	Vitamin C	0 mg
Fat-Saturated	2.15 g	Vitamin E	0.153 mg
Fat-Mono	2.38 g	Calcium	3.40 mg
Fat-Poly	0.227 g	Copper	0.119 mg
Cholesterol	58.9 mg	Iron	1.70 mg
Vit A-Carotene	0 re	Magnesium	24.7 mg
Vit A-Preformed	2.00 re	Phosphorus	193 mg
Vitamin A-Total	2.00 re	Potassium	337 mg
Thiamin-B1	0.079 mg	Selenium	27.5 mcg
Riboflavin-B2	0.147 mg	Sodium	52.0 mg
Niacin-B3	3.17 mg	Zinc	5.04 mg

Calories from protein:	66 %	Poly/Sat	= 0.1:1
Calories from carbohydrates:	0 %	Sod/Pot	= 0.2:1
Calories from fats:	34 %	Ca/Phos	= 0.0:1
		CSI	= 5.1

Bluefish, fillet, baked/broiled   *3 ounces*

Weight: 85.0 grams (3.00 oz.)   Water weight: 57.8 g

Calories	135	Pyridoxine-B6	0.492 mg
Protein	22.3 g	Cobalamin-B12	3.06 mcg
Carbohydrates	0 g	Folacin	8.50 mcg
Dietary Fiber	0 g	Pantothenic	0.498 mg
Fat-Total	6.97 g	Vitamin C	0.009 mg
Fat-Saturated	1.50 g	Vitamin E	0.850 mg
Fat-Mono	3.10 g	Calcium	24.7 mg
Fat-Poly	1.72 g	Copper	0.081 mg
Cholesterol	53.6 mg	Iron	0.595 mg
Vit A-Carotene	0 re	Magnesium	38.3 mg
Vit A-Preformed	12.8 re	Phosphorus	244 mg
Vitamin A-Total	12.8 re	Potassium	357 mg
Thiamin-B1	0.094 mg	Selenium	25.5 mcg
Riboflavin-B2	0.085 mg	Sodium	86.8 mg
Niacin-B3	1.62 mg	Zinc	0.833 mg

Calories from protein:	59 %	Poly/Sat	= 1.1:1
Calories from carbohydrates:	0 %	Sod/Pot	= 0.2:1
Calories from fats:	41 %	Ca/Phos	= 0.1:1
		CSI	= 4.2

Brandy   *1 ounce*

Weight: 28.0 grams (0.988 oz.)   Water weight: 21.6 g

Calories	68.5	Pyridoxine-B6	0 mg
Protein	0 g	Cobalamin-B12	0 mcg
Carbohydrates	10.5 g	Folacin	0 mcg
Dietary Fiber	0 g	Pantothenic	0 mg
Fat-Total	0 g	Vitamin C	0 mg
Fat-Saturated	0 g	Vitamin E	0 mg
Fat-Mono	0 g	Calcium	2.50 mg
Fat-Poly	0 g	Copper	0.008 mg
Cholesterol	0 mg	Iron	0.011 mg
Vit A-Carotene	0 re	Magnesium	0 mg
Vit A-Preformed	0 re	Phosphorus	1.00 mg
Vitamin A-Total	0 re	Potassium	1.00 mg
Thiamin-B1	0.002 mg	Selenium	0 mcg
Riboflavin-B2	0.002 mg	Sodium	1.00 mg
Niacin-B3	0.003 mg	Zinc	0.019 mg

Calories from protein:	0 %	Poly/Sat = 0.0:1	
Calories from carbohydrates:	61 %	Sod/Pot = 1.0:1	
Calories from fats:	0 %	Ca/Phos = 2.5:1	
Other calories (i.e. alcohol):	39 %		

Bread, French   *1 5×2-inch piece*

Weight: 35.0 grams (1.23 oz.)   Water weight: 11.9 g

Calories	100	Pyridoxine-B6	0.019 mg
Protein	3.30 g	Cobalamin-B12	0 mcg
Carbohydrates	17.7 g	Folacin	13.0 mcg
Dietary Fiber	0.620 g	Pantothenic	0.126 mg
Fat-Total	1.36 g	Vitamin C	0.001 mg
Fat-Saturated	0.293 g	Vitamin E	0.100 mg
Fat-Mono	0.440 g	Calcium	39.0 mg
Fat-Poly	0.455 g	Copper	0.051 mg
Cholesterol	0 mg	Iron	1.08 mg
Vit A-Carotene	0 re	Magnesium	7.30 mg
Vit A-Preformed	0 re	Phosphorus	30.0 mg
Vitamin A-Total	0 re	Potassium	32.0 mg
Thiamin-B1	0.160 mg	Selenium	8.30 mcg
Riboflavin-B2	0.120 mg	Sodium	203 mg
Niacin-B3	1.40 mg	Zinc	0.221 mg

Calories from protein:	14 %	Poly/Sat = 1.6:1	
Calories from carbohydrates:	74 %	Sod/Pot = 6.3:1	
Calories from fats:	13 %	Ca/Phos = 1.3:1	
		CSI = 0.3	

Bread crumbs
¼ cup

Weight: 25.0 grams (0.882 oz.)   Water weight: 1.75 g

Calories	97.5	Pyridoxine-B6	0.006 mg
Protein	3.25 g	Cobalamin-B12	0 mcg
Carbohydrates	18.2 g	Folacin	7.00 mcg
Dietary Fiber	1.01 g	Pantothenic	0.077 mg
Fat-Total	1.25 g	Vitamin C	0 mg
Fat-Saturated	0.375 g	Vitamin E	0.130 mg
Fat-Mono	0.400 g	Calcium	30.5 mg
Fat-Poly	0.250 g	Copper	0.050 mg
Cholesterol	1.25 mg	Iron	1.02 mg
Vit A-Carotene	0 re	Magnesium	7.75 mg
Vit A-Preformed	0 re	Phosphorus	35.2 mg
Vitamin A-Total	0 re	Potassium	38.0 mg
Thiamin-B1	0.087 mg	Selenium	3.00 mcg
Riboflavin-B2	0.087 mg	Sodium	184 mg
Niacin-B3	1.20 mg	Zinc	0.125 mg

Calories from protein:	13 %	Poly/Sat = 0.7:1	
Calories from carbohydrates:	75 %	Sod/Pot = 4.8:1	
Calories from fats:	12 %	Ca/Phos = 0.9:1	
		CSI = 0.4	

Brussels sprouts
½ cup cooked

Weight: 78.0 grams (2.75 oz.)   Water weight: 68.1 g

Calories	30.0	Pyridoxine-B6	0.155 mg
Protein	2.99 g	Cobalamin-B12	0 mcg
Carbohydrates	6.75 g	Folacin	46.8 mcg
Dietary Fiber	2.57 g	Pantothenic	0.280 mg
Fat-Total	0.398 g	Vitamin C	48.4 mg
Fat-Saturated	0.082 g	Vitamin E	0.665 mg
Fat-Mono	0.030 g	Calcium	28.0 mg
Fat-Poly	0.203 g	Copper	0.065 mg
Cholesterol	0 mg	Iron	0.940 mg
Vit A-Carotene	56.0 re	Magnesium	16.0 mg
Vit A-Preformed	0 re	Phosphorus	43.5 mg
Vitamin A-Total	56.0 re	Potassium	245 mg
Thiamin-B1	0.083 mg	Selenium	5.35 mcg
Riboflavin-B2	0.062 mg	Sodium	8.50 mg
Niacin-B3	0.473 mg	Zinc	0.250 mg

Calories from protein:	28 %	Poly/Sat = 2.5:1	
Calories from carbohydrates:	63 %	Sod/Pot = 0.0:1	
Calories from fats:	8 %	Ca/Phos = 0.6:1	
		CSI = 0.1	

Cabbage   *½ cup cooked*

Weight: 75.0 grams (2.65 oz.)   Water weight: 70.2 g

Calories	16.0	Pyridoxine-B6	0.048 mg
Protein	0.720 g	Cobalamin-B12	0 mcg
Carbohydrates	3.58 g	Folacin	15.5 mcg
Dietary Fiber	1.65 g	Pantothenic	0.047 mg
Fat-Total	0.188 g	Vitamin C	18.2 mg
Fat-Saturated	0.024 g	Vitamin E	0.021 mg
Fat-Mono	0.013 g	Calcium	25.0 mg
Fat-Poly	0.089 g	Copper	0.021 mg
Cholesterol	0 mg	Iron	0.292 mg
Vit A-Carotene	6.50 re	Magnesium	11.3 mg
Vit A-Preformed	0 re	Phosphorus	19.0 mg
Vitamin A-Total	6.50 re	Potassium	154 mg
Thiamin-B1	0.043 mg	Selenium	1.28 mcg
Riboflavin-B2	0.041 mg	Sodium	14.5 mg
Niacin-B3	0.172 mg	Zinc	0.120 mg

Calories from protein:	15 %	Poly/Sat = 3.7:1	
Calories from carbohydrates:	76 %	Sod/Pot = 0.1:1	
Calories from fats:	9 %	Ca/Phos = 1.3:1	
		CSI = 0.0	

Carrot   *½ cup cooked*

Weight: 78.0 grams (2.75 oz.)   Water weight: 68.2 g

Calories	35.0	Pyridoxine-B6	0.192 mg
Protein	0.850 g	Cobalamin-B12	0 mcg
Carbohydrates	8.18 g	Folacin	10.8 mcg
Dietary Fiber	2.61 g	Pantothenic	0.237 mg
Fat-Total	0.140 g	Vitamin C	2.00 mg
Fat-Saturated	0.027 g	Vitamin E	0.709 mg
Fat-Mono	0.007 g	Calcium	24.0 mg
Fat-Poly	0.069 g	Copper	0.105 mg
Cholesterol	0 mg	Iron	0.484 mg
Vit A-Carotene	1915 re	Magnesium	10.0 mg
Vit A-Preformed	0 re	Phosphorus	24.0 mg
Vitamin A-Total	1915 re	Potassium	177 mg
Thiamin-B1	0.027 mg	Selenium	0.884 mcg
Riboflavin-B2	0.044 mg	Sodium	52.0 mg
Niacin-B3	0.395 mg	Zinc	0.234 mg

Calories from protein:	9 %	Poly/Sat = 2.6:1	
Calories from carbohydrates:	88 %	Sod/Pot = 0.3:1	
Calories from fats:	3 %	Ca/Phos = 1.0:1	
		CSI = 0.0	

Catfish fillets

3 ounces uncooked

Weight: 85.0 grams (3.00 oz.) Water weight: 66.3 g

Calories	87.6	Pyridoxine-B6	0.128 mg
Protein	16.2 g	Cobalamin-B12	1.87 mcg
Carbohydrates	0 g	Folacin	7.65 mcg
Dietary Fiber	0 g	Pantothenic	0.398 mg
Fat-Total	2.98 g	Vitamin C	0.009 mg
Fat-Saturated	0.400 g	Vitamin E	0.510 mg
Fat-Mono	1.11 g	Calcium	54.4 mg
Fat-Poly	0.765 g	Copper	0.145 mg
Cholesterol	56.1 mg	Iron	0.340 mg
Vit A-Carotene	0 re	Magnesium	12.8 mg
Vit A-Preformed	0.255 re	Phosphorus	194 mg
Vitamin A-Total	0.255 re	Potassium	281 mg
Thiamin-B1	0.034 mg	Selenium	34.0 mcg
Riboflavin-B2	0.026 mg	Sodium	50.2 mg
Niacin-B3	1.45 mg	Zinc	0.221 mg

Calories from protein:	71 %	Poly/Sat = 1.9:1	
Calories from carbohydrates:	0 %	Sod/Pot = 0.2:1	
Calories from fats:	29 %	Ca/Phos = 0.3:1	
		CSI = 3.2	

Celery

1/4 cup cooked

Weight: 37.5 grams (1.32 oz.) Water weight: 35.6 g

Calories	5.50	Pyridoxine-B6	0.011 mg
Protein	0.190 g	Cobalamin-B12	0 mcg
Carbohydrates	1.32 g	Folacin	2.52 mcg
Dietary Fiber	0.610 g	Pantothenic	0.054 mg
Fat-Total	0.042 g	Vitamin C	1.77 mg
Fat-Saturated	0.010 g	Vitamin E	0.050 mg
Fat-Mono	0.008 g	Calcium	13.2 mg
Fat-Poly	0.020 g	Copper	0.012 mg
Cholesterol	0 mg	Iron	0.050 mg
Vit A-Carotene	4.05 re	Magnesium	4.50 mg
Vit A-Preformed	0 re	Phosphorus	9.00 mg
Vitamin A-Total	4.05 re	Potassium	133 mg
Thiamin-B1	0.010 mg	Selenium	0.412 mcg
Riboflavin-B2	0.011 mg	Sodium	24.2 mg
Niacin-B3	0.094 mg	Zinc	0.057 mg

Calories from protein:	12 %	Poly/Sat = 1.9:1	
Calories from carbohydrates:	82 %	Sod/Pot = 0.2:1	
Calories from fats:	6 %	Ca/Phos = 1.5:1	
		CSI = 0.0	

Cheese, Parmesan, grated   *1 teaspoon*

Weight: 1.67 grams (0.059 oz.)   Water weight: 0.295 g

Calories	7.68	Pyridoxine-B6	0.002 mg
Protein	0.702 g	Cobalamin-B12	0.025 mcg
Carbohydrates	0.063 g	Folacin	0.119 mcg
Dietary Fiber	0 g	Pantothenic	0.009 mg
Fat-Total	0.507 g	Vitamin C	0 mg
Fat-Saturated	0.322 g	Vitamin E	0.011 mg
Fat-Mono	0.149 g	Calcium	23.2 mg
Fat-Poly	0.012 g	Copper	0.001 mg
Cholesterol	1.31 mg	Iron	0.016 mg
Vit A-Carotene	0.321 re	Magnesium	0.839 mg
Vit A-Preformed	2.60 re	Phosphorus	13.6 mg
Vitamin A-Total	2.92 re	Potassium	1.79 mg
Thiamin-B1	0.001 mg	Selenium	0.060 mcg
Riboflavin-B2	0.006 mg	Sodium	31.4 mg
Niacin-B3	0.005 mg	Zinc	0.060 mg

Calories from protein:	37 %	Poly/Sat = 0.0:1	
Calories from carbohydrates:	3 %	Sod/Pot = 17.6:1	
Calories from fats:	60 %	Ca/Phos = 1.7:1	
		CSI = 0.4	

Cherry   *1 fresh*

Weight: 6.80 grams (0.240 oz.)   Water weight: 5.51 g

Calories	4.90	Pyridoxine-B6	0.002 mg
Protein	0.082 g	Cobalamin-B12	0 mcg
Carbohydrates	1.13 g	Folacin	0.280 mcg
Dietary Fiber	0.103 g	Pantothenic	0.009 mg
Fat-Total	0.065 g	Vitamin C	0.500 mg
Fat-Saturated	0.010 g	Vitamin E	0.061 mg
Fat-Mono	0.020 g	Calcium	1.000 mg
Fat-Poly	0.020 g	Copper	0.006 mg
Cholesterol	0 mg	Iron	0.030 mg
Vit A-Carotene	1.50 re	Magnesium	0.800 mg
Vit A-Preformed	0 re	Phosphorus	1.30 mg
Vitamin A-Total	1.50 re	Potassium	15.2 mg
Thiamin-B1	0.003 mg	Selenium	0 mcg
Riboflavin-B2	0.004 mg	Sodium	0 mg
Niacin-B3	0.030 mg	Zinc	0.004 mg

Calories from protein:	6 %	Poly/Sat = 2.0:1	
Calories from carbohydrates:	83 %	Sod/Pot = 0.0:1	
Calories from fats:	11 %	Ca/Phos = 0.8:1	
		CSI = 0.0	

Chicken, light meat only, cooked without added fat   *3 ounces*

Weight: 85.0 grams (3.00 oz.)   Water weight: 57.8 g

Calories	135	Pyridoxine-B6	0.279 mg
Protein	24.5 g	Cobalamin-B12	0.194 mcg
Carbohydrates	0 g	Folacin	3.04 mcg
Dietary Fiber	0 g	Pantothenic	0.487 mg
Fat-Total	3.52 g	Vitamin C	0 mg
Fat-Saturated	0.954 g	Vitamin E	0.425 mg
Fat-Mono	1.15 g	Calcium	10.9 mg
Fat-Poly	0.735 g	Copper	0.038 mg
Cholesterol	65.0 mg	Iron	0.796 mg
Vit A-Carotene	0 re	Magnesium	18.8 mg
Vit A-Preformed	6.68 re	Phosphorus	135 mg
Vitamin A-Total	6.68 re	Potassium	153 mg
Thiamin-B1	0.036 mg	Selenium	9.11 mcg
Riboflavin-B2	0.100 mg	Sodium	55.3 mg
Niacin-B3	6.62 mg	Zinc	1.01 mg

Calories from protein:	76 %	Poly/Sat = 0.8:1	
Calories from carbohydrates:	0 %	Sod/Pot = 0.4:1	
Calories from fats:	24 %	Ca/Phos = 0.1:1	
		CSI = 4.2	

Chicken, dark meat only, cooked without added fat   *3 ounces*

Weight: 85.0 grams (3.00 oz.)   Water weight: 56.0 g

Calories	163	Pyridoxine-B6	0.176 mg
Protein	22.1 g	Cobalamin-B12	0.188 mcg
Carbohydrates	0 g	Folacin	6.07 mcg
Dietary Fiber	0 g	Pantothenic	0.759 mg
Fat-Total	7.65 g	Vitamin C	0 mg
Fat-Saturated	2.08 g	Vitamin E	0.425 mg
Fat-Mono	2.77 g	Calcium	12.1 mg
Fat-Poly	1.78 g	Copper	0.064 mg
Cholesterol	74.7 mg	Iron	1.15 mg
Vit A-Carotene	0 re	Magnesium	17.0 mg
Vit A-Preformed	17.6 re	Phosphorus	122 mg
Vitamin A-Total	17.6 re	Potassium	154 mg
Thiamin-B1	0.047 mg	Selenium	10.4 mcg
Riboflavin-B2	0.172 mg	Sodium	63.2 mg
Niacin-B3	4.03 mg	Zinc	2.27 mg

Calories from protein:	56 %	Poly/Sat = 0.9:1	
Calories from carbohydrates:	0 %	Sod/Pot = 0.4:1	
Calories from fats:	44 %	Ca/Phos = 0.1:1	
		CSI = 5.8	

Corn kernels

½ cup cooked

Weight: 82.0 grams (2.89 oz.)   Water weight: 57.1 g

Calories	89.0	Pyridoxine-B6	0.138 mg
Protein	2.72 g	Cobalamin-B12	0 mcg
Carbohydrates	20.6 g	Folacin	38.1 mcg
Dietary Fiber	5.63 g	Pantothenic	0.720 mg
Fat-Total	1.05 g	Vitamin C	5.10 mg
Fat-Saturated	0.162 g	Vitamin E	0.402 mg
Fat-Mono	0.307 g	Calcium	1.64 mg
Fat-Poly	0.494 g	Copper	0.043 mg
Cholesterol	0 mg	Iron	0.500 mg
Vit A-Carotene	17.8 re	Magnesium	26.2 mg
Vit A-Preformed	0 re	Phosphorus	85.0 mg
Vitamin A-Total	17.8 re	Potassium	204 mg
Thiamin-B1	0.176 mg	Selenium	0.330 mcg
Riboflavin-B2	0.059 mg	Sodium	14.0 mg
Niacin-B3	1.32 mg	Zinc	0.394 mg

Calories from protein:	11 %	Poly/Sat = 3.0:1
Calories from carbohydrates:	80 %	Sod/Pot = 0.1:1
Calories from fats:	9 %	Ca/Phos = 0.0:1
		CSI = 0.2

Cornmeal, baked

1 tablespoon enriched

Weight: 8.62 grams (0.304 oz.)   Water weight: 0.949 g

Calories	31.4	Pyridoxine-B6	0.016 mg
Protein	0.681 g	Cobalamin-B12	0 mcg
Carbohydrates	0.067 g	Folacin	0.906 mcg
Dietary Fiber	0.250 g	Pantothenic	0.041 mg
Fat-Total	0.104 g	Vitamin C	0 mg
Fat-Saturated	0.012 g	Vitamin E	0.184 mg
Fat-Mono	0.025 g	Calcium	0.500 mg
Fat-Poly	0.056 g	Copper	0.006 mg
Cholesterol	0 mg	Iron	0.371 mg
Vit A-Carotene	3.81 re	Magnesium	4.06 mg
Vit A-Preformed	0 re	Phosphorus	8.56 mg
Vitamin A-Total	3.81 re	Potassium	10.4 mg
Thiamin-B1	0.029 mg	Selenium	0.581 mcg
Riboflavin-B2	0.019 mg	Sodium	0.063 mg
Niacin-B3	0.285 mg	Zinc	0.072 mg

Calories from protein:	9 %	Poly/Sat = 4.5:1
Calories from carbohydrates:	1 %	Sod/Pot = 0.0:1
Calories from fats:	3 %	Ca/Phos = 0.1:1
Other calories (i.e. alcohol):	87 %	CSI = 0.0

Cornstarch

1 teaspoon

Weight: 2.67 grams (0.094 oz.)   Water weight: 0.320 g

Calories	9.67	Pyridoxine-B6	0 mg
Protein	0.008 g	Cobalamin-B12	0 mcg
Carbohydrates	2.33 g	Folacin	0 mcg
Dietary Fiber	0.033 g	Pantothenic	0 mg
Fat-Total	0.016 g	Vitamin C	0 mg
Fat-Saturated	0.002 g	Vitamin E	0 mg
Fat-Mono	0.003 g	Calcium	0 mg
Fat-Poly	0.007 g	Copper	0.001 mg
Cholesterol	0 mg	Iron	0.013 mg
Vit A-Carotene	0 re	Magnesium	0.053 mg
Vit A-Preformed	0 re	Phosphorus	0.667 mg
Vitamin A-Total	0 re	Potassium	0 mg
Thiamin-B1	0 mg	Selenium	0.083 mcg
Riboflavin-B2	0.002 mg	Sodium	0 mg
Niacin-B3	0 mg	Zinc	0.001 mg

Calories from protein:	0 %	Poly/Sat =	4.4:1
Calories from carbohydrates:	98 %	Sod/Pot =	0.0:1
Calories from fats:	2 %	Ca/Phos =	−1.5:1
		CSI =	0.0

Crab, blue

3 ounces cooked

Weight: 85.0 grams (3.00 oz.)   Water weight: 62.9 g

Calories	71.6	Pyridoxine-B6	0.274 mg
Protein	17.7 g	Cobalamin-B12	8.42 mcg
Carbohydrates	0.421 g	Folacin	16.8 mcg
Dietary Fiber	0 g	Pantothenic	0.484 mg
Fat-Total	1.09 g	Vitamin C	1.68 mg
Fat-Saturated	0.211 g	Vitamin E	1.03 mg
Fat-Mono	0.286 g	Calcium	49.7 mg
Fat-Poly	0.463 g	Copper	0.893 mg
Cholesterol	65.7 mg	Iron	0.568 mg
Vit A-Carotene	0 re	Magnesium	6.74 mg
Vit A-Preformed	553 re	Phosphorus	207 mg
Vitamin A-Total	553 re	Potassium	403 mg
Thiamin-B1	0.122 mg	Selenium	49.7 mcg
Riboflavin-B2	0.083 mg	Sodium	48.0 mg
Niacin-B3	2.53 mg	Zinc	4.09 mg

Calories from protein:	86 %	Poly/Sat = 2.2:1
Calories from carbohydrates:	2 %	Sod/Pot = 0.1:1
Calories from fats:	12 %	Ca/Phos = 0.2:1
		CSI = 3.5

Crayfish, uncooked   *3 ounces meat*

Weight: 85.0 grams (3.00 oz.)   Water weight: 70.2 g

Calories	61.2	Pyridoxine-B6	0.179 mg
Protein	14.2 g	Cobalamin-B12	2.30 mcg
Carbohydrates	1.02 g	Folacin	7.65 mcg
Dietary Fiber	0 g	Pantothenic	0.349 mg
Fat-Total	1.19 g	Vitamin C	0.009 mg
Fat-Saturated	0.255 g	Vitamin E	0.936 mg
Fat-Mono	0.340 g	Calcium	65.5 mg
Fat-Poly	0.255 g	Copper	1.53 mg
Cholesterol	46.8 mg	Iron	1.28 mg
Vit A-Carotene	0 re	Magnesium	17.0 mg
Vit A-Preformed	0.255 re	Phosphorus	171 mg
Vitamin A-Total	0.255 re	Potassium	187 mg
Thiamin-B1	0.009 mg	Selenium	42.5 mcg
Riboflavin-B2	0.034 mg	Sodium	170 mg
Niacin-B3	1.62 mg	Zinc	1.53 mg

Calories from protein:	79 %	Poly/Sat = 1.0:1	
Calories from carbohydrates:	6 %	Sod/Pot = 0.9:1	
Calories from fats:	15 %	Ca/Phos = 0.4:1	
		CSI = 2.6	

Cream of tartar   *1 teaspoon*

Weight: 3.33 grams (0.118 oz.)   Water weight: 0.033 g

Calories	2.33	Pyridoxine-B6	0 mg
Protein	0 g	Cobalamin-B12	0 mcg
Carbohydrates	0.600 g	Folacin	0 mcg
Dietary Fiber	0 g	Pantothenic	0 mg
Fat-Total	0 g	Vitamin C	0 mg
Fat-Saturated	0 g	Vitamin E	0 mg
Fat-Mono	0 g	Calcium	0 mg
Fat-Poly	0 g	Copper	0 mg
Cholesterol	0 mg	Iron	0 mg
Vit A-Carotene	0 re	Magnesium	0 mg
Vit A-Preformed	0 re	Phosphorus	0 mg
Vitamin A-Total	0 re	Potassium	120 mg
Thiamin-B1	0 mg	Selenium	0 mcg
Riboflavin-B2	0 mg	Sodium	0 mg
Niacin-B3	0 mg	Zinc	0 mg

Calories from protein:	0 %	Poly/Sat = 0.0:1	
Calories from carbohydrates:	100 %	Sod/Pot = −0.0:1	
Calories from fats:	0 %	Ca/Phos = 0.0:1	

Egg white

one cooked

Weight: 33.0 grams (1.16 oz.)   Water weight: 26.1 g

Calories	16.0	Pyridoxine-B6	0.001 mg
Protein	3.35 g	Cobalamin-B12	0.018 mcg
Carbohydrates	0.410 g	Folacin	4.00 mcg
Dietary Fiber	0 g	Pantothenic	0.080 mg
Fat-Total	0 g	Vitamin C	0 mg
Fat-Saturated	0 g	Vitamin E	0 mg
Fat-Mono	0 g	Calcium	4.00 mg
Fat-Poly	0 g	Copper	0.013 mg
Cholesterol	0 mg	Iron	0.010 mg
Vit A-Carotene	0 re	Magnesium	3.00 mg
Vit A-Preformed	0 re	Phosphorus	4.00 mg
Vitamin A-Total	0 re	Potassium	45.0 mg
Thiamin-B1	0.002 mg	Selenium	4.44 mcg
Riboflavin-B2	0.090 mg	Sodium	50.0 mg
Niacin-B3	0.128 mg	Zinc	0.060 mg

Calories from protein:	89 %	Poly/Sat = 0.0:1	
Calories from carbohydrates:	11 %	Sod/Pot = 1.1:1	
Calories from fats:	0 %	Ca/Phos = 1.0:1	

Eggplant

3 ounces cooked

Weight: 85.0 grams (3.00 oz.)   Water weight: 78.0 g

Calories	23.8	Pyridoxine-B6	0.073 mg
Protein	0.707 g	Cobalamin-B12	0 mcg
Carbohydrates	5.63 g	Folacin	12.2 mcg
Dietary Fiber	3.19 g	Pantothenic	0.064 mg
Fat-Total	0.197 g	Vitamin C	1.11 mg
Fat-Saturated	0.037 g	Vitamin E	0.027 mg
Fat-Mono	0.017 g	Calcium	5.10 mg
Fat-Poly	0.079 g	Copper	0.092 mg
Cholesterol	0 mg	Iron	0.298 mg
Vit A-Carotene	5.42 re	Magnesium	11.2 mg
Vit A-Preformed	0 re	Phosphorus	18.6 mg
Vitamin A-Total	5.42 re	Potassium	211 mg
Thiamin-B1	0.065 mg	Selenium	0 mcg
Riboflavin-B2	0.017 mg	Sodium	2.55 mg
Niacin-B3	0.510 mg	Zinc	0.128 mg

Calories from protein:	10 %	Poly/Sat = 2.1:1	
Calories from carbohydrates:	83 %	Sod/Pot = 0.0:1	
Calories from fats:	7 %	Ca/Phos = 0.3:1	
		CSI = 0.0	

Flounder/Sole, baked without fat   *3 ounces*

Weight: 85.0 grams (3.00 oz.)   Water weight: 66.3 g

Calories	80.0	Pyridoxine-B6	0.284 mg
Protein	17.0 g	Cobalamin-B12	1.27 mcg
Carbohydrates	0 g	Folacin	10.0 mcg
Dietary Fiber	0 g	Pantothenic	0.429 mg
Fat-Total	1.00 g	Vitamin C	1.00 mg
Fat-Saturated	0.300 g	Vitamin E	1.61 mg
Fat-Mono	0.200 g	Calcium	13.0 mg
Fat-Poly	0.400 g	Copper	0.076 mg
Cholesterol	57.0 mg	Iron	0.300 mg
Vit A-Carotene	0 re	Magnesium	18.7 mg
Vit A-Preformed	10.0 re	Phosphorus	197 mg
Vitamin A-Total	10.0 re	Potassium	286 mg
Thiamin-B1	0.050 mg	Selenium	72.0 mcg
Riboflavin-B2	0.080 mg	Sodium	101 mg
Niacin-B3	1.70 mg	Zinc	0.723 mg

Calories from protein:	88 %	Poly/Sat = 1.3:1	
Calories from carbohydrates:	0 %	Sod/Pot = 0.4:1	
Calories from fats:	12 %	Ca/Phos = 0.1:1	
		CSI = 3.2	

Flour, dry roux   *1 tablespoon*

Weight: 7.81 grams (0.276 oz.)   Water weight: 0.938 g

Calories	28.4	Pyridoxine-B6	0.002 mg
Protein	0.819 g	Cobalamin-B12	0 mcg
Carbohydrates	5.94 g	Folacin	1.13 mcg
Dietary Fiber	0.219 g	Pantothenic	0.025 mg
Fat-Total	0.078 g	Vitamin C	0 mg
Fat-Saturated	0.012 g	Vitamin E	0.104 mg
Fat-Mono	0.006 g	Calcium	1.25 mg
Fat-Poly	0.034 g	Copper	0.010 mg
Cholesterol	0 mg	Iron	0.344 mg
Vit A-Carotene	0 re	Magnesium	1.64 mg
Vit A-Preformed	0 re	Phosphorus	6.81 mg
Vitamin A-Total	0 re	Potassium	7.44 mg
Thiamin-B1	0.042 mg	Selenium	2.38 mcg
Riboflavin-B2	0.026 mg	Sodium	0.156 mg
Niacin-B3	0.392 mg	Zinc	0.052 mg

Calories from protein:	12 %	Poly/Sat = 2.7:1	
Calories from carbohydrates:	86 %	Sod/Pot = 0.0:1	
Calories from fats:	3 %	Ca/Phos = 0.2:1	
		CSI = 0.0	

Garlic clove   *one*

Weight: 3.00 grams (0.106 oz.)   Water weight: 1.76 g

Calories	4.47	Pyridoxine-B6	0.100 mg
Protein	0.191 g	Cobalamin-B12	0 mcg
Carbohydrates	0.992 g	Folacin	0.092 mcg
Dietary Fiber	0.050 g	Pantothenic	0 mg
Fat-Total	0.015 g	Vitamin C	0.935 mg
Fat-Saturated	0.003 g	Vitamin E	0.000 mg
Fat-Mono	0.000 g	Calcium	5.42 mg
Fat-Poly	0.007 g	Copper	0.008 mg
Cholesterol	0 mg	Iron	0.051 mg
Vit A-Carotene	0 re	Magnesium	0.750 mg
Vit A-Preformed	0 re	Phosphorus	4.60 mg
Vitamin A-Total	0 re	Potassium	12.0 mg
Thiamin-B1	0.006 mg	Selenium	0.747 mcg
Riboflavin-B2	0.003 mg	Sodium	0.510 mg
Niacin-B3	0.021 mg	Zinc	0.265 mg

Calories from protein:	16 %	Poly/Sat = 2.7:1	
Calories from carbohydrates:	82 %	Sod/Pot = 0.0:1	
Calories from fats:	3 %	Ca/Phos = 1.2:1	
		CSI = 0.0	

Gelatin, unflavored   *1-ounce packet*

Weight: 7.00 grams (0.247 oz.)   Water weight: 0.910 g

Calories	25.0	Pyridoxine-B6	0.005 mg
Protein	6.00 g	Cobalamin-B12	0 mcg
Carbohydrates	0 g	Folacin	0 mcg
Dietary Fiber	1.00 g	Pantothenic	0 mg
Fat-Total	0 g	Vitamin C	0 mg
Fat-Saturated	0 g	Vitamin E	0 mg
Fat-Mono	0 g	Calcium	1.00 mg
Fat-Poly	0 g	Copper	0.031 mg
Cholesterol	0 mg	Iron	0 mg
Vit A-Carotene	0 re	Magnesium	2.31 mg
Vit A-Preformed	0 re	Phosphorus	0 mg
Vitamin A-Total	0 re	Potassium	2.00 mg
Thiamin-B1	0 mg	Selenium	2.04 mcg
Riboflavin-B2	0 mg	Sodium	6.00 mg
Niacin-B3	0 mg	Zinc	0 mg

Calories from protein:	100 %	Poly/Sat = 0.0:1	
Calories from carbohydrates:	0 %	Sod/Pot = 3.0:1	
Calories from fats:	0 %	Ca/Phos = 0.0:1	

Grape

1 seedless

Weight: 5.00 grams (0.176 oz.)   Water weight: 4.03 g

Calories	3.50	Pyridoxine-B6	0.005 mg
Protein	0.033 g	Cobalamin-B12	0 mcg
Carbohydrates	0.888 g	Folacin	0.350 mcg
Dietary Fiber	0.082 g	Pantothenic	0.001 mg
Fat-Total	0.029 g	Vitamin C	0.540 mg
Fat-Saturated	0.009 g	Vitamin E	0.032 mg
Fat-Mono	0.001 g	Calcium	0.530 mg
Fat-Poly	0.008 g	Copper	0.008 mg
Cholesterol	0 mg	Iron	0.013 mg
Vit A-Carotene	0.400 re	Magnesium	0.300 mg
Vit A-Preformed	0 re	Phosphorus	0.660 mg
Vitamin A-Total	0.400 re	Potassium	9.20 mg
Thiamin-B1	0.005 mg	Selenium	0.481 mcg
Riboflavin-B2	0.003 mg	Sodium	0.094 mg
Niacin-B3	0.015 mg	Zinc	0.003 mg

Calories from protein:	3 %	Poly/Sat = 0.9:1	
Calories from carbohydrates:	90 %	Sod/Pot = 0.0:1	
Calories from fats:	7 %	Ca/Phos = 0.8:1	
		CSI = 0.0	

Horseradish, prepared

1 teaspoon

Weight: 5.00 grams (0.176 oz.)   Water weight: 4.35 g

Calories	2.00	Pyridoxine-B6	0.004 mg
Protein	0.067 g	Cobalamin-B12	0 mcg
Carbohydrates	0.467 g	Folacin	0.583 mcg
Dietary Fiber	0.045 g	Pantothenic	0.003 mg
Fat-Total	0.010 g	Vitamin C	0.210 mg
Fat-Saturated	0.003 g	Vitamin E	0 mg
Fat-Mono	0.002 g	Calcium	3.00 mg
Fat-Poly	0.005 g	Copper	0.007 mg
Cholesterol	0 mg	Iron	0.033 mg
Vit A-Carotene	0 re	Magnesium	1.27 mg
Vit A-Preformed	0 re	Phosphorus	1.67 mg
Vitamin A-Total	0 re	Potassium	14.7 mg
Thiamin-B1	0.005 mg	Selenium	0 mcg
Riboflavin-B2	0.001 mg	Sodium	4.67 mg
Niacin-B3	0.021 mg	Zinc	0.059 mg

Calories from protein:	12 %	Poly/Sat = 1.6:1	
Calories from carbohydrates:	84 %	Sod/Pot = 0.3:1	
Calories from fats:	4 %	Ca/Phos = 1.8:1	
		CSI = 0.0	

Leek

3 ounces cooked

Weight: 85.0 grams (3.00 oz.)   Water weight: 77.2 g

Calories	26.3	Pyridoxine-B6	0.123 mg
Protein	0.689 g	Cobalamin-B12	0 mcg
Carbohydrates	6.48 g	Folacin	26.2 mcg
Dietary Fiber	2.78 g	Pantothenic	0.082 mg
Fat-Total	0.170 g	Vitamin C	3.60 mg
Fat-Saturated	0.023 g	Vitamin E	0.736 mg
Fat-Mono	0.003 g	Calcium	25.5 mg
Fat-Poly	0.095 g	Copper	0.074 mg
Cholesterol	0 mg	Iron	0.932 mg
Vit A-Carotene	3.93 re	Magnesium	11.9 mg
Vit A-Preformed	0 re	Phosphorus	14.4 mg
Vitamin A-Total	3.93 re	Potassium	73.9 mg
Thiamin-B1	0.021 mg	Selenium	4.17 mcg
Riboflavin-B2	0.018 mg	Sodium	8.50 mg
Niacin-B3	0.170 mg	Zinc	0.196 mg

Calories from protein:	9 %	Poly/Sat	= 4.1:1
Calories from carbohydrates:	86 %	Sod/Pot	= 0.1:1
Calories from fats:	5 %	Ca/Phos	= 1.8:1
		CSI	= 0.0

Lemon juice, fresh

1 teaspoon

Weight: 5.08 grams (0.179 oz.)   Water weight: 4.61 g

Calories	1.25	Pyridoxine-B6	0.003 mg
Protein	0.019 g	Cobalamin-B12	0 mcg
Carbohydrates	0.440 g	Folacin	0.656 mcg
Dietary Fiber	0.018 g	Pantothenic	0.005 mg
Fat-Total	0.015 g	Vitamin C	2.33 mg
Fat-Saturated	0.002 g	Vitamin E	0.011 mg
Fat-Mono	0.001 g	Calcium	0.375 mg
Fat-Poly	0.004 g	Copper	0.001 mg
Cholesterol	0 mg	Iron	0.002 mg
Vit A-Carotene	0.104 re	Magnesium	0.333 mg
Vit A-Preformed	0 re	Phosphorus	0.292 mg
Vitamin A-Total	0.104 re	Potassium	6.31 mg
Thiamin-B1	0.002 mg	Selenium	0.010 mcg
Riboflavin-B2	0.000 mg	Sodium	0.042 mg
Niacin-B3	0.005 mg	Zinc	0.002 mg

Calories from protein:	4 %	Poly/Sat	= 2.2:1
Calories from carbohydrates:	89 %	Sod/Pot	= 0.0:1
Calories from fats:	7 %	Ca/Phos	= 1.3:1
		CSI	= 0.0

Lettuce, iceberg   *1 leaf*

Weight: 20.0 grams (0.705 oz.)   Water weight: 19.2 g

Calories	2.60	Pyridoxine-B6	0.008 mg
Protein	0.202 g	Cobalamin-B12	0 mcg
Carbohydrates	0.418 g	Folacin	11.2 mcg
Dietary Fiber	0.270 g	Pantothenic	0.009 mg
Fat-Total	0.038 g	Vitamin C	0.780 mg
Fat-Saturated	0.005 g	Vitamin E	0.021 mg
Fat-Mono	0.001 g	Calcium	3.80 mg
Fat-Poly	0.020 g	Copper	0.006 mg
Cholesterol	0 mg	Iron	0.100 mg
Vit A-Carotene	6.60 re	Magnesium	1.80 mg
Vit A-Preformed	0 re	Phosphorus	4.00 mg
Vitamin A-Total	6.60 re	Potassium	31.6 mg
Thiamin-B1	0.009 mg	Selenium	0.714 mcg
Riboflavin-B2	0.006 mg	Sodium	1.80 mg
Niacin-B3	0.037 mg	Zinc	0.044 mg

Calories from protein:	29 %	Poly/Sat = 4.0:1	
Calories from carbohydrates:	59 %	Sod/Pot = 0.1:1	
Calories from fats:	12 %	Ca/Phos = 0.9:1	
		CSI = 0.0	

Lettuce, Romaine   *1 inner leaf*

Weight: 10.0 grams (0.353 oz.)   Water weight: 9.49 g

Calories	1.60	Pyridoxine-B6	0.055 mg
Protein	0.162 g	Cobalamin-B12	0 mcg
Carbohydrates	0.240 g	Folacin	13.6 mcg
Dietary Fiber	0.166 g	Pantothenic	0.020 mg
Fat-Total	0.020 g	Vitamin C	2.40 mg
Fat-Saturated	0.003 g	Vitamin E	0.040 mg
Fat-Mono	0.001 g	Calcium	3.60 mg
Fat-Poly	0.011 g	Copper	0.005 mg
Cholesterol	0 mg	Iron	0.110 mg
Vit A-Carotene	26.0 re	Magnesium	0.600 mg
Vit A-Preformed	0 re	Phosphorus	4.50 mg
Vitamin A-Total	26.0 re	Potassium	29.0 mg
Thiamin-B1	0.010 mg	Selenium	0.040 mcg
Riboflavin-B2	0.010 mg	Sodium	0.800 mg
Niacin-B3	0.050 mg	Zinc	0.033 mg

Calories from protein:	36 %	Poly/Sat = 3.7:1	
Calories from carbohydrates:	54 %	Sod/Pot = 0.0:1	
Calories from fats:	10 %	Ca/Phos = 0.8:1	
		CSI = 0.0	

Milk, skim

½ cup

Weight: 122 grams (4.32 oz.)   Water weight: 111 g

Calories	43.0	Pyridoxine-B6	0.049 mg
Protein	4.17 g	Cobalamin-B12	0.463 mcg
Carbohydrates	5.95 g	Folacin	7.00 mcg
Dietary Fiber	0 g	Pantothenic	0.403 mg
Fat-Total	0.220 g	Vitamin C	1.20 mg
Fat-Saturated	0.143 g	Vitamin E	0.000 mg
Fat-Mono	0.058 g	Calcium	151 mg
Fat-Poly	0.008 g	Copper	0.024 mg
Cholesterol	2.00 mg	Iron	0.050 mg
Vit A-Carotene	0 re	Magnesium	14.0 mg
Vit A-Preformed	74.5 re	Phosphorus	123 mg
Vitamin A-Total	74.5 re	Potassium	203 mg
Thiamin-B1	0.044 mg	Selenium	5.80 mcg
Riboflavin-B2	0.171 mg	Sodium	63.0 mg
Niacin-B3	0.108 mg	Zinc	0.457 mg

Calories from protein:	39 %	Poly/Sat	= 0.1:1
Calories from carbohydrates:	56 %	Sod/Pot	= 0.3:1
Calories from fats:	5 %	Ca/Phos	= 1.2:1
		CSI	= 0.2

Mirliton (chayote, vegetable pear)

3 ounces boiled

Weight: 85.0 grams (3.00 oz.)   Water weight: 79.4 g

Calories	20.2	Pyridoxine-B6	0 mg
Protein	0.526 g	Cobalamin-B12	0 mcg
Carbohydrates	4.33 g	Folacin	0 mcg
Dietary Fiber	0.494 g	Pantothenic	0.347 mg
Fat-Total	0.409 g	Vitamin C	6.80 mg
Fat-Saturated	0 g	Vitamin E	0 mg
Fat-Mono	0 g	Calcium	11.2 mg
Fat-Poly	0 g	Copper	0 mg
Cholesterol	0 mg	Iron	0.186 mg
Vit A-Carotene	0 re	Magnesium	10.1 mg
Vit A-Preformed	0 re	Phosphorus	24.5 mg
Vitamin A-Total	0 re	Potassium	147 mg
Thiamin-B1	0.022 mg	Selenium	0 mcg
Riboflavin-B2	0.034 mg	Sodium	0.532 mg
Niacin-B3	0.357 mg	Zinc	0 mg

Calories from protein:	9 %	Poly/Sat	= 0.0:1
Calories from carbohydrates:	75 %	Sod/Pot	= 0.0:1
Calories from fats:	16 %	Ca/Phos	= 0.5:1

Mushroom   *1 large raw*

Weight: 18.0 grams (0.635 oz.)   Water weight: 16.5 g

Calories	4.50	Pyridoxine-B6	0.018 mg
Protein	0.376 g	Cobalamin-B12	0 mcg
Carbohydrates	0.838 g	Folacin	4.14 mcg
Dietary Fiber	0.450 g	Pantothenic	0.396 mg
Fat-Total	0.076 g	Vitamin C	0.630 mg
Fat-Saturated	0.010 g	Vitamin E	0 mg
Fat-Mono	0.001 g	Calcium	0.900 mg
Fat-Poly	0.031 g	Copper	0.089 mg
Cholesterol	0 mg	Iron	0.224 mg
Vit A-Carotene	0 re	Magnesium	1.80 mg
Vit A-Preformed	0 re	Phosphorus	18.7 mg
Vitamin A-Total	0 re	Potassium	67.0 mg
Thiamin-B1	0.180 mg	Selenium	0 mcg
Riboflavin-B2	0.081 mg	Sodium	0.700 mg
Niacin-B3	0.742 mg	Zinc	0.131 mg

Calories from protein:	27 %	Poly/Sat = 3.1:1
Calories from carbohydrates:	61 %	Sod/Pot = 0.0:1
Calories from fats:	12 %	Ca/Phos = 0.0:1
		CSI = 0.0

Mustard, prepared   *1 teaspoon*

Weight: 5.21 grams (0.184 oz.)   Water weight: 4.17 g

Calories	3.92	Pyridoxine-B6	0.004 mg
Protein	0.246 g	Cobalamin-B12	0 mcg
Carbohydrates	0.333 g	Folacin	0 mcg
Dietary Fiber	0.021 g	Pantothenic	0 mg
Fat-Total	0.229 g	Vitamin C	0 mg
Fat-Saturated	0.001 g	Vitamin E	0.216 mg
Fat-Mono	0.208 g	Calcium	4.37 mg
Fat-Poly	0.001 g	Copper	0.021 mg
Cholesterol	0 mg	Iron	0.104 mg
Vit A-Carotene	0 re	Magnesium	2.50 mg
Vit A-Preformed	0 re	Phosphorus	3.83 mg
Vitamin A-Total	0 re	Potassium	6.75 mg
Thiamin-B1	0.004 mg	Selenium	1.21 mcg
Riboflavin-B2	0.010 mg	Sodium	65.2 mg
Niacin-B3	0.065 mg	Zinc	0.033 mg

Calories from protein:	22 %	Poly/Sat = 1.0:1
Calories from carbohydrates:	30 %	Sod/Pot = 9.7:1
Calories from fats:	47 %	Ca/Phos = 1.1:1
		CSI = 0.0

Oats, rolled

¼ cup baked

Weight: 20.0 grams (0.705 oz.)   Water weight: 1.56 g

Calories	77.7	Pyridoxine-B6	0.021 mg
Protein	3.25 g	Cobalamin-B12	0 mcg
Carbohydrates	13.6 g	Folacin	3.25 mcg
Dietary Fiber	1.28 g	Pantothenic	0.189 mg
Fat-Total	1.27 g	Vitamin C	0 mg
Fat-Saturated	0.235 g	Vitamin E	0.250 mg
Fat-Mono	0.450 g	Calcium	10.5 mg
Fat-Poly	0.520 g	Copper	0.083 mg
Cholesterol	0 mg	Iron	0.852 mg
Vit A-Carotene	1.00 re	Magnesium	30.0 mg
Vit A-Preformed	0 re	Phosphorus	96.0 mg
Vitamin A-Total	1.00 re	Potassium	71.0 mg
Thiamin-B1	0.111 mg	Selenium	5.95 mcg
Riboflavin-B2	0.023 mg	Sodium	0.750 mg
Niacin-B3	0.150 mg	Zinc	0.620 mg

Calories from protein:	16 %	Poly/Sat = 2.2:1	
Calories from carbohydrates:	69 %	Sod/Pot = 0.0:1	
Calories from fats:	15 %	Ca/Phos = 0.1:1	
		CSI = 0.2	

Okra

6 pods fresh-cooked

Weight: 63.8 grams (2.25 oz.)   Water weight: 57.3 g

Calories	20.4	Pyridoxine-B6	0.119 mg
Protein	1.19 g	Cobalamin-B12	0 mcg
Carbohydrates	4.60 g	Folacin	29.1 mcg
Dietary Fiber	1.40 g	Pantothenic	0.136 mg
Fat-Total	0.109 g	Vitamin C	10.4 mg
Fat-Saturated	0.028 g	Vitamin E	0 mg
Fat-Mono	0.018 g	Calcium	40.2 mg
Fat-Poly	0.029 g	Copper	0.055 mg
Cholesterol	0 mg	Iron	0.287 mg
Vit A-Carotene	36.7 re	Magnesium	36.0 mg
Vit A-Preformed	0 re	Phosphorus	36.0 mg
Vitamin A-Total	36.7 re	Potassium	205 mg
Thiamin-B1	0.084 mg	Selenium	0 mcg
Riboflavin-B2	0.035 mg	Sodium	3.00 mg
Niacin-B3	0.555 mg	Zinc	0.351 mg

Calories from protein:	20 %	Poly/Sat = 1.0:1	
Calories from carbohydrates:	76 %	Sod/Pot = 0.0:1	
Calories from fats:	4 %	Ca/Phos = 1.1:1	
		CSI = 0.0	

Onion, green   *¼ cup chopped green and white parts*

Weight: 25.0 grams (0.882 oz.)   Water weight: 23.0 g

Calories	6.50	Pyridoxine-B6	0.012 mg
Protein	0.435 g	Cobalamin-B12	0 mcg
Carbohydrates	1.39 g	Folacin	4.00 mcg
Dietary Fiber	0.660 g	Pantothenic	0.036 mg
Fat-Total	0.035 g	Vitamin C	11.3 mg
Fat-Saturated	0.006 g	Vitamin E	0.075 mg
Fat-Mono	0.005 g	Calcium	15.0 mg
Fat-Poly	0.013 g	Copper	0.015 mg
Cholesterol	0 mg	Iron	0.470 mg
Vit A-Carotene	125 re	Magnesium	5.00 mg
Vit A-Preformed	0 re	Phosphorus	8.00 mg
Vitamin A-Total	125 re	Potassium	64.0 mg
Thiamin-B1	0.017 mg	Selenium	0.300 mcg
Riboflavin-B2	0.035 mg	Sodium	1.00 mg
Niacin-B3	0.050 mg	Zinc	0.110 mg

Calories from protein:	23 %	Poly/Sat	= 2.3:1
Calories from carbohydrates:	73 %	Sod/Pot	= 0.0:1
Calories from fats:	4 %	Ca/Phos	= 1.9:1
		CSI	= 0.0

Onion, white   *¼ cup chopped cooked*

Weight: 52.5 grams (1.85 oz.)   Water weight: 48.4 g

Calories	14.5	Pyridoxine-B6	0.094 mg
Protein	0.475 g	Cobalamin-B12	0 mcg
Carbohydrates	3.29 g	Folacin	6.65 mcg
Dietary Fiber	0.765 g	Pantothenic	0.066 mg
Fat-Total	0.085 g	Vitamin C	3.00 mg
Fat-Saturated	0.014 g	Vitamin E	0.155 mg
Fat-Mono	0.012 g	Calcium	14.5 mg
Fat-Poly	0.033 g	Copper	0.021 mg
Cholesterol	0 mg	Iron	0.105 mg
Vit A-Carotene	0 re	Magnesium	5.50 mg
Vit A-Preformed	0 re	Phosphorus	12.0 mg
Vitamin A-Total	0 re	Potassium	79.5 mg
Thiamin-B1	0.022 mg	Selenium	0.725 mcg
Riboflavin-B2	0.004 mg	Sodium	4.00 mg
Niacin-B3	0.042 mg	Zinc	0.095 mg

Calories from protein:	12 %	Poly/Sat	= 2.4:1
Calories from carbohydrates:	83 %	Sod/Pot	= 0.1:1
Calories from fats:	5 %	Ca/Phos	= 1.2:1
		CSI	= 0.0

Orange

1 medium

Weight: 131 grams (4.62 oz.)   Water weight: 114 g

Calories	60.0	Pyridoxine-B6	0.079 mg
Protein	1.23 g	Cobalamin-B12	0 mcg
Carbohydrates	15.4 g	Folacin	39.7 mcg
Dietary Fiber	2.80 g	Pantothenic	0.328 mg
Fat-Total	0.160 g	Vitamin C	69.7 mg
Fat-Saturated	0.020 g	Vitamin E	0.314 mg
Fat-Mono	0.030 g	Calcium	52.0 mg
Fat-Poly	0.033 g	Copper	0.059 mg
Cholesterol	0 mg	Iron	0.136 mg
Vit A-Carotene	27.0 re	Magnesium	13.0 mg
Vit A-Preformed	0 re	Phosphorus	18.0 mg
Vitamin A-Total	27.0 re	Potassium	237 mg
Thiamin-B1	0.114 mg	Selenium	0.200 mcg
Riboflavin-B2	0.052 mg	Sodium	0.001 mg
Niacin-B3	0.369 mg	Zinc	0.090 mg

Calories from protein:	7 %	Poly/Sat = 1.6:1	
Calories from carbohydrates:	91 %	Sod/Pot = 0.0:1	
Calories from fats:	2 %	Ca/Phos = 2.9:1	
		CSI = 0.0	

Oysters, raw, Eastern

3 ounces

Weight: 85.0 grams (3.00 oz.)   Water weight: 72.3 g

Calories	56.7	Pyridoxine-B6	0.047 mg
Protein	7.09 g	Cobalamin-B12	14.0 mcg
Carbohydrates	2.83 g	Folacin	8.50 mcg
Dietary Fiber	0 g	Pantothenic	0.319 mg
Fat-Total	1.42 g	Vitamin C	8.50 mg
Fat-Saturated	0.496 g	Vitamin E	0.723 mg
Fat-Mono	0.177 g	Calcium	80.1 mg
Fat-Poly	0.496 g	Copper	9.36 mg
Cholesterol	42.5 mg	Iron	5.53 mg
Vit A-Carotene	0 re	Magnesium	41.1 mg
Vit A-Preformed	79.0 re	Phosphorus	122 mg
Vitamin A-Total	79.0 re	Potassium	103 mg
Thiamin-B1	0.120 mg	Selenium	48.5 mcg
Riboflavin-B2	0.152 mg	Sodium	62.0 mg
Niacin-B3	2.13 mg	Zinc	34.3 mg

Calories from protein:	50 %	Poly/Sat = 1.0:1	
Calories from carbohydrates:	20 %	Sod/Pot = 0.6:1	
Calories from fats:	22 %	Ca/Phos = 0.7:1	
Other calories (i.e. alcohol):	8 %	CSI = 2.6	

Oysters, raw, Pacific

3 ounces

Weight: 85.0 grams (3.00 oz.)   Water weight: 72.3 g

Calories	56.7	Pyridoxine-B6	0.047 mg
Protein	7.44 g	Cobalamin-B12	14.0 mcg
Carbohydrates	2.83 g	Folacin	8.50 mcg
Dietary Fiber	0 g	Pantothenic	0.319 mg
Fat-Total	1.77 g	Vitamin C	25.5 mg
Fat-Saturated	0.620 g	Vitamin E	0.723 mg
Fat-Mono	0.248 g	Calcium	71.6 mg
Fat-Poly	0.620 g	Copper	7.69 mg
Cholesterol	42.5 mg	Iron	5.95 mg
Vit A-Carotene	0 re	Magnesium	19.0 mg
Vit A-Preformed	79.0 re	Phosphorus	134 mg
Vitamin A-Total	79.0 re	Potassium	103 mg
Thiamin-B1	0.103 mg	Selenium	48.5 mcg
Riboflavin-B2	0.152 mg	Sodium	65.6 mg
Niacin-B3	2.13 mg	Zinc	26.4 mg

Calories from protein:	52 %	Poly/Sat = 1.0:1	
Calories from carbohydrates:	20 %	Sod/Pot = 0.6:1	
Calories from fats:	28 %	Ca/Phos = 0.5:1	
		CSI = 2.8	

Pear, Bartlett

1 whole

Weight: 166 grams (5.86 oz.)   Water weight: 139 g

Calories	98.0	Pyridoxine-B6	0.030 mg
Protein	0.650 g	Cobalamin-B12	0 mcg
Carbohydrates	25.1 g	Folacin	12.1 mcg
Dietary Fiber	4.80 g	Pantothenic	0.116 mg
Fat-Total	0.660 g	Vitamin C	6.60 mg
Fat-Saturated	0.037 g	Vitamin E	0.825 mg
Fat-Mono	0.139 g	Calcium	19.0 mg
Fat-Poly	0.156 g	Copper	0.188 mg
Cholesterol	0 mg	Iron	0.415 mg
Vit A-Carotene	3.30 re	Magnesium	9.00 mg
Vit A-Preformed	0 re	Phosphorus	18.0 mg
Vitamin A-Total	3.30 re	Potassium	208 mg
Thiamin-B1	0.033 mg	Selenium	0.990 mcg
Riboflavin-B2	0.066 mg	Sodium	1.00 mg
Niacin-B3	0.166 mg	Zinc	0.200 mg

Calories from protein:	2 %	Poly/Sat = 4.2:1	
Calories from carbohydrates:	92 %	Sod/Pot = 0.0:1	
Calories from fats:	5 %	Ca/Phos = 1.1:1	
		CSI = 0.0	

Peas, fresh

½ cup cooked

Weight: 80.0 grams (2.82 oz.)   Water weight: 62.3 g

Calories	67.0	Pyridoxine-B6	0.125 mg
Protein	4.28 g	Cobalamin-B12	0 mcg
Carbohydrates	12.5 g	Folacin	50.5 mcg
Dietary Fiber	3.84 g	Pantothenic	0.122 mg
Fat-Total	0.170 g	Vitamin C	11.4 mg
Fat-Saturated	0.031 g	Vitamin E	1.70 mg
Fat-Mono	0.015 g	Calcium	22.0 mg
Fat-Poly	0.081 g	Copper	0.138 mg
Cholesterol	0 mg	Iron	1.23 mg
Vit A-Carotene	47.7 re	Magnesium	31.5 mg
Vit A-Preformed	0 re	Phosphorus	93.5 mg
Vitamin A-Total	47.7 re	Potassium	217 mg
Thiamin-B1	0.207 mg	Selenium	4.40 mcg
Riboflavin-B2	0.119 mg	Sodium	2.00 mg
Niacin-B3	1.61 mg	Zinc	0.950 mg

Calories from protein:	25 %	Poly/Sat = 2.6:1	
Calories from carbohydrates:	73 %	Sod/Pot = 0.0:1	
Calories from fats:	2 %	Ca/Phos = 0.2:1	
		CSI = 0.0	

Pepper, black

⅛ teaspoon freshly ground

Weight: 0.267 grams (0.009 oz.)   Water weight: 0.028 g

Calories	0.679	Pyridoxine-B6	0 mg
Protein	0.029 g	Cobalamin-B12	0 mcg
Carbohydrates	0.173 g	Folacin	0 mcg
Dietary Fiber	0.035 g	Pantothenic	0 mg
Fat-Total	0.009 g	Vitamin C	0 mg
Fat-Saturated	0.004 g	Vitamin E	0 mg
Fat-Mono	0.004 g	Calcium	1.17 mg
Fat-Poly	0.004 g	Copper	0.003 mg
Cholesterol	0 mg	Iron	0.077 mg
Vit A-Carotene	0.050 re	Magnesium	0.500 mg
Vit A-Preformed	0 re	Phosphorus	0.458 mg
Vitamin A-Total	0.050 re	Potassium	3.37 mg
Thiamin-B1	0.000 mg	Selenium	0.013 mcg
Riboflavin-B2	0.001 mg	Sodium	0.125 mg
Niacin-B3	0.003 mg	Zinc	0.004 mg

Calories from protein:	13 %	Poly/Sat = 1.2:1	
Calories from carbohydrates:	78 %	Sod/Pot = 0.0:1	
Calories from fats:	9 %	Ca/Phos = 2.5:1	
		CSI = 0.0	

Pepper, green bell   *¼ cup chopped*

Weight: 34.0 grams (1.20 oz.)   Water weight: 32.2 g

Calories	6.00	Pyridoxine-B6	0.036 mg
Protein	0.210 g	Cobalamin-B12	0 mcg
Carbohydrates	1.32 g	Folacin	4.95 mcg
Dietary Fiber	0.375 g	Pantothenic	0.008 mg
Fat-Total	0.110 g	Vitamin C	37.9 mg
Fat-Saturated	0.016 g	Vitamin E	0.122 mg
Fat-Mono	0.007 g	Calcium	1.50 mg
Fat-Poly	0.060 g	Copper	0.024 mg
Cholesterol	0 mg	Iron	0.300 mg
Vit A-Carotene	13.2 re	Magnesium	3.50 mg
Vit A-Preformed	0 re	Phosphorus	5.00 mg
Vitamin A-Total	13.2 re	Potassium	44.0 mg
Thiamin-B1	0.018 mg	Selenium	0.272 mcg
Riboflavin-B2	0.012 mg	Sodium	0.500 mg
Niacin-B3	0.123 mg	Zinc	0.041 mg

Calories from protein:	12 %	Poly/Sat = 3.6:1	
Calories from carbohydrates:	74 %	Sod/Pot = 0.0:1	
Calories from fats:	14 %	Ca/Phos = 0.3:1	
		CSI = 0.0	

Pineapple, fresh   *½ cup chunks*

Weight: 77.5 grams (2.73 oz.)   Water weight: 67.0 g

Calories	38.0	Pyridoxine-B6	0.067 mg
Protein	0.300 g	Cobalamin-B12	0 mcg
Carbohydrates	9.60 g	Folacin	8.20 mcg
Dietary Fiber	1.35 g	Pantothenic	0.124 mg
Fat-Total	0.330 g	Vitamin C	11.9 mg
Fat-Saturated	0.025 g	Vitamin E	0.081 mg
Fat-Mono	0.037 g	Calcium	5.50 mg
Fat-Poly	0.113 g	Copper	0.085 mg
Cholesterol	0 mg	Iron	0.287 mg
Vit A-Carotene	2.00 re	Magnesium	10.5 mg
Vit A-Preformed	0 re	Phosphorus	5.50 mg
Vitamin A-Total	2.00 re	Potassium	87.5 mg
Thiamin-B1	0.071 mg	Selenium	0.426 mcg
Riboflavin-B2	0.028 mg	Sodium	1.00 mg
Niacin-B3	0.325 mg	Zinc	0.060 mg

Calories from protein:	3 %	Poly/Sat = 4.5:1	
Calories from carbohydrates:	90 %	Sod/Pot = 0.0:1	
Calories from fats:	7 %	Ca/Phos = 1.0:1	
		CSI = 0.0	

Pork lean, loin   *3 ounces broiled*

Weight: 85.0 grams (3.00 oz.)   Water weight: 48.5 g

Calories	196	Pyridoxine-B6	0.402 mg
Protein	27.2 g	Cobalamin-B12	0.630 mcg
Carbohydrates	0 g	Folacin	5.08 mcg
Dietary Fiber	0 g	Pantothenic	0.588 mg
Fat-Total	8.91 g	Vitamin C	0.340 mg
Fat-Saturated	3.07 g	Vitamin E	0.304 mg
Fat-Mono	4.02 g	Calcium	4.25 mg
Fat-Poly	1.07 g	Copper	0.070 mg
Cholesterol	83.9 mg	Iron	0.782 mg
Vit A-Carotene	0 re	Magnesium	25.5 mg
Vit A-Preformed	2.36 re	Phosphorus	208 mg
Vitamin A-Total	2.36 re	Potassium	357 mg
Thiamin-B1	0.977 mg	Selenium	15.5 mcg
Riboflavin-B2	0.262 mg	Sodium	66.1 mg
Niacin-B3	4.71 mg	Zinc	1.90 mg

Calories from protein:	58 %	Poly/Sat = 0.4:1	
Calories from carbohydrates:	0 %	Sod/Pot = 0.2:1	
Calories from fats:	42 %	Ca/Phos = 0.0:1	
		CSI = 7.3	

Potato, baked with skin   *3 ounce*

Weight: 85.0 grams (3.00 oz.)   Water weight: 60.6 g

Calories	92.6	Pyridoxine-B6	0.295 mg
Protein	1.96 g	Cobalamin-B12	0 mcg
Carbohydrates	21.5 g	Folacin	9.35 mcg
Dietary Fiber	1.64 g	Pantothenic	0.472 mg
Fat-Total	0.084 g	Vitamin C	11.0 mg
Fat-Saturated	0.022 g	Vitamin E	0.042 mg
Fat-Mono	0.002 g	Calcium	8.42 mg
Fat-Poly	0.037 g	Copper	0.259 mg
Cholesterol	0 mg	Iron	1.16 mg
Vit A-Carotene	0 re	Magnesium	23.2 mg
Vit A-Preformed	0 re	Phosphorus	48.4 mg
Vitamin A-Total	0 re	Potassium	355 mg
Thiamin-B1	0.091 mg	Selenium	0.758 mcg
Riboflavin-B2	0.028 mg	Sodium	6.74 mg
Niacin-B3	1.40 mg	Zinc	0.274 mg

Calories from protein:	8 %	Poly/Sat = 1.7:1	
Calories from carbohydrates:	91 %	Sod/Pot = 0.0:1	
Calories from fats:	1 %	Ca/Phos = 0.2:1	
		CSI = 0.0	

Raisins   *1 tablespoon seedless*

Weight: 10.3 grams (0.364 oz.)   Water weight: 1.59 g

Calories	30.9	Pyridoxine-B6	0.026 mg
Protein	0.332 g	Cobalamin-B12	0 mcg
Carbohydrates	8.19 g	Folacin	0.412 mcg
Dietary Fiber	0.900 g	Pantothenic	0.005 mg
Fat-Total	0.047 g	Vitamin C	0.344 mg
Fat-Saturated	0.015 g	Vitamin E	0.030 mg
Fat-Mono	0.002 g	Calcium	5.06 mg
Fat-Poly	0.014 g	Copper	0.032 mg
Cholesterol	0 mg	Iron	0.216 mg
Vit A-Carotene	0.081 re	Magnesium	3.38 mg
Vit A-Preformed	0 re	Phosphorus	9.94 mg
Vitamin A-Total	0.081 re	Potassium	77.4 mg
Thiamin-B1	0.016 mg	Selenium	0.563 mcg
Riboflavin-B2	0.009 mg	Sodium	1.19 mg
Niacin-B3	0.084 mg	Zinc	0.033 mg

Calories from protein:	4 %	Poly/Sat	= 0.9:1
Calories from carbohydrates:	95 %	Sod/Pot	= 0.0:1
Calories from fats:	1 %	Ca/Phos	= 0.5:1
		CSI	= 0.0

Rice, long-grain, no fat or sodium added   *½ cup cooked*

Weight: 102 grams (3.62 oz.)   Water weight: 74.4 g

Calories	111	Pyridoxine-B6	0.051 mg
Protein	2.05 g	Cobalamin-B12	0 mcg
Carbohydrates	24.8 g	Folacin	2.05 mcg
Dietary Fiber	0.325 g	Pantothenic	0.236 mg
Fat-Total	0.102 g	Vitamin C	0 mg
Fat-Saturated	0.031 g	Vitamin E	0.231 mg
Fat-Mono	0.031 g	Calcium	10.2 mg
Fat-Poly	0.041 g	Copper	0.083 mg
Cholesterol	0 mg	Iron	1.43 mg
Vit A-Carotene	0 re	Magnesium	11.3 mg
Vit A-Preformed	0 re	Phosphorus	28.7 mg
Vitamin A-Total	0 re	Potassium	28.7 mg
Thiamin-B1	0.111 mg	Selenium	9.75 mcg
Riboflavin-B2	0.010 mg	Sodium	0 mg
Niacin-B3	1.02 mg	Zinc	0.420 mg

Calories from protein:	8 %	Poly/Sat	= 1.3:1
Calories from carbohydrates:	92 %	Sod/Pot	= 0.0:1
Calories from fats:	1 %	Ca/Phos	= 0.4:1
		CSI	= 0.0

Roux, blond or brown

1 tablespoon

Weight: 7.81 grams (0.276 oz.)   Water weight: 0.938 g

Calories	28.4	Pyridoxine-B6	0.002 mg
Protein	0.819 g	Cobalamin-B12	0 mcg
Carbohydrates	5.94 g	Folacin	1.13 mcg
Dietary Fiber	0.219 g	Pantothenic	0.025 mg
Fat-Total	0.078 g	Vitamin C	0 mg
Fat-Saturated	0.012 g	Vitamin E	0.104 mg
Fat-Mono	0.006 g	Calcium	1.25 mg
Fat-Poly	0.034 g	Copper	0.010 mg
Cholesterol	0 mg	Iron	0.344 mg
Vit A-Carotene	0 re	Magnesium	1.64 mg
Vit A-Preformed	0 re	Phosphorus	6.81 mg
Vitamin A-Total	0 re	Potassium	7.44 mg
Thiamin-B1	0.042 mg	Selenium	2.38 mcg
Riboflavin-B2	0.026 mg	Sodium	0.156 mg
Niacin-B3	0.392 mg	Zinc	0.052 mg

Calories from protein:	12 %	Poly/Sat = 2.7:1	
Calories from carbohydrates:	86 %	Sod/Pot = 0.0:1	
Calories from fats:	3 %	Ca/Phos = 0.2:1	
		CSI = 0.0	

Shrimp

3 ounces shelled, boiled

Weight: 85.0 grams (3.00 oz.)   Water weight: 53.2 g

Calories	92.7	Pyridoxine-B6	0.085 mg
Protein	20.2 g	Cobalamin-B12	0.850 mcg
Carbohydrates	0 g	Folacin	12.8 mcg
Dietary Fiber	0 g	Pantothenic	0.255 mg
Fat-Total	1.28 g	Vitamin C	0.001 mg
Fat-Saturated	0.241 g	Vitamin E	1.28 mg
Fat-Mono	0.241 g	Calcium	272 mg
Fat-Poly	0.666 g	Copper	0.468 mg
Cholesterol	125 mg	Iron	1.87 mg
Vit A-Carotene	0 re	Magnesium	93.6 mg
Vit A-Preformed	15.3 re	Phosphorus	230 mg
Vitamin A-Total	15.3 re	Potassium	340 mg
Thiamin-B1	0.026 mg	Selenium	45.9 mcg
Riboflavin-B2	0.026 mg	Sodium	153 mg
Niacin-B3	3.15 mg	Zinc	3.15 mg

Calories from protein:	88 %	Poly/Sat = 2.8:1	
Calories from carbohydrates:	0 %	Sod/Pot = 0.4:1	
Calories from fats:	12 %	Ca/Phos = 1.2:1	
		CSI = 6.5	

Spinach   *½ cup cooked*

Weight: 90.0 grams (3.17 oz.)   Water weight: 82.1 g

Calories	20.5	Pyridoxine-B6	0.218 mg
Protein	2.67 g	Cobalamin-B12	0 mcg
Carbohydrates	3.38 g	Folacin	131 mcg
Dietary Fiber	2.47 g	Pantothenic	0.130 mg
Fat-Total	0.235 g	Vitamin C	20.0 mg
Fat-Saturated	0.038 g	Vitamin E	2.00 mg
Fat-Mono	0.006 g	Calcium	122 mg
Fat-Poly	0.097 g	Copper	0.156 mg
Cholesterol	0 mg	Iron	3.21 mg
Vit A-Carotene	737 re	Magnesium	78.5 mg
Vit A-Preformed	0 re	Phosphorus	50.0 mg
Vitamin A-Total	737 re	Potassium	419 mg
Thiamin-B1	0.085 mg	Selenium	1.35 mcg
Riboflavin-B2	0.212 mg	Sodium	63.0 mg
Niacin-B3	0.441 mg	Zinc	0.685 mg

Calories from protein:	41 %	Poly/Sat = 2.6:1	
Calories from carbohydrates:	51 %	Sod/Pot = 0.2:1	
Calories from fats:	8 %	Ca/Phos = 2.4:1	
		CSI = 0.0	

Squash   *½ cup cooked*

Weight: 90.0 grams (3.17 oz.)   Water weight: 84.3 g

Calories	18.0	Pyridoxine-B6	0.058 mg
Protein	0.815 g	Cobalamin-B12	0 mcg
Carbohydrates	3.88 g	Folacin	18.1 mcg
Dietary Fiber	1.50 g	Pantothenic	0.123 mg
Fat-Total	0.280 g	Vitamin C	4.60 mg
Fat-Saturated	0.057 g	Vitamin E	0.126 mg
Fat-Mono	0.020 g	Calcium	24.0 mg
Fat-Poly	0.118 g	Copper	0.092 mg
Cholesterol	0 mg	Iron	0.320 mg
Vit A-Carotene	25.8 re	Magnesium	22.0 mg
Vit A-Preformed	0 re	Phosphorus	34.5 mg
Vitamin A-Total	25.8 re	Potassium	173 mg
Thiamin-B1	0.039 mg	Selenium	2.08 mcg
Riboflavin-B2	0.037 mg	Sodium	1.00 mg
Niacin-B3	0.461 mg	Zinc	0.355 mg

Calories from protein:	15 %	Poly/Sat = 2.1:1	
Calories from carbohydrates:	73 %	Sod/Pot = 0.0:1	
Calories from fats:	12 %	Ca/Phos = 0.7:1	
		CSI = 0.1	

Strawberries

½ cup fresh

Weight: 74.5 grams (2.63 oz.)   Water weight: 68.2 g

Calories	22.5	Pyridoxine-B6	0.044 mg
Protein	0.455 g	Cobalamin-B12	0 mcg
Carbohydrates	5.25 g	Folacin	14.0 mcg
Dietary Fiber	1.64 g	Pantothenic	0.253 mg
Fat-Total	0.275 g	Vitamin C	42.2 mg
Fat-Saturated	0.015 g	Vitamin E	0.150 mg
Fat-Mono	0.038 g	Calcium	10.5 mg
Fat-Poly	0.138 g	Copper	0.036 mg
Cholesterol	0 mg	Iron	0.283 mg
Vit A-Carotene	2.00 re	Magnesium	8.00 mg
Vit A-Preformed	0 re	Phosphorus	14.0 mg
Vitamin A-Total	2.00 re	Potassium	123 mg
Thiamin-B1	0.015 mg	Selenium	0 mcg
Riboflavin-B2	0.049 mg	Sodium	1.00 mg
Niacin-B3	0.171 mg	Zinc	0.097 mg

Calories from protein:	7 %	Poly/Sat = 9.2:1	
Calories from carbohydrates:	83 %	Sod/Pot = 0.0:1	
Calories from fats:	10 %	Ca/Phos = 0.8:1	
		CSI = 0.0	

Thyme

⅛ teaspoon dried

Weight: 0.179 grams (0.006 oz.)   Water weight: 0.014 g

Calories	0.500	Pyridoxine-B6	0 mg
Protein	0.016 g	Cobalamin-B12	0 mcg
Carbohydrates	0.115 g	Folacin	0 mcg
Dietary Fiber	0.033 g	Pantothenic	0 mg
Fat-Total	0.013 g	Vitamin C	0 mg
Fat-Saturated	0.005 g	Vitamin E	0 mg
Fat-Mono	0.001 g	Calcium	3.37 mg
Fat-Poly	0.002 g	Copper	0.002 mg
Cholesterol	0 mg	Iron	0.221 mg
Vit A-Carotene	0.679 re	Magnesium	0.375 mg
Vit A-Preformed	0 re	Phosphorus	0.375 mg
Vitamin A-Total	0.679 re	Potassium	1.46 mg
Thiamin-B1	0.001 mg	Selenium	0.013 mcg
Riboflavin-B2	0.001 mg	Sodium	0.083 mg
Niacin-B3	0.009 mg	Zinc	0.011 mg

Calories from protein:	10 %	Poly/Sat = 0.4:1	
Calories from carbohydrates:	71 %	Sod/Pot = 0.1:1	
Calories from fats:	19 %	Ca/Phos = 9.0:1	
		CSI = 0.0	

Tomato   *1 whole fresh medium*

Weight: 123 grams (4.34 oz.)   Water weight: 116 g

Calories	24.0	Pyridoxine-B6	0.094 mg
Protein	1.09 g	Cobalamin-B12	0 mcg
Carbohydrates	5.34 g	Folacin	11.5 mcg
Dietary Fiber	2.00 g	Pantothenic	0.304 mg
Fat-Total	0.260 g	Vitamin C	21.6 mg
Fat-Saturated	0.037 g	Vitamin E	0.860 mg
Fat-Mono	0.039 g	Calcium	9.00 mg
Fat-Poly	0.107 g	Copper	0.095 mg
Cholesterol	0 mg	Iron	0.590 mg
Vit A-Carotene	139 re	Magnesium	14.0 mg
Vit A-Preformed	0 re	Phosphorus	28.0 mg
Vitamin A-Total	139 re	Potassium	255 mg
Thiamin-B1	0.074 mg	Selenium	0.615 mcg
Riboflavin-B2	0.062 mg	Sodium	10.0 mg
Niacin-B3	0.738 mg	Zinc	0.130 mg

Calories from protein:	16 %	Poly/Sat	= 2.9:1
Calories from carbohydrates:	76 %	Sod/Pot	= 0.0:1
Calories from fats:	8 %	Ca/Phos	= 0.3:1
		CSI	= 0.0

Tripe, beef, raw   *3 ounces cooked*

Weight: 85.0 grams (3.00 oz.)   Water weight: 73.5 g

Calories	50.9	Pyridoxine-B6	0 mg
Protein	9.88 g	Cobalamin-B12	0.779 mcg
Carbohydrates	0 g	Folacin	0.898 mcg
Dietary Fiber	0 g	Pantothenic	0 mg
Fat-Total	1.20 g	Vitamin C	1.71 mg
Fat-Saturated	0.608 g	Vitamin E	0 mg
Fat-Mono	0.392 g	Calcium	74.9 mg
Fat-Poly	0.021 g	Copper	0.054 mg
Cholesterol	44.9 mg	Iron	1.17 mg
Vit A-Carotene	0 re	Magnesium	5.99 mg
Vit A-Preformed	0 re	Phosphorus	47.9 mg
Vitamin A-Total	0 re	Potassium	15.0 mg
Thiamin-B1	0.003 mg	Selenium	0 mcg
Riboflavin-B2	0.084 mg	Sodium	38.9 mg
Niacin-B3	0.030 mg	Zinc	1.47 mg

Calories from protein:	79 %	Poly/Sat	= 0.0:1
Calories from carbohydrates:	0 %	Sod/Pot	= 2.6:1
Calories from fats:	21 %	Ca/Phos	= 2.9

Trout, sea trout fillet

3 ounces cooked

Weight: 85.0 grams (3.00 oz.)   Water weight: 53.6 g

Calories	116	Pyridoxine-B6	0.556 mg
Protein	20.6 g	Cobalamin-B12	4.25 mcg
Carbohydrates	0 g	Folacin	6.80 mcg
Dietary Fiber	0 g	Pantothenic	1.48 mg
Fat-Total	3.40 g	Vitamin C	0.001 mg
Fat-Saturated	1.04 g	Vitamin E	0.190 mg
Fat-Mono	1.18 g	Calcium	8.16 mg
Fat-Poly	0.592 g	Copper	0.040 mg
Cholesterol	61.2 mg	Iron	0.248 mg
Vit A-Carotene	0 re	Magnesium	44.1 mg
Vit A-Preformed	59.5 re	Phosphorus	200 mg
Vitamin A-Total	59.5 re	Potassium	537 mg
Thiamin-B1	0.054 mg	Selenium	76.5 mcg
Riboflavin-B2	0.151 mg	Sodium	38.3 mg
Niacin-B3	6.40 mg	Zinc	0.442 mg

Calories from protein:	73 %	Poly/Sat = 0.6:1	
Calories from carbohydrates:	0 %	Sod/Pot = 0.1:1	
Calories from fats:	27 %	Ca/Phos = 0.0:1	
		CSI = 4.1	

Turkey, ground

3 ounces cooked white

Weight: 85.0 grams (3.00 oz.)   Water weight: 51.0 g

Calories	191	Pyridoxine-B6	0.221 mg
Protein	22.1 g	Cobalamin-B12	1.91 mcg
Carbohydrates	0 g	Folacin	2.38 mcg
Dietary Fiber	0 g	Pantothenic	0.262 mg
Fat-Total	11.1 g	Vitamin C	0.009 mg
Fat-Saturated	3.83 g	Vitamin E	0.298 mg
Fat-Mono	4.59 g	Calcium	24.7 mg
Fat-Poly	2.72 g	Copper	0.060 mg
Cholesterol	71.4 mg	Iron	1.41 mg
Vit A-Carotene	0 re	Magnesium	17.0 mg
Vit A-Preformed	0 re	Phosphorus	164 mg
Vitamin A-Total	0 re	Potassium	201 mg
Thiamin-B1	0.068 mg	Selenium	25.5 mcg
Riboflavin-B2	0.230 mg	Sodium	97.8 mg
Niacin-B3	5.11 mg	Zinc	2.93 mg

Calories from protein:	47 %	Poly/Sat = 0.7:1	
Calories from carbohydrates:	0 %	Sod/Pot = 0.5:1	
Calories from fats:	53 %	Ca/Phos = 0.2:1	
		CSI = 7.4	

Turkey ham   *3 ounces*

Weight: 85.0 grams (3.00 oz.)   Water weight: 61.2 g

Calories	109	Pyridoxine-B6	0.237 mg
Protein	16.1 g	Cobalamin-B12	1.92 mcg
Carbohydrates	1.27 g	Folacin	5.97 mcg
Dietary Fiber	0 g	Pantothenic	0.970 mg
Fat-Total	4.48 g	Vitamin C	0 mg
Fat-Saturated	1.42 g	Vitamin E	0.543 mg
Fat-Mono	1.12 g	Calcium	7.46 mg
Fat-Poly	1.12 g	Copper	0.101 mg
Cholesterol	47.7 mg	Iron	2.33 mg
Vit A-Carotene	0 re	Magnesium	17.9 mg
Vit A-Preformed	0 re	Phosphorus	206 mg
Vitamin A-Total	0 re	Potassium	243 mg
Thiamin-B1	0.060 mg	Selenium	6.71 mcg
Riboflavin-B2	0.224 mg	Sodium	818 mg
Niacin-B3	4.10 mg	Zinc	2.36 mg

Calories from protein:	59 %	Poly/Sat = 0.8:1
Calories from carbohydrates:	5 %	Sod/Pot = 3.4:1
Calories from fats:	37 %	Ca/Phos = 0.0:1
		CSI = 3.8

Turnips   *½ cup cubes cooked*

Weight: 78.0 grams (2.75 oz.)   Water weight: 73.0 g

Calories	14.0	Pyridoxine-B6	0.052 mg
Protein	0.550 g	Cobalamin-B12	0 mcg
Carbohydrates	3.83 g	Folacin	7.10 mcg
Dietary Fiber	1.72 g	Pantothenic	0.111 mg
Fat-Total	0.060 g	Vitamin C	9.00 mg
Fat-Saturated	0.006 g	Vitamin E	0.012 mg
Fat-Mono	0.004 g	Calcium	18.0 mg
Fat-Poly	0.033 g	Copper	0.031 mg
Cholesterol	0 mg	Iron	0.170 mg
Vit A-Carotene	0 re	Magnesium	6.00 mg
Vit A-Preformed	0 re	Phosphorus	15.0 mg
Vitamin A-Total	0 re	Potassium	106 mg
Thiamin-B1	0.021 mg	Selenium	0.540 mcg
Riboflavin-B2	0.018 mg	Sodium	39.0 mg
Niacin-B3	0.233 mg	Zinc	0.083 mg

Calories from protein:	12 %	Poly/Sat = 5.5:1
Calories from carbohydrates:	85 %	Sod/Pot = 0.4:1
Calories from fats:	3 %	Ca/Phos = 1.2:1
		CSI = 0.0

Turnip greens

½ cup cooked

Weight: 72.0 grams (2.54 oz.)   Water weight: 67.4 g

Calories	14.5	Pyridoxine-B6	0.129 mg
Protein	0.820 g	Cobalamin-B12	0 mcg
Carbohydrates	3.14 g	Folacin	85.5 mcg
Dietary Fiber	1.80 g	Pantothenic	0.197 mg
Fat-Total	0.165 g	Vitamin C	19.7 mg
Fat-Saturated	0.038 g	Vitamin E	1.23 mg
Fat-Mono	0.011 g	Calcium	99.0 mg
Fat-Poly	0.065 g	Copper	0.182 mg
Cholesterol	0 mg	Iron	0.575 mg
Vit A-Carotene	396 re	Magnesium	16.0 mg
Vit A-Preformed	0 re	Phosphorus	20.5 mg
Vitamin A-Total	396 re	Potassium	146 mg
Thiamin-B1	0.032 mg	Selenium	0.650 mcg
Riboflavin-B2	0.052 mg	Sodium	20.5 mg
Niacin-B3	0.296 mg	Zinc	0.145 mg

Calories from protein:	19 %	Poly/Sat = 1.7:1	
Calories from carbohydrates:	72 %	Sod/Pot = 0.1:1	
Calories from fats:	9 %	Ca/Phos = 4.8:1	
		CSI = 0.0	

Vinegar, cider

1 teaspoon

Weight: 5.00 grams (0.176 oz.)   Water weight: 4.70 g

Calories	0.604	Pyridoxine-B6	0.000 mg
Protein	0 g	Cobalamin-B12	0 mcg
Carbohydrates	0.296 g	Folacin	0 mcg
Dietary Fiber	0 g	Pantothenic	0 mg
Fat-Total	0 g	Vitamin C	0.000 mg
Fat-Saturated	0 g	Vitamin E	0 mg
Fat-Mono	0 g	Calcium	0.292 mg
Fat-Poly	0 g	Copper	0.003 mg
Cholesterol	0 mg	Iron	0.029 mg
Vit A-Carotene	0 re	Magnesium	0.050 mg
Vit A-Preformed	0 re	Phosphorus	0.250 mg
Vitamin A-Total	0 re	Potassium	5.00 mg
Thiamin-B1	0 mg	Selenium	0.022 mcg
Riboflavin-B2	0 mg	Sodium	0.042 mg
Niacin-B3	0 mg	Zinc	0.006 mg

Calories from protein:	0 %	Poly/Sat = 0.0:1	
Calories from carbohydrates:	100 %	Sod/Pot = 0.0:1	
Calories from fats:	0 %	Ca/Phos = 1.2:1	

Watercress

½ cup fresh

Weight: 17.0 grams (0.600 oz.)   Water weight: 16.2 g

Calories	2.00	Pyridoxine-B6	0.022 mg
Protein	0.390 g	Cobalamin-B12	0 mcg
Carbohydrates	0.220 g	Folacin	34.0 mcg
Dietary Fiber	0.470 g	Pantothenic	0.053 mg
Fat-Total	0.020 g	Vitamin C	7.30 mg
Fat-Saturated	0.005 g	Vitamin E	0.170 mg
Fat-Mono	0.001 g	Calcium	20.0 mg
Fat-Poly	0.006 g	Copper	0.015 mg
Cholesterol	0 mg	Iron	0.030 mg
Vit A-Carotene	79.9 re	Magnesium	4.00 mg
Vit A-Preformed	0 re	Phosphorus	10.0 mg
Vitamin A-Total	79.9 re	Potassium	56.0 mg
Thiamin-B1	0.015 mg	Selenium	0 mcg
Riboflavin-B2	0.020 mg	Sodium	7.00 mg
Niacin-B3	0.034 mg	Zinc	0.030 mg

Calories from protein:	60 %	Poly/Sat = 1.2:1	
Calories from carbohydrates:	34 %	Sod/Pot = 0.1:1	
Calories from fats:	7 %	Ca/Phos = 2.0:1	
		CSI = 0.0	

Wine, red

4 ounces

Weight: 118 grams (4.16 oz.)   Water weight: 104 g

Calories	85.0	Pyridoxine-B6	0.040 mg
Protein	0.229 g	Cobalamin-B12	0.016 mcg
Carbohydrates	2.06 g	Folacin	2.40 mcg
Dietary Fiber	0 g	Pantothenic	0.041 mg
Fat-Total	0 g	Vitamin C	0 mg
Fat-Saturated	0 g	Vitamin E	0 mg
Fat-Mono	0 g	Calcium	9.20 mg
Fat-Poly	0 g	Copper	0.024 mg
Cholesterol	0 mg	Iron	0.508 mg
Vit A-Carotene	0 re	Magnesium	15.0 mg
Vit A-Preformed	0 re	Phosphorus	16.0 mg
Vitamin A-Total	0 re	Potassium	131 mg
Thiamin-B1	0.006 mg	Selenium	0 mcg
Riboflavin-B2	0.033 mg	Sodium	6.30 mg
Niacin-B3	0.095 mg	Zinc	0.110 mg

Calories from protein:	1 %	Poly/Sat = 0.0:1	
Calories from carbohydrates:	10 %	Sod/Pot = 0.0:1	
Calories from fats:	0 %	Ca/Phos = 0.6:1	
Other calories (i.e. alcohol):	89 %		

Wine, white   *4 ounces*

Weight: 119 grams (4.20 oz.)   Water weight: 107 g

Calories	79.0	Pyridoxine-B6	0.024 mg
Protein	0.120 g	Cobalamin-B12	0 mcg
Carbohydrates	0.720 g	Folacin	0.230 mcg
Dietary Fiber	0 g	Pantothenic	0.029 mg
Fat-Total	0 g	Vitamin C	0 mg
Fat-Saturated	0 g	Vitamin E	0 mg
Fat-Mono	0 g	Calcium	11.0 mg
Fat-Poly	0 g	Copper	0.012 mg
Cholesterol	0 mg	Iron	0.390 mg
Vit A-Carotene	0 re	Magnesium	11.0 mg
Vit A-Preformed	0 re	Phosphorus	7.00 mg
Vitamin A-Total	0 re	Potassium	73.0 mg
Thiamin-B1	0.002 mg	Selenium	0 mcg
Riboflavin-B2	0.006 mg	Sodium	5.00 mg
Niacin-B3	0.080 mg	Zinc	0.080 mg

Calories from protein:	1 %	Poly/Sat = 0.0:1	
Calories from carbohydrates:	4 %	Sod/Pot = 0.1:1	
Calories from fats:	0 %	Ca/Phos = 1.6:1	
Other calories (i.e. alcohol):	96 %		

Wine, champagne   *4 ounces*

Weight: 119 grams (4.20 oz.)   Water weight: 102 g

Calories	91.0	Pyridoxine-B6	0.024 mg
Protein	0.180 g	Cobalamin-B12	0 mcg
Carbohydrates	2.50 g	Folacin	0.180 mcg
Dietary Fiber	0 g	Pantothenic	0.036 mg
Fat-Total	0 g	Vitamin C	0 mg
Fat-Saturated	0 g	Vitamin E	0 mg
Fat-Mono	0 g	Calcium	6.50 mg
Fat-Poly	0 g	Copper	0.008 mg
Cholesterol	0 mg	Iron	0.389 mg
Vit A-Carotene	0 re	Magnesium	10.1 mg
Vit A-Preformed	0 re	Phosphorus	8.00 mg
Vitamin A-Total	0 re	Potassium	95.0 mg
Thiamin-B1	0 mg	Selenium	0 mcg
Riboflavin-B2	0.012 mg	Sodium	7.30 mg
Niacin-B3	0.080 mg	Zinc	0.112 mg

Calories from protein:	1 %	Poly/Sat = 0.0:1	
Calories from carbohydrates:	11 %	Sod/Pot = 0.1:1	
Calories from fats:	0 %	Ca/Phos = 0.8:1	
Other calories (i.e. alcohol):	88 %		

Wine, dry sherry   *4 ounces*

Weight: 142 grams (5.01 oz.)   Water weight: 109 g

Calories	142	Pyridoxine-B6	0.010 mg
Protein	0.120 g	Cobalamin-B12	0 mcg
Carbohydrates	1.68 g	Folacin	0.120 mcg
Dietary Fiber	0 g	Pantothenic	0 mg
Fat-Total	0 g	Vitamin C	0 mg
Fat-Saturated	0 g	Vitamin E	0 mg
Fat-Mono	0 g	Calcium	10.6 mg
Fat-Poly	0 g	Copper	0.103 mg
Cholesterol	0 mg	Iron	0.259 mg
Vit A-Carotene	0 re	Magnesium	9.80 mg
Vit A-Preformed	0 re	Phosphorus	13.0 mg
Vitamin A-Total	0 re	Potassium	89.0 mg
Thiamin-B1	0.008 mg	Selenium	0 mcg
Riboflavin-B2	0.012 mg	Sodium	11.0 mg
Niacin-B3	0.120 mg	Zinc	0.102 mg

Calories from protein:	0 %	Poly/Sat = 0.0:1	
Calories from carbohydrates:	5 %	Sod/Pot = 0.1:1	
Calories from fats:	0 %	Ca/Phos = 0.8:1	
Other calories (i.e. alcohol):	95 %		

Yogurt, nonfat   *½ cup*

Weight: 113 grams (4.00 oz.)   Water weight: 96.5 g

Calories	63.5	Pyridoxine-B6	0.060 mg
Protein	6.50 g	Cobalamin-B12	0.700 mcg
Carbohydrates	8.70 g	Folacin	14.0 mcg
Dietary Fiber	0 g	Pantothenic	0.730 mg
Fat-Total	0.204 g	Vitamin C	1.00 mg
Fat-Saturated	0.131 g	Vitamin E	0 mg
Fat-Mono	0.056 g	Calcium	226 mg
Fat-Poly	0.006 g	Copper	0.033 mg
Cholesterol	2.00 mg	Iron	0.102 mg
Vit A-Carotene	0.250 re	Magnesium	21.5 mg
Vit A-Preformed	2.25 re	Phosphorus	177 mg
Vitamin A-Total	2.50 re	Potassium	289 mg
Thiamin-B1	0.054 mg	Selenium	4.00 mcg
Riboflavin-B2	0.265 mg	Sodium	86.5 mg
Niacin-B3	0.140 mg	Zinc	1.10 mg

Calories from protein:	42 %	Poly/Sat = 0.0:1	
Calories from carbohydrates:	56 %	Sod/Pot = 0.3:1	
Calories from fats:	3 %	Ca/Phos = 1.3:1	
		CSI = 0.2	

Yogurt, coffee/vanilla

½ cup

Weight: 113 grams (4.00 oz.)

Water weight: 101 g

Calories	96.5	Pyridoxine-B6	0.051 mg
Protein	5.60 g	Cobalamin-B12	0.600 mcg
Carbohydrates	15.6 g	Folacin	11.5 mcg
Dietary Fiber	0 g	Pantothenic	0.625 mg
Fat-Total	1.41 g	Vitamin C	0.850 mg
Fat-Saturated	0.920 g	Vitamin E	0 mg
Fat-Mono	0.386 g	Calcium	194 mg
Fat-Poly	0.045 g	Copper	0.045 mg
Cholesterol	5.70 mg	Iron	0.079 mg
Vit A-Carotene	2.00 re	Magnesium	18.0 mg
Vit A-Preformed	13.0 re	Phosphorus	153 mg
Vitamin A-Total	15.0 re	Potassium	248 mg
Thiamin-B1	0.047 mg	Selenium	2.50 mcg
Riboflavin-B2	0.228 mg	Sodium	75.0 mg
Niacin-B3	0.121 mg	Zinc	0.940 mg

Calories from protein:	23 %	Poly/Sat	= 0.0:1
Calories from carbohydrates:	64 %	Sod/Pot	= 0.3:1
Calories from fats:	13 %	Ca/Phos	= 1.3:1
		CSI	= 1.2

INDEX